A Contested Caribbean Indigeneity

CRITICAL CARIBBEAN STUDIES

Focused particularly in the twentieth and twenty-first centuries,
although attentive to the context of earlier eras, this series encourages
interdisciplinary approaches and methods and is open to scholarship
in a variety of areas, including anthropology, cultural studies, diaspora and transnational studies, environmental studies, gender and
sexuality studies, history, and sociology. The series pays particular
attention to the four main research clusters of Critical Caribbean
Studies at Rutgers University, where the coeditors serve as members
of the executive board: Caribbean Critical Studies Theory and the
Disciplines; Archipelagic Studies and Creolization; Caribbean Aesthetics, Poetics, and Politics; and Caribbean Colonialities.

Giselle Anatol, *The Things That Fly in the Night: Female Vampires in
Literature of the Circum-Caribbean and African Diaspora*
Alaí Reyes-Santos, *Our Caribbean Kin: Race and Nation in the Neo-
liberal Antilles*
Milagros Ricourt, *The Dominican Racial Imaginary: Surveying the
Landscape of Race and Nation in Hispaniola*
Katherine A. Zien, *Sovereign Acts: Performing Race, Space, and
Belonging in Panama and the Canal Zone*
Frances R. Botkin, *Thieving Three-Fingered Jack: Transatlantic Tales
of a Jamaican Outlaw, 1780–2015*
Melissa A. Johnson, *Becoming Creole: Nature and Race in Belize*
Carlos Garrido Castellano, *Beyond Representation in Contemporary
Caribbean Art: Space, Politics, and the Public Sphere*

A Contested Caribbean Indigeneity

~

Language, Social Practice, and Identity
within Puerto Rican Taíno Activism

SHERINA FELICIANO-SANTOS

R

Rutgers University Press

New Brunswick, Camden, and Newark, New Jersey, and London

Library of Congress Cataloging-in-Publication Data
Names: Feliciano-Santos, Sherina, author.
Title: A contested Caribbean indigeneity : language, social practice, and identity
within Puerto Rico Taíno activism / Sherina Feliciano-Santos.
Description: New Brunswick, NJ : Rutgers University Press, [2021] | Series: Critical
Caribbean studies | Includes bibliographical references and index.
Identifiers: LCCN 2020020793 | ISBN 9781978808171 (paperback) alk. paper |
ISBN 9781978808188 (hardcover) alk. paper | ISBN 9781978808195 (epub) |
ISBN 9781978808201 (mobi) | ISBN 9781978808218 (pdf)
Subjects: LCSH: Taino Indians—Puerto Rico—Ethnic identity. |
Taino Indians—Puerto Rico—Political activity. | National characteristics,
Puerto Rican. | Jíbaro (Puerto Rican identity) | Indian activists—Puerto Rico. |
Ethnicity—Puerto Rico.
Classification: LCC F1969 .F39 2021 | DDC 305.80097295—dc23
LC record available at https://lccn.loc.gov/2020020793

A British Cataloging-in-Publication record for this book
is available from the British Library.

♾ The paper used in this publication meets the requirements of the American
National Standard for Information Sciences—Permanence of Paper for Printed
Library Materials, ANSI Z39.48-1992.

www.rutgersuniversitypress.org

Manufactured in the United States of America

For all of mis amores from before, now, and the future:
Abuelito, Abuelita, Abuela Adela, Mami, Daddy, Allen, Eric,
Liza, Zoelle, Jonathan, Mateo, and Isaac. Siempre.

Contents

Prologue

I remember when my paternal great-grandmother, Mamá Vicenta, would come visit my *abuelito* and *abuelita*'s house in San Sebastián, Puerto Rico. My strongest memories of that time are of Mamá Vicenta as she unraveled her bun, letting loose a cascade of long white hair. I remember watching as she combed through that pale mane, leaving it to lie on her shoulders and her back, grazing her waist. Each night after this ritual, she would get into bed, clasp her rosary to her chest, and read the Bible. It was her hair, though, that fascinated me. My own hair was very curly, and I was captivated by our differences. When I would ask why her hair was so straight and mine so curly, my family would explain, "Es que ella es india" (She is Indian). I would look at her and think, *She does look* india.

I recall having my appearance dissected and analyzed from a young age—my hair, my nose, my legs, my lips, my skin color. Everything about me was susceptible to analysis, a sign of my ancestry made flesh. My curly hair, full lips, and thinner legs were from Africa, people would say; my big nose from Europe; my olive-tan skin color and other features a mixture of both. I remember encountering an exercise in a social studies textbook in elementary school that encouraged this kind of categorization. Three faces—one Taíno Indigenous, one African, and one Spanish—were illustrated with key physical descriptions listed under each image. Under the Taíno face, characteristics included "copper-colored skin" and "straight black hair." In Puerto Rico—along with the other Caribbean islands of Cuba, Hispaniola, Jamaica, and the Bahamas—the Taíno were the pre-Columbian inhabitants thought to have become extinct through the European conquest and colonization. The African face was described as having "thick, full lips" and "curly hair." The Spanish face was distinguished by its "fair skin" and "long aquiline nose." Each student was supposed to identify the physical characteristics they had inherited from each of these racialized heritages.

My family had moved "back" to the island a few years earlier, when I was nine. I had finally learned to navigate the school system and was called "americanita" less often. I thought that I understood how to be a *more Puerto Rican* Puerto Rican, and I saw the textbook's exercise as furthering this essential education—teaching me about my Puerto Rican heritage by teaching me how to figure out race in Puerto Rico. The range of so-called racialized looks in my family was broad, but I had never dissected how these differences related to the different (recognized) ethnic and racial heritages on the island. I completed the social studies exercise with a certain amount of satisfaction, classifying my whole family: "Well, my dad looks Spanish; my mother, like me, is a mixture of African and Spanish; my dad's father looks Taíno; my dad's mother is a mix of Taíno and Spanish; my mom's mother is also a mixture of African and Spanish; my mom's father looks Taíno; and my three siblings are also mixtures like me, but some are more Spanish and others are more African." My elementary-school self was satisfied with my analysis and with the book's conclusion: we are all Puerto Rican, and all Puerto Ricans have all of these three ancestries.

As I grew older, other messages about race reached me. In Puerto Rico, I learned that my hair was bad, that my legs were too skinny, that my nose was too big. These comments were not meant to be mean-spirited. They were matter-of-fact observations, often accompanied by advice: my hair could be relaxed and straightened, I could exercise to grow my calves, I could stay out of the sun to maintain the lighter version of my skin tone. My body could be managed, improved. I could be made more beautiful. Underlying it all, of course, were racialized assumptions about beauty. I remembered my great-grandmother's long, straight hair. *If only I had her hair*, I thought, *I might be deemed as pretty at the girls with the straight "Taíno" or wavy "Spanish" hair.* The racialized and racist beauty hierarchy in Puerto Rico positioned my hair, and its index-ical Blackness, as less desirable than the straight and wavy hair that indexed Spanish and Taíno heritage. After I had my hair relaxed and straightened for the first time, at twelve, I looked in the mirror, in awe of my altered reflection. What would it be like to have hair like this *all* the time, without any effort? I soon learned why my mother feared the rain, sweating, and the humidity of living on a tropical island. The illusion needed to be managed and maintained. It was exhausting.

When I was sixteen, I started leaving my hair curly. This was before the explosion of curly hair care products in the early 2000s and their mass marketing by 2010. In the town of San Sebastián, Puerto Rico, in 1996, you would make do with hair products designed either for naturally straight hair or for straightening naturally curly hair. Herbal Essences had released a hair gel that, when combined with a conditioner that I would leave in, allowed me to have controlled curls that my mom would let me leave the house with—most of the time. I knew that if we went to my mom's mother's house in Vieques, my hair would need to be managed.

Abuela Adela was tough, forceful. Never Abuelita. Abuela Adela. I would take her in only through glimpses, not wanting her to catch my staring—my intent study of what this silent but pow-erful woman's physical presence might reveal. She spoke so little about her past, and the little bit of information I could glean about Abuela Adela only made her more confusing. My mother often mentioned that Adela's mother looked "Spanish," with her green eyes and wavy light-brown hair. Adela had three brothers, all from different fathers, and they too were fair like Adela's mother. Adela, however, had darker skin and curly hair. Adela grew up unrecog-nized by her father, a wealthy foreman for one of the large sugar mills that existed in Vieques before the navy and marine bases appropriated two-thirds of the island. Adela's father did not look Spanish. They described him to me as being *"mulato."*

Adela did not like it when we wore our hair wild and curly. When we did, she would comment on the beauty of her daughters and granddaughters with *good* hair. Neither my mom nor I were in that esteemed group. While we looked the most like Adela, we did not inherit the traits from our fathers that she valued the most—my dad's gray-blue eyes or my maternal grandfather's straight hair. So before a visit to Vieques, I straightened my hair.

I learned about the circumstances that formed Adela's personality in bits and pieces, most of which I uncovered in the process of doing the research that would lead to this book. In phone conversations with my mother throughout college and graduate school, I would share things that I had learned about Vieques and Puerto Rican migration that helped me make sense of Adela. Then my mom would ask Adela if she knew about an event, a person, a place. Adela would answer the question, sometimes offering an extra detail, an illuminating stray piece of the puzzle that was her history. It was a point of pride for Adela that she had graduated from high school. When she was young, in order to get money from her father, she had to go to the sugar mill every week when his wife and other children wouldn't see her. She never took her father's last name because when he decided that he would finally recognize her as his child, she said it was too little, too late.

Sometimes our probing earned us a name that we could use to track down more details of Adela's past. I once uncovered some documents that claimed Adela's grandfather was born in Guadeloupe and her grandmother was born in Portugal. I called my mother. She called Adela, who was unsurprised. She already knew, and she didn't care. Adela gave my mom a few more details, then moved on to another topic.

As I worked on this project, I often thought about how I have experienced race and ethnicity in Puerto Rico. I mulled over my exchanges with Adela, mediated through my mom. What would we have never known about Adela, and our family histories, had we not asked? Would it have mattered? Do all the still-missing pieces matter? Does it matter if we know more about my great-grandfather, the man who didn't recognize my grandmother as his daughter? My mother and her six siblings were Viequenses. Being Viequense was what mattered. Without my scholarly digging, I would have only had what Adela and my mother and her siblings gave me: the bits and pieces of our family's history—the stories they knew, the stories they cherished, the stories of the ways they were scarred, the stories that allowed them to make sense of who they were and who they could become. Those stories told me who they were and who I was. Sometimes I wondered about the stories that were told to the children, grandchildren, and great-grandchildren of Adela's father. How do they, through those stories, make sense of who they are?

These reflections about my own family, about the stories I heard again and again and the stories I would never hear, have guided my scholarly pursuits. How do the stories told by families whose histories and trajectories are not recoverable through archives and documents—whose pasts, simultaneously memorialized and over-looked, are not reflected in the broader and more widespread histories of the island—impact how Puerto Rican people understand who they are?

In 2004, when I first read about Taíno mobilization in Puerto Rico, I was skeptical. I had learned that the Taíno were "extinct" and was so confident in this monolithic historical "truth" that I assumed that "claiming" to be Taíno was akin to "claiming" to be an extraterrestrial being. I soon had my assumptions checked. My PhD advisor, Barb Meek, introduced me to the concept of settler colonialism, through which colonial societies discursively erased Indigenous cultures in order to accomplish the physical settling of Indigenous lands. She forced me to think about Puerto Rican history not as a truth but as a positioned narrative that draws on notions of truth to accomplish its political and economic goals. I had to reconsider decolonization narratives not only in terms of Puerto Rico's colonization by the United States but also in terms of the more complicated forms of hegemony that frame the relationships between Puerto Rican elites and the complex of marginalized groups on the island. I started to think seriously about the histories told from below, and rather than check these narratives against the standard historical canon, I checked the historical canon against the histories told from below. Rather than assume my own family history—illegitimate children, migrations to non-standard places, insecurities about our legitimate belonging—was an aberration, I started to expect dissonance between my family's history and the larger narrative of Puerto Rico. After all, my family was working in sugar fields and picking coffee, moving to the United States and St. Croix to work in factories and open small shops. They would never have the chance to write history books in their own image, so in the history books that others had time to write, the complexity of their lives would be flattened, their messy and distinct stories amalgamated and ironed into a bland, noble simplicity that bore little resemblance to any truth they would have recognized.

I returned to Puerto Rico in the summer of 2006 to start my dissertation fieldwork about Puerto Rican Taíno mobilization. When I told old friends from school about the project, they said I was crazy. Their resistance told me I was on to something. Why were they so committed to the myth that no Taíno had existed since the 1500s, when the period of Taíno survival was even a matter of debate among Puerto Rican historians (Brau 1983 [1917]; Curtis and Scarano 2011)? What was at stake? These friends, after they finished telling me about the insanity of claiming to be Taíno, often told me that their *abuelas* were india. But that did not make them indias. "She made *casabe*," they would say. "She called cotton *sarobei* and ate out of *ditas* and *jatacas*. She knew about healing plants." They continued to offer me evidence of just how india their grandmothers and great-grandmothers were. Were they like me, looking at my great-grandmother—born around 1911, without formal education, a mother at sixteen—and assuming her stories were about *looking* like an india, not about being one? Did they also consult the authority of their history textbooks and use that to explain that because we were all a mixture, we couldn't claim to be exclusively any one thing?

In spite of my friends' dismissiveness, I spent the next two years interviewing and spending time with different groups who mobilized on behalf of Indigenous rights and recognition in Puerto Rico. After that, I sporadically kept in touch with people from different groups, but I wouldn't see many of them again until 2018 in New York, where I attended a National Museum of the American Indian exhibit on Taíno survival. In the time I have been writing, thinking about, and revisiting the Taíno who opened their lives to me, I have found a consistency in their narratives. They listened to their grandparents' stories and shared them with their own children. They anchored their identities in these stories. These identities were not always compatible with or reducible to sanctioned historical narratives, so they disregarded their history books in favor of their families' narratives. They held on to those stories of survival, and in turn, those stories of survival survived in them.

My father's mother, my abuelita, the grandmother I grew up with, passed away while I was in New York for the Smithsonian exhibit in September 2018. I was having coffee with several Taíno elders when I received the call. I broke into tears. Abuela Shashira hugged me, and a distant scrap of memory flashed before my mind's eye. Years earlier, Shashira and I had stopped by my parents' house in San Sebastián on the way back from a festival in Las Marías. My grandmother came down from her house, which was above ours, and introduced herself. When Shashira left, my grandmother wondered why I was spending so much time with another abuela, an abuela who wasn't even mine. I explained that I was spending time with her because of my project—I was learning about the Taíno.

My grandmother bristled. "Well, you could spend time with me," she said. "I know how to make casabe, I know about healing plants, I know about Indian things too. My mother was india too."

Both confused and surprised at the revelation, I asked her, "Why didn't you ever tell me?"

She responded, "Because you never asked."

As Shashira embraced me all those years later, all those miles away, I reflected on that moment and what I had learned from that exchange with my abuelita. I had asked her about her own identity, and while she did not consider herself india, she claimed her mother's india knowledge and told me how my abuelito, her husband, loved casabe with *bacalao*. She made it for him often but, assuming that I would find such food old fashioned, never for me. In 2018, I wondered about all the questions I had never asked, about the stories that died with my grandmother. What knowledge, passed from generation to generation, would not be passed on to my own children? What else had I lost through my disregard?

In Puerto Rico and in the world, my mistake is writ large. What have we lost through our disregard? And how might taking Taíno narratives seriously now help us recoup some of the deficit we have created, helping us understand Puerto Rican and Caribbean history more broadly? This book is my attempt to begin the process of recovering some of the stories, the ways of making meaning that have for too long been dismissed by a world that preferred for the Taíno to have disappeared five hundred years ago. In these pages, I try to make sense of the possibilities, ambiguities, and processes involved in being and becoming Taíno. What can the experiences of being Taíno allow us to understand about how we anchor our own sense of what it means to be who we are? What kinds of becoming could result from this reflection? What new ways of being could emerge from our constellations of identifications?

In 2005, a film called *Taínos: La última tribu* premiered in Puerto Rico. In the film, an archaeology student explores Cueva de la Mora in Comerío and encounters a hidden Taíno tribe that has survived intact, unchanged, and "unmixed" for five hundred years. This imagined Taíno tribe reveals the expectations against which real-life Taíno, and Indigenous claims more broadly, are evaluated. If the Taíno were truly Indigenous, the argument seems to go, they would look, behave, and speak as they did in pre-Columbian times. In order to demonstrate their survival, the experience of colonial "encounter" and "discovery" would have to be re-created.

These fantastical and absurd expectations stand in stark relief against Taíno narratives of continuity and survival, which exist not in tribes hidden away from time and from the rest of humanity but in groups of people who use mobile phones, drive cars, and live in concrete or wooden homes with modern appliances. The Taíno I met have maintained their identity not by holing up in a cave to pass the centuries but by continuing to share the oral histories and knowledge that have been passed down through generations. They recognize each other in their practices, dances, and spiritual beliefs. Their narratives reflect the colonial histories of the island, the displacements of their ancestors, and the fragility of their survival. Their narratives reflect not linguistic continuity and isolation but adaptation, linguistic transformation, and dogged survival in the face of supposed extinction.

Abbreviations and Acronyms

CGT	Consejo General de Taíno (General Council of Taíno)
DIVEDCO	División de Educación de la Comunidad (Division of Community Education)
DRNA	Departamento de Recursos Naturales y Ambientales (Department of Natural and Environmental Resources)
ELA	Estado Libre Asociado (Free Associated State Commonwealth of Puerto Rico)
GK	Guaka-Kú
ICP	Instituto de Cultura Puertorriqueña (Puerto Rican Institute of Culture)
LGTK	Liga Guakía Taína-ké (League of the Good Land/Earth)
MIJB	Movimiento Indígena Jíbaros Boricua (Jíbaro Boricua Indigenous Movement)
MOVIJIBO	Movimiento Indígena Chib'al'o [Jíbaro]-Boricua (Chib'al'o [Jíbaro]-Boricua Indigenous Movement)
OECH	Oficina de Estatal de Conservación Histórica (State Office of Historic Preservation)
PIP	Partido Independentista Puertorriqueño (Puerto Rican Independence Party)
PNP	Partido Nuevo Progresista (New Progressive Party)
PPD	Partido Popular Democrático (Popular Democratic Party)
TN	Taíno Nation
UCTP	United Confederation of Taíno People
USACE	U.S. Army Corps of Engineers

Note on Transcription Conventions

[word]	Brackets around words or parts of a word indicate overlapping talk.
wor-	A dash indicates a truncated word.
word=	An equal sign indicates latching.
WORD	A word or part of a word in all capital letters indicates loudness.
((gesture))	Double parentheses around words indicate extralinguistic information.
wo::rd	A colon in a word indicates the lengthening of the last sound; each colon is equivalent to about 0.1 seconds.
word	Underlining indicates emphasis.
word	Bolding indicates the focus of the transcript.
{?}	A question mark between curly brackets indicates uncertain or unclear talk.
.	A period indicates a falling intonation contour.
,	A comma indicates a continuing intonation contour.
?	A question mark indicates a rising intonation contour.
(#s)	A number in parentheses followed by *s* indicates seconds of silence.

Adapted from Duranti (2004) and Ochs and Capps (2001).

A Contested Caribbean Indigeneity

Introduction

This book examines the historical, institutional, and interactional dimensions of Taíno/Boricua activism in Puerto Rico. I use the term *Taíno/Boricua* to encompass the distinct and sometimes competing forms of identification that Indigenous Puerto Ricans claim. Among Indigenous Puerto Ricans, self-designations range from the more widely known term *Taíno* to the less common, though no less important, *Canjíbaro* or *Jíbaro-Boricua*. The former is often aligned with an Arawakan Indigenous genealogy. The latter is often tied to a Mayan one that rejects the validity of the Taíno designation altogether. Since *Jíbaro-Boricua* was the term used by the groups that mobilize on behalf of a Mayan genealogy during my research, it is the designation I use for them throughout this work.

I consider how the presumed extinction of the Taíno/Boricua on the island has served to limit their claims to Indigeneity as well as the role they can play in public policy debates concerning the management of Indigenous human remains and sacred sites. I show how Taíno/Boricua activists address and reconfigure widespread historical narratives within everyday interactions and seek to reposition the histories that erase them. Their efforts have led to the recent public emergence of Taíno/Boricua as an increasingly visible social identification in Puerto Rico. In my terminological choices regarding Taíno/Boricua language and culture, I have attempted to be careful in choosing terms that reframe the potential vitalities of Taíno/Boricua cultural and linguistic forms away from extinction (Perley 2012).

The first section of the book engages with the competing historical narratives regarding Taíno/Boricua extinction. A careful analysis of the social and historical phenomena involved in a Taíno/Boricua reckoning of Indigeneity sheds light on the narratives told about the entire Caribbean. In *The Repeating Island*, Antonio Benítez-Rojo (1996) argues that scholars need to critically examine what has been taken for granted in Caribbean discourses and open up to heterogeneous narratives that circulate alongside each other. The chapters in this section explore how Puerto Rican Taíno/Boricua see the extinction narrative as simply one of the many stories told by the people of Puerto Rico. These chapters put standard versions of Puerto Rican history in conversation with social actors whose politics, understandings of the past, and hopes for the future have been formed along trajectories that diverge from that of scholars, other public figures, and the general Puerto Rican population. This section considers the sources, evaluative criteria, and ideas of authority and legitimacy that undergird Taíno/Boricua historical narratives, and in doing so, it examines the memories shared by Puerto Rican Taíno/Boricua alongside historical documents and explores the different ways in which Taíno and non-Taíno interpret the ambiguities and silences in the historical archive.

The second section explores the discourses surrounding the Puerto Rican nation and ethnoracial regimes in Puerto Rico. A discussion of history and historical memory in Puerto Rico must necessarily be grounded in a discussion of Puerto Rican cultural nationalism and national figures. This section focuses on two figurations of national belonging: the Jíbaro and the racial triad. After examining the emergence, circulation, and impact of these emblematic expressions of being Puerto Rican, these chapters consider how the discourses of *jibaridad* and the racial triad work to configure and ideologically demarcate possibilities and impossibilities in ethnoracial claims and identifications. It is within this contextualization that the book considers the emergence, complications, and challenges of the Taíno/Boricua mobilization in Puerto Rico. The chapters in this section take a critical look at the discourses of jíbaridad and the racial triad that frame the notion of Taíno/Boricua among Puerto Ricans.

The last section of the book concerns Taíno/Boricua heritage and political mobilization. Each chapter highlights different organizations and their work on Taíno/Boricua language, Taíno/Boricua genealogies, Taíno/Boricua material culture, Taíno/Boricua politics, and Taíno/Boricua spirituality. Ethnographic insight into different dimensions of Taíno/Boricua social action shows that it is neither cohesive nor interconnected. Rather, by focusing on the everyday lives of Taíno/Boricua activists, the chapters in this section describe in careful detail the investments, stories, and motivations of different women and men as they construct Taíno/Boricua as an inhabitable and relevant ethnic category of identification in Puerto Rico and beyond.

As a whole, this book extends current considerations regarding Taíno/Boricua in Puerto Rico by offering an in-depth discussion of the movement that combines ethnographic fieldwork with a rigorous analysis of oral histories, historical archives, media representations, and scholarly discourse of Puerto Ricanness and Taíno/Boricuaness.

~

As a linguistic anthropologist, I drew on ethnographic research methods of participant observation, interviews, and extensive recordings of talk and interactions. I spent two years among different Puerto Rican Taíno/Boricua groups, including a trip to New York City to meet two active groups whose members also largely identified as Puerto Rican Taíno.[1] The book's analysis in chapters 4–7 reflects my field and analytical training as a linguistic anthropologist in its attention to interaction as a site for productive analysis and insight. These chapters in particular contain several transcripts of interactions that I recorded, transcribed, and translated when necessary. In my writing, I attempt to foreground my positionality as a Puerto Rican woman who was often assumed to be Taíno/Boricua even when I did not exclusively identify with that category. Additionally, I am careful to present the different oral histories, narratives, and perspectives that circulate among my Taíno/Boricua research consultants.

The approaches to Taíno identity and language I observed during my research are best likened to lines in the sand that were drawn, erased, and redrawn by different groups at different times rather than clearly demarcated walls. Throughout the book, I tell the story of how I met each group in order to illustrate the tensions between their approaches and to introduce myself as a social actor in this research. I was born in the United States but grew up largely in Puerto Rico, where the majority of my family lived from 1989 through 2017. When I returned home in the summer of 2004 after my first year of graduate school, I encountered a series of news pieces on the "neo-Taíno."[2] Like most Puerto Ricans, I had been taught in school that the Taíno suffered a massive genocide in the fifteenth and sixteenth centuries, so I was surprised—and admittedly skeptical—to read that people in the twenty-first century were claiming to be Taíno. Fascinated by the politics and the possibility, I embarked on this project.

I started my field research, which largely consisted of participant observation and audio and video recordings, in the summer of 2006. In August, my younger sister told me she was taking an anthropology class at the University of Puerto Rico (UPR) taught by a Taíno activist, a woman called Yarey.[3] She became my first research consultant and my introduction to many of the groups I would later work with. Yarey was a cultural anthropologist who was committed to her Indigenous heritage and also wanted to establish her own Indigenous organization among persons from her parents' communities in the southeastern region of the island, the Liga Guakía Taína-ké (LGTK). Through that process, she—and I through her—became acquainted with members from other more established groups.

Intergroup politics became apparent as I began my research. The Consejo General de Taínos (CGT), having mobilized in the '70s, was one of the oldest and largest Taíno organizations in Puerto Rico and was based in the northern and metropolitan areas near San Juan. While not broadly known throughout the island, in part due to the widespread belief that the Taíno have been extinct, they are quite well known among Puerto Rican Indigenous organizations. When I first met Abuela Shashira, one of their elders, she immediately highlighted some points of contention between different Taíno groups. This happened when I was introduced to virtually all the groups I would eventually work with. There was often a complaint or criticism of another group's politics, methods, and/or goals. Disagreements that fell along group lines included matters such as the role of women in Taíno leadership, genealogies of current Taíno groups, access to institutional resources, media coverage and the right to speak on behalf of all Taíno, and organizational authority.

One evening, I received a call from the head of another group, the Movimiento Indígena Jíbaro Boricua (MIJB), based on the northwest coast. Tito Guajataca wanted to introduce me to the "genuine natives" of the island—those who knew not to call themselves Taíno and instead went by Jíbaros or Boricuas. He believed that the true natives had a Mayan background and that their true language was related to Yucatec Maya.

I met the leader of Guaka-Kú (GK), Tuján, when we drove to the southeastern community where Yarey was working. Tuján was a mystical middle-aged man who lived in and cared for a cave full of petroglyphs. While he was friends with another very spiritual member of CGT, Tuján was not part of the CGT. He only shared his knowledge of Taíno culture and practices in limited ways with select people.

My own identifications and allegiances often became the topic of conversation. I was asked if I identified as Taíno/Boricua and treated as an initiate by the groups I worked with even though I always responded in the negative. I remained open about my views but was also careful not to side with any one group. As I explained to them at the time, I focused my energies on making sense of how such conflicts, distinctions, and occasional agreements affected the project of a Taíno language.

Throughout my research, I encountered around five hundred people within approximately eight organizations that actively claimed an Indigenous Caribbean identity. The 2010 U.S. Census shows the island's population to be 3,725,789 persons, of which 3,351 (.09 percent) identified as Taíno alone and 9,399 (0.25 percent) identified as Taíno alone or in combination with other categories.[4] I met many people who claimed to be indio without necessary affiliating with activist organizations or calling themselves Taíno. Since not everyone in Puerto Rico who considers themselves Indigenous to the island uses the term *Taíno*, I use the term *Taíno/Boricua* to speak generally about Indigenous activists in Puerto Rico and *Taíno* or *Jíbaro-Boricua* when speaking of specific groups or citing the relevant literature. Quite a few organizations I encountered during my fieldwork rejected the scripts of Indigeneity as Taínoness. Rather, they organize as Jíbaro-Boricuas with the goal of reinterpreting and reframing the Jíbaro as an Indigenous figure.[5] The Jíbaro is a national archetype, celebrated as encapsulating the essential character of Puerto Ricans. As an everyday descriptor, it is much more narrowly used to describe the rural and ostensibly less "modern" and less educated population of the island (Scarano 1996). While the persons who organize the Jíbaro-Boricua Indigenous organizations largely seek to recruit people who would be described as jíbaros who might also consider themselves indios, the term's association with the former category of Jíbaro also leads to tensions.

Taíno activists live all over the island (Puerto Rico is about 100 miles × 35 miles) and often drive to meet at a particular leader or elder's home for organizational matters or at particular sacred sites for ceremonies. I understood current Taíno/Boricua organizations to function as a modern tribal association with somewhat standardized modes of governance across groups. Most groups had a clear leader who might sometimes call themselves a cacique or cacica. All groups had elders, called abuelos and abuelas, who might have previously held leadership positions. Most organizations also had teachers, known as *tequinas*, and spiritual healers, who are sometimes known as *behiques* or *bohiques*. Some organizations focused more on ceremonial matters, while others were known for their artistic performances. Some organized around political issues, some were more prone to take on protests, while yet others worked with governmental and nongovernmental institutions to obtain resources to buttress their educational efforts.

There were also organizations throughout the Greater Antilles and in the Caribbean diaspora in the United States. I did not have the opportunity to meet and spend time with every single group; this book reflects the groups that I was able to get to know over the course of my research.

PART 1

Competing Historical Narratives regarding Taíno Extinction

1

The Stakes of Being Taíno

The Taíno resurgence has been documented throughout the Caribbean, challenging historical and national narratives premised on their extinction (Forte 2005; Guitar 2002). Recent work has considered the discursive aspects of the Taíno resurgence as it relates to racial and political paradigms in Puerto Rico (Haslip-Viera 2001; Martínez-San Miguel 2011). Other research has addressed surviving Taíno social and cultural practices and their relationship to Indigenous-identifying populations (Berman Santana 2005; Castanha 2011; González 2018; Guitar 2002; Yaremko 2009). Taíno activists are aware of the historical discourses that have positioned the Taíno as an extinct and therefore impossible identity to claim (Brusi Gil de Lamadrid and Godreau 2007; Haslip-Viera 2013; Rouse 1993). Taíno activists are particularly attentive to scholarly discourse on Taíno ethnicity that presumes the truth of the extinction narratives and argues that the Taíno Indigenous movement in Puerto Rico is about either the denial of African influence on the island or an attempt to obtain governmental recognition and, subsequently, land rights through the use of a nationally legitimated identity (Borrero 2001, 150).

Many people today claim to have maintained Taíno culture and self-identifications through their family lineages, although their assertions are questioned by those in the Caribbean who do not identify or believe that others could identify as Taíno—in fact, the Taíno have no official governmental recognition. To understand the levels of opposition and incredulity the Taíno movement has provoked in Puerto Rico, I consider how the widely circulated and hegemonic narratives of the Puerto Rican nation rely on the Taíno extinction narrative, prefiguring the Taíno as an impossible category of affiliation. I also consider how work on Puerto Rican nationalism is often critical of the hegemonizing discourses that characterize nation building in Puerto Rico (Duany 2002b; Guerra 1998; Haslip-Viera 2009; Hernández Hiraldo 2006) yet also sometimes reproduces the assumptions contained within this discourse—for example, that since Taíno survival is not documented, Taíno identity is not possible (Brusi Gil de Lamadrid and Godreau 2007; Haslip-Viera 2001, 2013, 2014, 2019).

Rather than consider whether Taíno/Boricua claims are true or false, this book aims to take an analytical step back to instead propose the concept of contested epistemologies of possibility—different theories of knowledge that consider how we know what we know and, based on that knowledge, what can be possible—to frame debates about the Taíno/Boricua more broadly. I argue that an analysis of Puerto Rican Taíno/Boricua mobilization must carefully engage with how Taíno/Boricua come to know about their past as a people. Approaching semiotic ambiguity as a site of possibility, erasure, negotiation over meaning, and emergence for different interpretive paradigms, I analyze how Taíno/Boricua histories circulate, how their activities are framed, how Taíno/Boricua frame belonging, and what futures Taíno/Boricua work toward building. Ethnographic attention to face-to-face interactions reveals the complex ways Taíno/Boricua negotiate their claims to identity with governments, other social actors, and academic institutions. In this sense, interactional and institutional recalibrations emerge as important sites where people highlight ambiguities in discourse to facilitate their own identity claims.

Cultural Reclamation and Indigenous Movements Worldwide

The Taíno/Boricua in Puerto Rico are among a number of groups around the world who are seen as making unwarranted claims to Indigenous identity. For example, Brian D. Haley and Larry R.

Wilcoxon (1997, 5–6) address the claims of the "neo-Chumash," a group from California's central coast. The authors argue that among those who claim Chumash ancestry, some people—to whom they refer as "neo-Chumash" or "Chumash traditionalists"—have tenuous links to identifiable or documented Chumash heritage and conclude that "the neo-Chumash pose a challenge: Their example appears to be a clear case of whole-cloth fabrication, yet the reasons for their ethnogenesis are rarely ascertained" (2005, 433).

Studies such as Haley and Wilcoxon's (1997, 2005) fall within a larger body of literature that critically considers the complexities of current articulations of American Indian identity. From "playing Indian" (Deloria 1999) to "wannabe Indians" (Green 1988) to accusations of "ethnic fraud" (Gonzales 1998), the question of who can claim to be Indian is hotly debated. Philip J. Deloria (1999, 12) argues that the Indian persona has been donned in social protest by European Americans as part of a larger "misrule tradition" since the American Revolution. Rayna Green (1988, 46) discusses not only how people have put on the American Indian mask for protest but also the increase in what she considers to be tenuous claims to an Indian identity, which she views as rooted in a larger racial politics. Bonita Lawrence (2004), on the other hand, considers how some current claims to being Indian might have been preceded by erasures—highlighting the complicated histories of race, classification, and censuses that might have silenced claims to Indigeneity for people with mixed Afro-Indigenous backgrounds. Angela Gonzales (1998, 203) argues that concomitant with ethnic pride and revival movements more broadly, some new claims to American Indian identity are couched in an emerging understanding of race and ethnicity that has "become voluntary and a matter of personal volition." Because claiming to be Taíno/Boricua is often understood as a personal choice rather than a product of other historically documented forms of affiliation and assessment of difference, some scholars understand this claim to be inauthentic and problematic (see essays in Haslip-Viera 2001).

The question of what it means to be Indigenous—and who can claim Indigeneity—resonates around the world (Anderson

2007; Clifford 2013; de la Cadena and Orin Starn 2009; Hathaway 2010). Surveying the literature in Latin America, Africa, and Asia, Michael Hathaway argues that Indigeneity is "a social and political category . . . that repositions groups out of local and domestic struggles, and into a position of transnational solidarities, rights, and participation in a dynamic social movement." He approaches Indigeneity as a "process of continuing emergence, rather than . . . reemergence" (2010, 303). Elizabeth A. Povinelli (2002) considers the challenges of Indigenous activism with a focus on process and emergence and the ambiguities inherent therein. Here is a call for an ethnography of the trajectories of social phenomena—a study of emergence, materialization, and transformation that attends to the heterogeneities, tensions, and ambiguities that pervade any sociocultural context. Povinelli also explores the tensions embedded in making claims to Indigeneity for the Belyuen people in Australia, who, in order to legally evidence their claims for land rights, are pressured to prove their locality on colonial terms. Other cases have shown similar constraints on the expression of Indigenous claims. For example, linguistic anthropologist Laura Graham (2002) finds Amazonian Indigenous leaders in Brazil and Venezuela caught in a linguistic catch-22: use "authenticating" native languages and struggle to communicate with national governments or use national languages (either Spanish or Portuguese) and stand accused of being inauthentic. Linguistic anthropologist Bernard Perley criticizes "institutional definitions of Indianness" that "privilege formal political economies of identity management, often at the expense of the community informal and experiential management of identity" (2011, 175). Instead, in order to ensure that acts of language maintenance and recovery are analyzed in terms that reflect Indigenous agencies and sovereignties, Myaamia linguist Wesley Leonard proposes the concept of linguistic reclamation, which points to the right of Indigenous groups to self-determine and "recognize their right to learn, use, ultimately pass on their language" (2007). My work here reflects this stance by engaging with the acts of cultural and linguistic reclamation that the Taíno/Boricua participate in on their terms while also recognizing the pressures they encounter in making themselves institutionally and interactionally legible and audible (Conklin 1997; Graham 2002; Povinelli 2002).

In studies of Latin American Indigenous activism, cultural anthropologists Jean E. Jackson and Kay B. Warren call for researchers to engage with the communities they study, considering "their contrasting subject positions as insiders or outsiders, Indigenous or not, and as fellow citizens with Indigenous nationals or not" (2002, 4). My own subject position consistently informs my understanding of the Taíno/Boricua communities whose emergence, and all the tensions and ambiguities contained therein, is chronicled and examined in this book.

Puerto Rican Forms of Nationalism and Nation-Building

For most of the sixteenth century through the twentieth century, Puerto Rico was a Spanish colony. These centuries were generally characterized by Spanish settler colonization, using the island's land and labor to support Spain's incursions into the rest of the western Caribbean and the Americas (Scarano 1989). Reflected in the limited availability of documents and histories of the island written during the seventeenth and some of the eighteenth century is a momentary diminution in Spanish investment in its Puerto Rican colony, perhaps due in part to a rising interest in Spain's continental colonies and their promise of mining wealth and large swaths of land. The Haitian Revolution, which left a void in sugar production, and Spain's loss of its continental colonies may have reignited interest in its island colonies during the eighteenth and nineteenth centuries. The American era of independence also reverberated in Puerto Rico, where local elites pushed for self-rule on the island, ultimately gaining a more autonomous government in 1898. But at the same time, the United States, solidifying its own burgeoning power, waged the Spanish-American War, ousted Spain from its remaining colonies, and assumed sovereignty over the island.

So ended Puerto Rico's three months of relative freedom, and so began the U.S. government's efforts to export its political, cultural, and linguistic frameworks to the island.

The fifty-year period between the U.S. takeover and the implementation of the commonwealth was characterized, among other things, by the struggle to establish a Puerto Rican–led government and to find a language policy that could balance Puerto Rico's desire to preserve the Spanish vernacular and the United States' Americanization efforts. In 1900, through the Foraker Act, the United States appointed a U.S. governor and civil government. By 1912, English had been imposed as the language of instruction at all levels, and educators with sufficient English skills were given major salary increases. Weary of these language policies, teachers organized the first Puerto Rican teachers' union in 1912 (López Yustos 1997). In 1917, the United States conceded citizenship to Puerto Ricans through the Jones Act of Puerto Rico (Trías Monge 1997).[1] In 1927, the education commissioner banned the celebration of Puerto Rican holidays in schools. At a union assembly that year, some teachers argued that schools needed to become agents of "Puerto Ricanization" instead of Americanization (Negrón de Montilla 1975; see also DuBord 2007).

Puerto Rico's constitution was ratified in 1952, officially making the island a commonwealth of the United States, which was to be a temporary solution to the debate between statehood and independence for Puerto Rico.[2] Politically, this meant that the island was granted a relative amount of political autonomy while ultimately being held accountable to the decisions of the U.S. Congress. In this new political system, the island could organize its government according to how Puerto Ricans perceived their political, social, and economic needs. These included a temporary resolution that accommodated teacher requests for the Spanish vernacular to be the medium of instruction at all grade levels, with English permanently relegated to being taught as a foreign language (Parker and Parker 1978, 15).

Throughout the '50s and '60s, the dire economic situation in Puerto Rico encouraged the mass labor migration of Puerto

Ricans to urban industrial manufacturing centers like Chicago and New York and to farming communities outside Philadelphia and Hawaii, forming diasporic communities that primarily spoke English and Spanglish (Pérez 2004). Many of these mostly English-speaking migrants would return to the island and experience language-based exclusions (Acevedo 2004; Duany 2002a; Zentella 1990).

In addition to maintaining an ongoing commitment to the Spanish language, Puerto Rican cultural nationalism, which developed in response to U.S. efforts to establish cultural dominance, romanticized the Taíno as a national legacy—a shared bygone heritage of the island (Duany 2002b).[3] The Taíno served as a powerful national symbol of authentic Puerto Ricanness precisely because they were said to be extinct, leaving all Puerto Ricans free to claim Taíno as one of their cultural roots and jibaridad as their cultural heritage (Curet 2015; A. Dávila 2001; Galarza 2007). By the '60s, these forms of cultural nationalism had become so entrenched that even pro-statehood candidates made clear that they would protect the primacy of the Spanish language in Puerto Rico if the island were to join the United States as the fifty-first state.

However, both Nuyoricans and Afro–Puerto Ricans on the island contested the prevailing national narrative by bringing attention to Afro–Puerto Rican and Nuyorican forms of identity and positing critiques of the hegemony of a homogenous definition of Puerto Ricanness (Flores, Attinasi, and Pedraza 1981; Gonzalez 1980; Zenón Cruz 1975). While African heritage in Puerto Rico was marginally celebrated, Blackness itself was erased as a form of identity, though it was still recognized as a basis for racist interaction, prejudice, and social marginalization.

During the '70s, proindependence movements swept the island. Activists were concerned with the evident permanence of the supposedly temporary commonwealth status and skeptical of the impact of the neocolonial industrialization that had been implemented in Puerto Rico. At the same time, Puerto Ricans on the island and in the New York City diaspora began to organize around their Taíno identity. Meanwhile, the imagined and supposedly extinct Taíno flourished as a national icon of Puerto Ricanness, appearing everywhere from late-night television, where in the '90s, model Noris "La Taína" Díaz was celebrated for her embodiment of Taíno and Puerto Rican ideals of beauty; to the clothing, handbags, car stickers, and restaurants whose petroglyphic symbols touted a Taíno connection; to the local (and now defunct) newspaper *El Mundo*, in which a comic called *Turey el Taíno* debuted in 1989.

With the dawn of a new millennium came increasing instability and unrest on the island—changes in the tax code, the Great Recession, debt crisis, stagnant wages and layoffs, rising crime and drug use, increasing criminalization of poor communities, university strikes, a devastating hurricane, and a series of disastrous earthquakes (Bonilla and Lebrón 2019; Caban 2017; Cortés 2018; Feliciano and Green 2017; Goldstein 2016; Lebrón 2016a, 2016b; Lloréns 2018b; Rivera 1997; Rodríguez-Díaz 2018). As Puerto Ricans questioned the government structures that had failed them, discourses interrogating the island's hegemonic narratives of culture, race, and ethnicity gained traction. Many Puerto Ricans also became more vocal in proclaiming their Afro–Puerto Rican, Afro-Taíno, and Taíno/Boricua identifications. In 2018, the National Museum of the American Indian curated an exhibit in New York called *Taíno: Native Heritage and Identity in the Caribbean*. What had once been a foregone conclusion in hegemonic narratives about the island—that the Taíno were extinct—had been challenged in a national U.S. exhibit.

The theoretical framework of this book builds on ambiguity in the emergence and materialization of sociocultural identity categories such as race and considers the different epistemologies that sustain distinct narratives of Taíno/Boricua existence. These ambiguities challenge homogenous narratives that rely on colonial logics of erasure, displacement, and replacement to instead consider the multiple historical possibilities of the past as they become materialized in the present and mark the potentiality of the future.

Semiotic Ambiguity, Emergence, and Interactional Materialization

Literary critic William Empson defines *ambiguity* as "any verbal nuance, however slight, which gives room for alternative reactions to the same piece of language" (1966 [1930], 1) Ambiguity in how the ethnoracial terms—such as *native*, *Jíbaro*, and *indio*—used in historical documents are interpreted result in discrepancies in how contemporary social actors understand the past. Chapters 2 and 3 explore the (hegemonic) processes through which particular interpretations take hold, circulate, and are imposed as legitimate and authoritative. I also consider a variety of interrelated social progressions that are involved in creating, maintaining, or challenging the historical interpretations that influence Taíno mobilization.

Discourses of Taíno extinction often rely on governmental and disciplinary interventions to silence, erase, and trivialize alternative interpretations and understandings of Puerto Rican historical trajectories. As linguistic anthropologists Judith T. Irvine and Susan Gal have argued with regard to language ideologies, "Erasure is the process in which ideology, in simplifying the sociolinguistic field, renders some persons or activities (or sociolinguistic phenomena) invisible. Facts that are inconsistent with the ideological scheme either go unnoticed or get explained away" (2000, 38). A focus on "the interplay of multiple perspectives" allows us to "see historically how effects of truth are produced within discourses which in themselves are neither true nor false" (Foucault 1980, 118; see also Clifford and Marcus 1986; Taussig 1986, 288). It is within this analytical framework that I examine how Taíno/Boricua activists articulate themselves and their historical trajectories in response to institutionally sanctioned versions of the island's history and how, in turn, Taíno/Boricua activists' attempts at public visibility become problematized as inauthentic and motivated by an interest in land.

Taíno/Boricua claims occur within a context that presumes them to be extinct and are, to some extent, contingent on the willingness of non-Taíno-identifying Puerto Ricans to engage with them. Taíno/Boricua activists' efforts to gain recognition foreground the fact that "every plan, scenario, and conception is always already situated in a social, political and historical moment" (Tedlock and Mannheim 1995, 11). From this perspective, subject positions and the linguistic forms through which they become negotiated are dialogical and emergent in interactional situations. With respect to the emergent aspects of social interaction, I draw from sociologist Anthony Giddens's (1976, 1977; Giddens and Cassell 1993, 102) interpretive schemas "to make sense not only of what others say, but of what they mean: the constitution of 'sense' as an intersubjective accomplishment of mutual understanding in an ongoing exchange." Giddens's schemas, like sociologist Erving Goffman's (1974) discussion of frames, foreground the negotiation and dialogism of interaction, given that they account for the role of both the personal trajectories of interactions and the contexts in which such interactions take place in organizing experience, interpretation, and meaning.

Epistemologies of Possibility

Works in Black and Chicana feminist theory have been fundamental to my thinking about the overlapping and complex relationships between difference and identity. These authors' critiques of White feminist theory emphasize the need to account for the multiple and different types of oppression experienced by non-White women. Scholars such as Patricia Hill Collins (1986), Audre Lorde (2012 [1984]), bell hooks (2000 [1984], 2014 [1981]), Gloria Anzaldúa (1987), and Cherríe Moraga (Moraga and Anzaldúa 1981), among others, have recognized the distinct ontological and epistemological frameworks that shape the experiences of being and knowing for women of different racialized and ethnicized backgrounds. Additionally, they account for the unique experiences afforded to varying kinds of identification. For example, they highlight the ontological significance of being visibly identifiable—that is, marked—as distinct versus being able to "pass" (Stanley and Wise 2013). These disparities in experience, they argue, have political and academic importance, and an exploration of the experiences of alternatively oppressed populations, along with a theoretical framework and approach that account for their subsequently particular ways of being and knowing, is essential to any study of identity and identification.

Applying these insights to Taíno/Boricua political action helps disentangle the multiple experiences of disparity, marginalization, and oppression that have resulted from the most dominant racial discourses in Puerto Rico while attempting to avoid the reproduction of settler-colonial and White supremacist logics that pit marginalized groups against each other yet still recognizing that the experience of marginalization may look dissimilar across diversely identifying and looking groups and persons. By grounding the analysis of Taíno/Boricua identifcation in their experiences and drawing on other recent research on race and racialization in Puerto Rico, my work acknowledges the heterogeneous experiences of oppression held by differently colored, knowing, trajectoried, and identifying Puerto Rican social actors despite their sharing of a similar national discursive and ideological environment and context. In this recognition of heterogeneity—sometimes cacophonic and dissonant, other times more harmonious—I attempt to make sense of the pressures to conform to discourses that rely on Taíno extinction. I try to show how these pressures may have emerged from the power dynamics established by settler-colonial frames and logics of suppression—that is, singular narratives and modes of knowing often written by and for the benefit of those with economic and political wherewithal (Bourdieu 1999; Trouillot 1995; Foucault 1980). The power in such discourses and the narratives they facilitate lies in their ability to define what is and is not knowable and experienceable and, importantly, in their ability to define political and economic futures. For the Taíno/Boricua, defining their futures often involved readjusting peoples' expectations regarding Taíno/Boricua histories of survival over multiple interactions and encounters. Thus attention to "intertextual misunderstanding and heterogeneity" in these encounters revealed the interactional work involved in constituting (or not) Taíno/Boricua sociocultural communities and political possibilities (Nevins 2010, 5).

Feminist theory's attention to temporality has also influenced my approach to identity. To examine the forms of endurance and resilience that preceded the more explicit forms of resistance and struggle that the Taíno/Boricua have engaged in over the past centuries and decades, I draw on the work of feminist philosopher Elizabeth A. Grosz and sociocultural anthropologist Elizabeth A. Povinelli. Grosz's attention to the temporal dimensions that ground ontological and epistemological theories moves analytical approaches of subjective experience away from being to becoming. The notion of becoming stresses chance, randomness, open-endedness, multiplicity, and the potential for future selves and political forms. Grosz's concept of chance is grounded in a recognition of the multiplicity of causal-like events and the complexity of their effects, each with their own temporal continuities and entanglements that may be separate from their own "causes" and "effects" (1999, 4). By showing how the temporal ontologies of becoming are based in the multiple aspects and complex dynamics of chance, Grosz moves away from privileging predictability and stability in our notions of truth—of what is—to highlighting the importance of the many visions of what might be and become.

Povinelli argues for a move toward not just an ontology but a sociology of potentiality. In *Economies of Abandonment*, she offers a framework for the analysis of "social projects that attempt to capacitate an alternative set of human and posthuman worlds" (2011, 7). In this context, social projects are understood as emerging from any number of potential forces, often in social spaces that are not recognized, acknowledged, or valued within the current political framework—spaces of abandonment. These social spaces are maintained not through support from the state but in spite of it, often out of its view. Povinelli wonders, What is demanded of those who seek "alternative forms of life in the gale force of curtailing social winds" (10)? How do potential social projects endure? In the case of the Taíno, what events, however small or unwritten, have prompted them to make claims on the state and coalesce into a social project with an alternative view of the potential futures that are possible? What happens when they become sufficiently acknowledged so as to necessitate more explicit forms of resistance, and how do they negotiate recognition on their terms? Philosopher Alphonso Lingis highlights the "liberating futurity" of defiant political struggle, which does not rely on actual lived outcomes but instead strives toward a future where the struggle "has produced more than was ever foreseeable" (Grosz 1999, 10).

For the Taíno/Boricua, their endurance and their vision of a future are grounded in alternative trajectories, logics, and ways of knowing, which have often been couched within and illegible to more widespread discourses of the Puerto Rican nation. Their claimed experiences and filial trajectories as Taíno/Boricua have often been positioned as ignorant and confused. Borrowing again from Povinelli, the concept of social tense is useful for investigating how different groups and populations become temporally placed while considering the timing and potentiality of their temporality—that is, in understanding the limits and potential "when" of a population (see also Rosa 2016). In this grammar of time, the Taíno/Boricua and their actions are often situated in the preterit perfect in mainstream narratives of Puerto Rico, with an irrealis mood in the current era. That is, they are not only located in the past but also considered to have been completed in the past, with no place in the present or future. For the Taíno/Boricua, the temporality of their social action is in the present tense, connected to the past, and with clear hopes for the future. They have been, they are, and they will be. It is from this position that Taíno/Boricua agencies can be grounded and understood.

Drawing on this approach to temporality and time, the book considers different ways of knowing and making sense of the relationships between events and trajectories and the temporal logics that undergird Taíno/Boricua subjectivity and political action and their influence on Taíno/Boricua ontological experiences. I use the concept of epistemologies of possibility to highlight the ways of knowing that circulate among many Taíno/Boricua and are grounded in the possibility of other kinds of political futures. An attention to ways of knowing and modes of becoming helps analytically move away from static conceptions of the relationship among the past, present, and future grounded in a singular truth to instead conceptualize such claims as demands over the future trajectories of Taíno/Boricua and, more generally, Puerto Rican political and social action. This book thus looks at how ideologies of language and discourses of belonging are grounded in different epistemes of the possible. The theories of knowledge that frame and generate Taíno/Boricua acts of linguistic and cultural reclamation are traced, analyzed, and compared to highlight rather than foreclose the possibilities inherent to their undertaking. A study of Taíno/Boricua forms of mobilization underlines how debates about identity and identity-building projects are not just about identity claims but also about the theories, frameworks, and vehicles that define what is known and knowable and how to interpret such knowledge to construct genealogical belongings in the past, the present, and the future.

In this way, this project is grounded in the possibility of multiple interpretations of the past and the present in ways that are sometimes incoherent to one another and that may materialize in different visions and possibilities for the future. And in a multiply colonized context like Puerto Rico, the vectors of power that push toward certain narratives are also complex. What may be framed as liberating in one context may be oppressive in another. Furthermore, if chance and contingency are key aspects of social, cultural, and political life, how do positions congeal and agree?

Interactional and Institutional Recalibrations

In her work on Kaska language revitalization in the Yukon, Barbra Meek considers how social reproduction and structures materialize from otherwise contingent and disrupted situations. Meek further argues that incongruities in interactional schema and the frames, ideologies, discourses, and concomitant interactional disjunctures they precipitate "create opportunities for re-setting patterns, for re-schematizing some system of semiotic value, for transforming everyday communicative practices and expectations" (2012, 95). I connect this insight to the historical and ideological processes of erasure, silencing, and trivialization that have led to such inconsistencies. Likewise, Meek addresses how social structures and social reproduction materialize through socialized practices of extrapolation that erase moments of disjuncture and disruption in language socialization and interaction. From this perspective, moments of disjuncture are essential to understanding the complicated role of interaction and social practice in the surfacing of new conversational styles and routines—and, I argue, to the negotiation of emergent identities and histories. A focus on how ambiguities, incongruities, and disjunctures are managed lends insight into the role of enregisterment in regimenting or interrupting texts and discourses, which, in turn, illuminates how particular modalities of power are exercised (Agha 2005; Gal 2005; Irvine 2005; Meek 2012). Attention to ideologies of origin (Woolard 2002; Gal and Woolard 1995), the deployment of histories and genealogies of language (Inoue 2002; Irvine 2008), and the reconstruction and study of linguistic and sociocultural trajectories (Errington 2001; Irvine 2004; Philips 2004; Silverstein and Urban 1996) help disentangle how acts of ethnic and linguistic reclamation (re)construct genealogies of origin in order to legitimate efforts and, in turn, how such genealogies direct future trajectories of social action.

In terms of the materialization of particular ethnic alignments in interaction, I am influenced by Mary Bucholtz and Kira Hall's (2005) understanding of social identity. They argue that identity as a social category needs to be understood as an interactional achievement that can mark practices and people as similar to some and differentiated from others. This is accomplished through what they call the interpersonal tactics of identity, a series of meaningful practices and processes that serve to establish resemblances or distinctions, to authenticate or denaturalize social positions, and to authorize or make illegitimate particular forms of social action. Through this focus, identity is understood as an element of interactional situations, compelling us to analyze subject positions as always socially and culturally located. Thus social actors manufacture ethnic identities that materialize as forms of related-ness that rely on the constant managing of discursive alignments in interaction.

For the Taíno/Boricua, producing the discursive alignments needed to ground a recognizable identity depends on the recapture and resocialization of Indigenous concepts, figures, and practices. Analyses of interactions among Taíno/Boricua activists reveal the linguistic practices involved in constructing social alignments and relatedness more generally. Language, as it concerns how people talk and explicitly configure it as a medium of interactions and symbolic resistance, is a key site for understanding identity, belonging, and differentiation. By thinking of building a shared Taíno/Boricua ethnic identification as creating forms of related-ness among social actors, I link the cohesion that ethnic identifi-cation entails with the variable levels of unity and disunity it may allow for in practice (see Nash 2005). This project, though focused on Taíno resurgence, applies to any context in which people rede-fine themselves by reconfiguring their relatedness to each other via institutionalizing or de-regimenting different modes of belonging. Considering the linguistic aspects of these processes, I account for the sorts of disruptions to which any such project of identity reconfiguration is susceptible: historical disruptions, considering Puerto Rico's colonial histories; political disruptions, given the growing acknowledgment of Indigenous rights; and interactional disruptions, especially in terms of the potential misunderstand-ings to which all interactions—locally or globally—are vulnerable. The next section explores how the project of constructing Puerto Ricanness has set up the frameworks and criteria of evaluation that impact how family histories and ideas about the Taíno became framed and made commonplace in Puerto Rico.

2

Historical Discourses and Debates about Puerto Rico's Indigenous Trajectory

The Taínos of the Caribbean islands are extinct.
—Anthony M. Stevens-Arroyo, *The Cave of the Jagua*

These so-called Taínos maintain an attitude of supremacy over the other Puerto Ricans. They consider themselves the only authentic "Boricuas." They want to be conceded privileges and prerogatives that would be denied to everyone else. They assume an attitude of rejection and confrontation toward those who, with valid reasons, do not recognize their allegations of "ancestral Taíno heritage." ... We cannot, nor should we, recognize what they are not, nor give legitimacy to a claim that has no foundation.
—Teresa Tió, director of the Instituto de Cultura Puertorriqueña, July 2005 (Kuilán-Torres 2005)

Our very surroundings—the foods with which we grew up; our house a bohío [hut] of straw, shrubbery, and yagua [large leaf of a type autochthonous tree]; the containers in which we took our food—spoke to me more of the Taíno Indians and of the Blacks than of the Spanish.
—Tina Casanova (Rodríguez 2005)

I looked out of Yarey's car window, terrified of the steep drop off the mountain road that connected the two municipalities, Yabucoa and Maunabo, where we did most of our research. But in spite of my fear, I was amazed by the view. Though I had grown up in Puerto Rico, I hadn't spent much time in this part of the island, and the scenery felt at once both foreign and familiar. The view was amazing because it was breathtaking but also because it was a reminder that this island, which felt so much like home—so known, and often so small—could still hold surprises and revelations. In some ways, my encounters with the Taíno/Boricua often resonated with that same sensation of surprise. The people I encountered throughout my research did not necessarily stand out from any other Puerto Ricans I had met throughout my life on the island. But as I got to know them, I was often astonished to find that in a place where most people I knew had converged on an overlapping version of shared historical events, of our historical memory—often regardless of their political partisanship, socio-economic view, or racialized positioning in society—the Taíno/Boricua I encountered had such a radically different sense of the island's history.

Though I did not have a driver's license throughout my research (and still hate to drive), I spent a lot of time in transit. Yarey would pick me up from my apartment in Río Piedras to drive to Yabucoa and Maunabo, or sometimes Comerío. I would take the *tren urbano* to Bayamón to meet Yarey or Abuela Shashira. I would get on public cars from the Río Piedras station to Trujillo Alto to meet Anaca and to Las Piedras to meet Tuján. I would drive with the abuela to Jácanas in Ponce or to el Museo del Cemí in Jayuya. My brother would drive me from my parents' house in San Sebastián to Camuy to meet with Tito, who would in turn drive me throughout the Guajataca region to meet the campesinos who were not a part of any organization but were proud to call themselves indios. My then boyfriend (now husband), Jonathan, would take me to Ponce and Orocovis to meet with people and groups whom I would recruit into my research. In contrast to my childhood memories of being in cars to see family or go shopping, these drives did not feel repetitive or known. Somehow, as I traversed Puerto Rico during my research with the Taíno/Boricua, the landscape of the island became renewed and (re)knowable.

On one occasion, as we crossed the Puente del Indio in Vega Baja, the abuela told me the story behind the name. She explained how the remains of Taíno were found underneath the bridge, and she expressed frustration that she had no say in the process of their exhumation as the bridge was built. On another occasion, Yarey and I stopped in Comerío and ended up walking through the *campo*, led by a man with a machete, to a cave filled with Taíno petroglyphs. With Tito, I often found myself riding down unmarked roads that led to small wooden homes with slatted floors, the kind that are often represented in nostalgic images of a preindustrial Puerto Rico, except these were inhabited and full of contemporary life—TVs, electric stoves, refrigerators, and modern furniture. With Tuján, I walked through many a forest, layered with the mysticism and sense of the supernatural that he seemed to feel everywhere. During my years among the Taíno/Boricua, I learned to accept this feeling of my island as at once known and foreign, small but also heterogeneous, almost cacophonous in the different ways people had come to know and to sense this place and their place within it.

As I traveled over those roads—winding and steep, long and flat, hillside and oceanside—experiencing them anew, I began to question all my preconceived notions about the island and its diverse inhabitants. Did I hold stereotypes that erased the knowledge, values, trajectories, and potential of the people I encountered on my travels? And to what extent did previous work on the Taíno/Boricua also reflect racial scripts rather than the Taíno/Boricua lived experience? In this chapter, I try to set aside those scripts and stereotypes to explore the Taíno/Boricua through the histories they construct, the trajectories and values they claim, and the ways of knowing through which they frame their experience of the island.

Discrepant Historical Threads

To disentangle the historical threads that have led some to claim that the Taíno/Boricua are long extinct and others to claim the opposite, I consider the different narratives of Puerto Rican history that inform each position and explore how particular versions of Puerto Rican history became dominant—the established scripts from which "common-sense" notions of history became conventionalized. Publicly circulating denials of Taíno/Boricua survivals have not succeeded in extinguishing Taíno/Boricua activists' claims, though they have impeded Taíno/Boricua access to institutional resources and forms of sovereignty. Instead, Taíno/Boricua activists' historical claims often exist alongside, crosscut, or stand in opposition to the more widely circulating versions of Puerto Rican history concerning their survival. I want to focus on each version of Puerto Rican history as the product of different trajectories that coexist on asymmetrically authorized terms.

To this end, I examine how Taíno/Boricua activists and others recount memories of their Indigenous upbringing, and I contrast their narratives with more conventional interpretations of Puerto Rican events and figures. Many of the Taíno/Boricua activists I interviewed considered more broadly circulating historical accounts too distant and too broad to tell the island's stories. The reminiscences shared by many Taíno/Boricua activists interrupted and expanded those standard narratives. Drawing on linguistic anthropologist Barbra Meek, I consider Taíno/Boricua sociocultural reclamation as a process that, like language revitalization, "attempts to repair the rips and tears, the disjunctures, resulting from an enduring colonial history focused on termination" (2012).[1] For my Indigenous research consultants, such repairs depended on sharing their own recollections and, in doing so, potentially reconfiguring expectations and representations of Puerto Rican histories. My analysis of Taíno/Boricua efforts to renovate Puerto Rican history requires a consideration of the role of memory and politics in the construction and contestation of past discourses, of the spaces that remain when nation-level processes of erasure take place, and of how sign relations embedded in local cultural categories and accounts become maintained in such spaces. This chapter examines how layers of colonial rule and midcentury attempts to establish Puerto Rico as a nation in a colonial context reinscribed the extinction narrative.

When reading historical documents and collecting oral histories, the ambiguities and incongruities involved in the story of Taíno/Boricua survival become clear. For example, some of the records I discuss throughout this chapter mention a native population and some do not. When a native population *is* mentioned, it is with immensely ambiguous terms whose referents differs from author to author. This vagueness has been compounded by contemporary readings of historical terms, which often vary according to each reader's understanding of Puerto Rican trajectories. Given the incongruity of accounts of Puerto Rican histories throughout my fieldwork, and especially the personal nature of many of the oral recollections shared by Taíno/Boricua, attempting to reconcile the accounts presented a challenge. Rather than try to resolve the dissonance, I approached the sources that informed my present-day research collaborators' understandings of their personal histories as part of a contested, ambiguous, and incongruous discursive formation—as heterogeneous constellations of discourse (Mannheim 1998; Philips 2004). I put the Taíno/Boricua case in conversation with other settler-colonial narratives, including some from the United States and Australia, to consider the ways that collective histories of settler nationhood erase Indigenous groups' ability to establish their own rights to lands (Collins 2014 [1998]; Dippie 1982; Fitzgerald 2007; O'Brien 2010).

As in other settler-colonial contexts (Dippie 1982; O'Brien 2010), I ask what the silencing and erasure of Indigenous voices have accomplished for nation building in Puerto Rico. Shona Jackson argues that it is the relationship into which Blacks and Indigenous peoples "are placed under colonialism that is definitive for Caribbean modernity" (2012, 5). Settler-colonial narratives render unimaginable the complex and contemporaneous colonial relationships of Blackness and Indigeneity. The settler-colonial assumption that the Indigenous genocide was complete, that the Taíno were replaced by enslaved Africans, has impacted the subjectivities understood to be possible for non-European populations. However, while the accounts of Puerto Rican history that erase the Taíno/ Boricua have been hegemonic on the island, they have not been successful at silencing Taíno/Boricua recollections in every respect. The processes involved in homogenizing historical narratives are always partial, positioned, and problematic (Benítez-Rojo 1996). My attention to Puerto Rico's colonial histories in the context of the resurgence of the Taíno/Boricua movement complements discussions that take place at the juncture between history and social practices, with attention to how alternative narratives configure different sets of social and genealogical relationships (Asad 1991; Chatterjee 1993; Dirlik 1996; Kenny 1999; Stoler 2008; Trouillot 1995). By contrasting widespread historical narratives with the Taíno/Boricua recollections I encountered throughout my field research, I clarify the spaces for reschematization that remain and within which many Taíno/Boricua activists respond to discourses that endeavor to erase them.

Whose History? Conventional Narrations of the Taíno and the Nation

In conventional histories of Puerto Rico, the designation of Taíno is often reserved for the aboriginal inhabitants of Puerto Rico prior to Spanish conquest and colonization. In these histories, Taíno political, social, and cultural organization was largely decimated in the early sixteenth century through warfare, disease, slavery, and assimilation (Alegría 1969; Picó 1986; Scarano 1993). Presumed extinct, the Taíno are often discussed either in terms of their material culture, a matter to be discussed by archaeologists (Curet 1992; Keegan and Carlson 2010; Rouse 1993), or in their role as distant ancestors of all Puerto Ricans (Gómez Acevedo and Ballesteros Gaibrois 1978, 1993). Such assumptions are encapsulated in a passage I found in an elementary school workbook:

> Hasta aquí hemos narrado la historia del origen, costumbres, creencias y forma de vida de un pueblo sencillo, pacífico y amante de la naturaleza. Con la llegada de los exploradores españoles a

Boriquén en 1493 y el comienzo de la conquista por Juan Ponce de León a partir de 1508 la vida del pueblo taíno es trastocada. El descubrimiento para ellos significó enfermedades, la pérdida de la libertad o de la vida y su eventual exterminio como pueblo. Pero su herencia permanece viva en el puertorriqueño y cada día descubrimos nuevas evidencias que así lo confirman. (Colón Peña 2001, 22)

Up to this point, we have narrated the origin, customs, beliefs, and form of life of a simple, peaceful, and nature-loving people. With the arrival of the Spanish explorers to Boriquén in 1493 and Juan Ponce de León's conquest beginning in 1508, the life of the Taíno people is disrupted. The discovery for them meant illnesses, the loss of liberty or life, and their eventual extermination as a people. But their heritage remains alive in the Puerto Rican, and each day we find new evidence that confirms it is so.

In 1509, Spain authorized Ponce de León to partition and distribute the Taíno among Spanish officials under the *encomienda* system with the expectation that they pan rivers for gold and work in agriculture. As taught in the schoolbooks of my youth and of today, in 1511, the Taíno drowned Spaniard Diego Salcedo as he tried to cross the Guaorabo River. After discovering that the Spanish were mortal, the Taíno battled the invaders in what is known as the Taíno rebellion of 1511 (Fernández Méndez 1976, 1995a, 1995b; Stevens-Arroyo 2006). The Taíno were largely unsuccessful, and Spanish pacification of the island took the shape of the further enslavement of the remaining Indigenous population.

The Spanish priest Bartolomé de las Casas interrupted the explicit enslavement of the Indigenous populations in the Spanish Americas. His description of the treatment of Indigenous populations, published in 1552 as "A Short Account of the Destruction of the Indies," was influential in Spain's passage of the New Laws of 1542, which abolished the encomienda system of Indigenous slavery in the Spanish colonies. According to the statute, the partition and distribution of the Taíno were no longer legal. Whether

diminished through migration to other islands, genocide, or flee-
ing and hiding in the mountainous region of the island, the population of Taíno that might have survived in Puerto Rico after
these events remains unclear and is still debated among historians.
What is evident from the archival record is that at this point, there
is an explicit shift in the discourse about Taíno survival that might
have reflected the colonizers' inability to continue using the Taíno
as unpaid labor, either due to the change in the legal framework
or because they were unable to find them. Additionally, during the
sixteenth century, the number of enslaved Africans on the island
was relatively low, so sources of forced labor were diminished
overall. Consider the following excerpt from a 1582 letter from Sir
Captain Jhoan Melgarejo, then governor of the island, to King
Felipe II of Spain:

> Cessó esta grangería respeto de acabarse los yndios y de encar-
> ecerse los negros . . . y si su majestad hiziese merced de mandar
> a esta isla myl negros y venderlos a los vezinos, en muy breve
> tiempo se le pagarán y los vezinos quedarán ricos y las Reales
> rentas se aumentarían en gran manera. (Fernández Méndez
> 1995a, 126)

> This profit source ceased because the Indians were finished and
> the Blacks were scarce . . . and if your majesty did the mercy
> of sending to the island one thousand Blacks and sold them to
> the residents, in very little time it will be paid, and the residents
> would be rich, and the Royal rents would greatly increase.

Melgarejo casually mentions that the Indians were "finished" in the
context of asking the king for more enslaved African labor so that
the Spanish residents of the island, and the king himself, might
profit from gold in the rivers. This request was echoed in a 1644
letter from the bishop of Puerto Rico to an official of the Council
of the Indies, the administrative arm of the Spanish kingdom in
the Indies, requesting more labor to exploit the island's resources:

Así mismo hay en la Isla grandes minas de oro, cristal y cobre, que no se benefician por haber faltado los indios naturales. (178)

In this way, there are on the Island great gold, crystal, and copper mines that do not benefit for lacking the natural Indians.

What exactly were these missives to Spain communicating about the native population of the island? Was Indian labor "finished," or had the people succumbed to the ravages of disease, warfare, and enslavement? And if the aim of these colonial officials' correspondence was to encourage the crown to send enslaved Africans to the island, wouldn't they have been inclined to downplay the Indigenous population regardless of its actual size?

Censuses during the Spanish colonial period are no more helpful in determining the actual Indigenous population. Indigenous populations were noted in Puerto Rico's census of 1777 (1,756 indios) and 1787 (2,032 indios; Brau 1983 [1917]; Fernández Méndez 1995), but it is unclear who would have been counted as an indio (O. Wagenheim 1998) by census takers. There was also the distinct possibility that some Indians did not want to be counted (Castanha 2004). As author Stan Steiner writes, "A man hiding in the hills from the swords of the Conquistadors was not likely to report his wife and his children to the census taker" (1974, 16).

According to Puerto Rican historian Loida Figueroa, "Our country's natives seem to have been typed as Indians until the beginning of the nineteenth century when Governor don Toribio Montes, faced with the difficulty of fixing ethnic origins, banded all the non-Whites together under the title of free colored people (pardos)" (1971, 59). In fact, the term *pardos* was already being used by brigadier general Alexander O'Reilly in 1765, when he was sent by King Carlos III of Spain to assess the state of Puerto Rico's defenses. His census included separate categories for "blancos" (Whites), "pardos," "morenos libres" (free Blacks), and "esclavos" (slaves) (Fernández Méndez 1995a, 251). He wrote,

Los blancos ninguna repugnancia hallan en estar mezclados con los pardos. Todos los pueblos a excepción de Puerto Rico, no tienen de vivientes de continuo que el Cura, los demás existen siempre en el campo a excepción de todos los domingos que los inmediatos a la Iglesia acuden a Misa, y los tres días de Pascua en que concurren todos los feligreses generalmente. Para aquellos días tienen unas casas que parecen palomares, fabricadas sobre pilares de madera con vigas y tablas. (242)

The Whites are not repulsed at being mixed with the pardos. All the towns with the exception of Puerto Rico [the then name of the municipality of San Juan] do not have houses near the church; the rest are always in the countryside with the exception of every Sunday, when those near the church go to Mass, and the three days of Easter, when all the faithful generally go. For those days, they have some homes that look like pigeon lofts, fabricated over wooden piers with beams and boards.

Many Taíno/Boricua activists interpret this description of pardos as describing Taíno/Boricua homes and practices and supporting their assertion that many Indigenous people stayed far from the centers of government and economy. They draw on such readings to debate the history of the Taíno/Boricua during and beyond the postencomienda period.

Whose History? Less Conventional Historical Tellings

El verdadero genocidio es decir que no existimos, que estamos extintos. ¿No ven que estoy aquí? ¿Que no he muerto?

The true genocide is to say that we do not exist, that we are extinct. Do they not see that I am here? That I have not died?
—Katsí, interviewed August 2008

The Taíno/Boricua activists I worked with were suspicious of written histories. Their skepticism stemmed from several convictions:

that mainstream historians had no knowledge of the existence of an Indigenous population, that they might have knowledge of Indigenous populations but also have a vested interest in not including Indigenous voices in their narratives, and that Taíno/ Boricua voices may have been excluded because they had not yet organized or articulated themselves as Indigenous.[2] Juan Manuel Delgado, a Puerto Rican oral historian, responds to what he considers to be the denials of Taíno survival by most historians:

Tomaron al pie de la letra cada información, cada opinión, cada especulación, cada censo de almas; tomaron todo lo dicho sin cuestionamiento de clase alguna, sin una actitud crítica ante lo que el conquistador escribió sobre el papel. En cierta medida estos historiadores enterraron a los indios. . . . Entonces, ¿dónde podemos encontrar esa historia parte del rompecabeza de esa historia que es nuestra y que nos sirve para contrarrestar la versión oficial? La respuesta es sencilla, la podemos encontrar en la historia oral, en la historia narrada por nuestra propia gente. (1977, 41)

They took each piece of information, each opinion, each speculation, each census of souls literally; they took all that was said without any kind of question, without a critical attitude to what the conquistador wrote on paper. By some measures, these historians buried the Indians. . . . Then where can we find that history or part of the puzzle of that history that is ours and that serves us to counter the official version? The answer is simple: we can find it in the oral history, in the history narrated by our own people.

The Taíno/Boricua claim that institutionalized renderings of history erase their actual survival. This survival, they argue, was facilitated through religious, historical, and cultural knowledge and cosmologies passed through oral histories and ceremonial practices in Taíno/Boricua families. They maintain that this knowledge was kept secret due to the possible political and social consequences of asserting an Indigenous background. When I asked what these consequences might have been, they explained that their families feared being separated, killed, and enslaved, so they moved to the mountains and far reaches of the island after the abolition of the encomienda system in the sixteenth century. While not completely isolated from other Puerto Ricans, they were able, they argued, to maintain certain practices and beliefs along with their sense of being Indigenous.

This version of Taíno/Boricua history in Puerto Rico has been most thoroughly expounded in a book by native Boricua activist-scholar Anthony Castanha (2011).[3] The description of Taíno/Boricua survival into the present found in Castanha's work often echoes and agrees with many of my research collaborators. Taíno/Boricua survival from genocide, they argue, was aided by the topography of the island and the location of government centers away from the island's mountainous interior, which led to the colloquial name for these areas: Las Indieras (the place of the Indians; see also Steiner 1974). Though now Las Indieras refers to a section of the Maricao municipality in the midwestern region of the island, Castanha and other Taíno/Boricua activists contend that in the recent past, it referred to the totality of the central mountainous region of the island, which the Taíno/Boricua think explains the large population of people with Indigenous phenotypical features in this area, along with the high concentration of people who continue to make Indigenous foods, the somewhat higher use of Taíno/Boricua-derived vocabulary, and other practices often associated with Taíno/Boricua culture. They cite as additional evidence the fact that few towns in Puerto Rico were founded during the sixteenth and seventeenth centuries, and most towns were not founded until the late eighteenth through the nineteenth centuries: "Many fled to mountain regions where Indian people had already been living for hundreds if not thousands of years in the yucayekes of, for example, Guama, Otoao, Coabey, Jatibonico, Guaynabo, Turabo and Cayeco" (Castanha 2008).

Las Indieras was often cited by many Taíno/Boricua as a stronghold of Taíno/Boricua Indian presence in Puerto Rico; it was understood as the place where the Taíno/Boricua organized their lives—hidden away, at least for a while (Castanha 2011; Fernández

Méndez 1976; Steiner 1974). In a 1977 newspaper article called "¿Dónde están nuestros indios?" (Where are our Indians?) Juan Manuel Delgado reveals that in oral narratives, elders corroborated that there were still people who were understood to be and classified as Indian in the nineteenth century, many of whom lived in Las Indieras. Activists drew from these histories when they spoke to me about Taíno/Boricua survival. These trajectories and narratives are also subject to critique, and they are told alongside—and sometimes in contradiction to—more conventional ones. For example, in an interview conducted in a rural setting on the island, an elder Indigenous activist and leader (who I will discuss in more depth in chapter 3), Tito, noted,

> Tú dices, "¡Caramba! Este hombre es extraordinariamente inteligente. ¿Por qué se salió? ¿Por qué no tiene chavos pa' ir pa' la escuela?" No . . . en la escuela había comida, un atractivo. Las escuelas, son un sistema de colonización . . . cuando Estados Unidos entro aquí, le dijo a las mamás, "Les podemos dar escuela a tus nenes, pero no me los traigas con la ropa indígena. Toma 'Army Surplus' ropa sobrante del ejército de los gringos. Vístemelos así entonces yo te les doy escuela."

> You say, "Darn! This man is extraordinarily intelligent. Why did he leave? Because he didn't have money to go to school?" No . . . at school there was food, an attraction. The schools are a colonization system . . . when the United States entered here, they said to the mothers, "We can give school to your kids, but don't bring them with the Indigenous clothing. Take 'Army Surplus' clothes remaining from the gringo army. Dress them up this way for me, and then I will give them school."

Tito articulates a theory that schools, as institutions of the state, worked to erase Indigenous knowledge and self-awareness among Puerto Ricans. By positing schools as colonization systems and positioning himself as someone who rejected schooling, he establishes that his awareness as an Indigenous person was never colonized and that he is, therefore, an authoritative, legitimate, and authentic source of Indigenous histories.

Prophetic Sources of Knowledge

Taíno/Boricua forms of knowing are not solely grounded in personal memory or family histories. Some Taíno/Boricua social actors, though not all, substantiate their claims through spiritual forms of knowing. The circulation of the prophecy of Aura Surey was key for how many self-identified Taíno understood Indigenous silences in the historical record and how they positioned their own roles as historical actors (Feliciano-Santos 2017). I was introduced to *la profecía*, as people call it, by three different Taíno-identifying groups: the Liga Guakía Taína-ké (LGTK), the Consejo General de Taínos (CGT), and the Guaka-Kú (GK), who understand it as a more accurate source for understanding Taíno survival and reemergence than conventional histories. La profecía lends Taíno activists a different framework through which to interpret the historical silences on the Taíno—not as extinction but as being in hiding and as survival. The wording of the prophecy is understood to reflect the language of Aura Surey, as mediated by a Taíno spiritual leader, Margarita Nogueras Vidal. Margarita is bilingual, and she self-published the prophecy in both Spanish and English, from which the following is quoted verbatim:

> If you have chosen to read this, the energy of Aura Surey (Morning Star, Venus) is calling upon you to reflect and to see your true essence as one that is connected with the totality of creation. You, I and all are connected to the "drama" of the past and the future which is embodied in the Present. . . .
>
> Aura Surey in the Indigenous Tradition of Boriké is Morning Star in our Ancestral Language. According to oral tradition Aura Surey is considered to be part of our past. It was through this essence that prophecy was decreed to come [to] pass in the twenty fourth generation of the descendants of this Land. . . .

This message arose from the heart of the Mother of Creation and has been birthed into the timeless sphere of body, Mind and Spirit to rekindle the flame of the "Awakening" of Boriké and their descendents thereof.[4]

Communicated by an elder spirit who was seen as a "truer" source of knowledge about the Taíno, the prophecy foments distrust of the historical record and functions as a different Taíno epistemology that grounds knowledge not in the historical record but in spirituality. Sociocultural anthropologists Robin Wright and Jonathan Hill note how nineteenth-century millenarian movements in the Northwest Amazon "became elevated to a sacred cosmological postulate" that refused "to cooperate with the external, dominating order of the white men" (1986, 31). Prophecy allows people to position their Taíno identity and agency not in a bygone past but in the current moment; not in an external order but in their beliefs and ways of knowing.

The prophecy works as an interpretive frame through which to understand contemporary events—as the result of a greater spiritual energy that animated all the Taíno, whether they were aware of being Taíno or not. Part of the process of recognizing oneself as Taíno within the LGTK, the General Council of Taíno (CGT), and GK is to learn how to identify spiritual cues in one's daily life. The identification and analysis of personal spiritual cues could then lend further insight into la profecía's inner workings, into one's own role in the Taíno reemergence, and into the how and when of Taíno future paths.

The prophecy of Aura Surey is only one notable example; in general, many Taíno/Boricua place authority and legitimacy, and seek to understand and buttress their own identity, in spiritual and filial forms of knowing—a grandmother's memories or practices, a communication from a spirit—rather than in academic theory and products.

Although the survival of Taíno/Boricua people is debated in Puerto Rico, the survival of Taíno practices is widely accepted and even celebrated. These range from domestic practices like cooking and gardening/farming to the use of many Taíno-derived words in contemporary Spanish (and English). This Indigenous heritage was even highlighted in a film created and disseminated by the Division of Community Education (DIVEDCO), *La buena herencia* (Tirado 1967), in which Taíno practices are cited as part of Puerto Rico's so-called good heritage:

> Con cada nuevo día, con cada nuevo sol tibio y purpura, una misma pregunta repetida de siglos: ¿qué somos? ¿quiénes somos? ¿dónde hallar nuestra raíz y nuestra sabia [*sic*]?

> With each new day, with each new warm and purple sun, one same question is repeated over centuries: What are we? Who are we? Where do we find our root and wisdom?

The film argues that although Taíno people no longer remain, they have left a legacy that all Puerto Ricans can claim as their own. These sorts of legacies are often promoted in the media. For example, in a 2008 segment titled "Herencia lengua taína," the host of *Boricuazo*—a popular news show that highlighted Puerto Rican contributions to science, culture, and the media—emphasized the Taíno legacy to the Spanish language as it is spoken today, including words from Taíno that have been totally incorporated into Spanish (and English), such as *jamaca* (*hamaca*/hammock), *juracán* (*huracán*/hurricane), *canoa* (*canoa*/canoe), and *cacique* (cacique/chieftain), among others. There are other Taíno words that are idiosyncratic to contemporary Caribbean Spanish: *macuto* (knapsack), *batey* (yard / ceremonial ground), *soberao* (ground of the home), and *bejuco* (vine).

The emphasis on Taíno as a shared inheritance whose source is located in the past is apparent in books geared toward teaching

42 A Contested Caribbean Indigeneity

Puerto Rican children about the Taíno, which root them firmly in the past tense. These books ask, "What kind of society did the Taínos have? What was their legacy toward our language? What were their religious beliefs?" (Muratti 2005). They also describe the Taíno as a common ancestor for all Puerto Ricans: "Vamos juntos a divertirnos y aprender sobre nuestros antepasados, los taínos" (Maldonado 2001 [1998]; Let's all have fun and learn about our ancestors, the Taíno). This focus on a common national heritage rather than a potential contemporary identification has been deployed in various versions of Puerto Rican nationalism, a practice that has been criticized by contemporary Taíno/Boricua groups and Puerto Rican scholars who note that the celebration of Taíno heritage often comes at the expense of trivializing the African legacies to the island.

Asserting Survival

I sat across from a Taíno elder at her kitchen table and asked how she knew she was Taíno. She had tears in her eyes as she answered:

> Listen and listen well. I don't think there are pure indios, and I know that the indios now have changed. The indios now are a mix of different things, but . . . the world has changed. When I was a just a baby, my mother died. Her sister, she took care of me, and she was my mother then. She said that she was an india, that my mother was an india, and that I was an india. She walked barefoot. My father, he was not any good, and he took me away from my mother and gave me to a wealthy family. I worked at a very wealthy family's home, and they would tell people that they adopted me, but really, they fed me less food than they fed their dogs. You know what it is that they feed better food to the dogs! That is why it is hard for me to read and write; I never did more than the third or fourth grade. It was because I was not like them; I was an india to them.[5]

How do we judge these stories against the officially sanctioned histories? Is being something based on the *feeling* of what it is to be something? Is it about a lived history or a consciousness of being something? Can one be something and not know it?

In the 1970s, historian Stan Steiner interviewed Ricardo Alegría, who has been lauded as the preeminent scholarly expert on Taíno culture and Puerto Rican anthropology. Alegría told Steiner that the Taíno people "disappeared as a cultural group in the first century of the Spanish conquest" and concluded, "Unfortunately, there are no more Indians on the island of Puerto Rico" (1974, 16). Steiner also interviewed a man named Don Pedro Matos Matos, who told him, "Our Indians did not die away the way you think. If you look in the faces of the jíbaros, you know somewhere the Indian history is living. . . . A man may not know he is Indian. A man may know and may not admit he is Indian. But it does not matter. The ignorance of your father and mother does not change who you are" (1974, 16).

In the next chapter, I consider the role of the archetypal Puerto Rican peasant figure of the Jíbaro in articulating, albeit problematically, both Taíno survival and Puerto Rican nationhood. Drawing on historical documents and analyses, I explore the ambiguities that emerge in constructing the Jíbaro as an icon of Puerto Ricanness and as a juncture of Indigenous continuity in Puerto Rico.

PART 2

The Puerto Rican Nation and Ethnoracial Regimes in Puerto Rico

3

Jíbaros and Jibaridades,
Ambiguities and Possibilities

The first time I heard someone called jíbaro, I was in the fourth grade. It was just after I had moved to San Sebastián from Chicago. "Tan jíbara ella siempre con esa ropa" (She is always so jíbara [adj.] with those clothes). It wasn't a compliment. But I was soon confronted with another image of the jíbaro—or rather, the Jíbaro—a celebrated figure meant to represent the nation, to instill pride. The jíbaros I knew looked nothing like the Jíbaros in our schoolbooks, and they were mocked instead of celebrated. This contradiction intrigued me. Was being a jíbaro supposed to be good or bad?

When Tito invited me to conduct research about his Indigenous community, he was careful to tell me that *Taíno* was not the correct term to describe his group. They were Jíbaro-Boricuas. Jíbaros, he explained, had been the true inheritors and maintainers of Indigenous ways. These jíbaros, Tito said, had nothing to do with the White peasant Jíbaro in our schoolbooks that became a national symbol. They were the multicolor jíbaros *pobres del campo*, who had a wealth of knowledge regarding the island's continuous Indigenous history. I made arrangements to meet Tito at his house, which was not that far from my parents' house in San Sebastián. He lived in a cozy wooden cottage on stilts, known in Puerto Rico as a *casa típica*, on the top of a hill in rural Camuy. His windows were wide open—no glass, but with shutters to keep out the rain. With a crosswind through the windows, there were no mosquitos or flies in Tito's house, and there were no couches, beds, chairs, or tables either—only hammocks. Tito lived out his image of an Indigenous Jíbaro-Boricua, a version of a jíbaro that my classmates might have recognized, though for Tito, the word was a badge of honor rather than a schoolyard slur.

Ambiguous Jibaridades

The concept of the jíbaro in Puerto Rico is rife with tension. Scholarly literature has often described the figure of the Jíbaro as a problematic archetype of Puerto Ricanness. For many of the activists I met, the jíbaro is an Indigenous figure, not just a national myth, and the Jíbaro archetype represents a folklorized appropriation of local Indigenous lives.

The accounts and recollections presented by my Indigenous research consultants and the travel writers discussed below obtain some of their argumentative force by drawing on what linguistic anthropologist Jane Hill calls "characteristic formulas" that "develop a small set of major rhetorical themes" (2002, 69). The mythologizing of Puerto Ricanness in terms of the Jíbaro archetype is one characteristic formula. The idea of the jíbaro as an Indigenous figure is another.

The lexical origin of the word is highly debated. Some argue that *jíbaro* is derived from ancient Castilian (*giba* [hump; arguably hill] + *ero* [man of] = *gíbaro* [man of the hills]; Roberts 1999). Others maintain that it was imported from the Spanish corruption of the name of the Shuar people in South America and then used to designate Puerto Rico's "savages" (Córdova 2005; Torres-Robles 1999; Scarano 1996, 1999), while others contend that it is an Indigenous Taíno term (Alvarez Nazario 1996). Debates about the origin of the word often go hand in hand with ideas about the ancestry of the people it describes.

An eighteenth-century painting depicting Spanish castes found in Mexico lends some insight. The Spanish caste system was used to sort, organize, and classify the results of what was understood as racial mixing, largely among Africans, Spanish, and Indigenous peoples in Spanish colonies. There were regional and temporal variations on the specific classifications, but it is not a stretch to imagine that the "Gíbaro" in figure 3.1 bears at least some relation to the Puerto Rican Jíbaro. The painting depicts the Gíbaro as the child of a "Lobo" with a "China." Both the Lobo and the China were understood as resulting from other "interracial" couplings. Within Spanish colonial understandings of race, the names given to each caste (or mixture) reveal the idea of what a person in that group might look like and their place in the racial hierarchy. For example, in the image below, castes two and three show how the child of a mestizo man and a Spanish woman, the "Castizo," could have a child with a Spanish person, and that child could be considered Spanish. Similarly, if someone like the Chino, a child of a Morisco (themselves the child of a *Mulato* and a Spanish person) and a Spanish person, had a child with an Indian person, that child would be a "Salta Atrás." Salta Atrás, or "jump back," refers to how these children were moving away from being considered Spanish and thus placed lower on the racial hierarchy and in the general social order. Terms like *Morisco* (Moorish) and *Chino* (Chinese) reveal how certain determinations of racial caste were made by virtue of what the imagined appearance of different forms racial mixture might be. In figure 3.2, I diagram the various combinations that were understood to result in a "Gíbaro" person.[1]

This classification points to *Gíbaro* as describing a person with Indigenous, Black, and Spanish backgrounds, a description that would generally be consistent with current racial ideologies of Puerto Ricans as a generally racially mixed population.[2] In early documentation of the term *Jíbaro* in Puerto Rico, the word was used to describe the island's rural inhabitants or peasantry, often highlighting what were perceived as the negative aspects of these populations.[3] For example, in a 1745 travel account by an anonymous source compiled by historian Manuel Moreno Alonso (not to be confused with writer Manuel A. Alonso), the Jíbaros are described as follows:

FIGURE 3.1. *Las Castas.* Casta painting containing complete set of sixteen casta combinations (racial classifications in Spanish colonies in the Americas), Anonymous, eighteenth century. Oil on canvas, 148 cm × 104 cm. Museo Nacional del Virreinato, Tepotzotlán, Mexico.

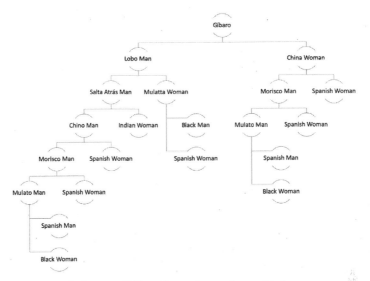

FIGURE 3.2. A diagram of Gíbaro lineage in accordance with the caste classification system in the eighteenth-century painting above.

Toda [Puerto Rico] está llena de intricadas arboledas, que fructifican plátanos, cocos, tamarintos, zapotes y otros semejantes, faltándola el principal, que es el pan, pues el que tienen aquellos infelices moradores, llamado casave, no es capaz comerles los europeos, y querían supliese los plátanos asados que ellos acostumbran comer. . . .

Los hombres llamados givaros [*sic*] son amulatados, y las hembras propiamente agitanadas; no traen éstas más ropas que camisa y guardapiés muy largos por su descalzas, gastando solo los zapatos para bailar el zapateado que es su estilo y lo hacen bizarramente. Yo noté la gran devoción que tienen a las ánimas los más de estos habitantes, prueba de ser buenos cristianos, manifestándola en que rrogavan [*sic*] y daban a por fía a los padres misioneros que venían en el navío, sus cortos bienes de limosna para que dijesen misas por ellas que me admiró bastante. Sus habitaciones son de quatro lados, y tablas que tienen dispersas entre las arboledas. (1983 [1745], 21, 37)

All [Puerto Rico] is full of intricate woods, that give fruit
to plantains, coconuts, tamarinds, sapotas, and other similar
[fruits], the most important thing was missing though, which
is the bread, as what those unfortunate inhabitants have, called
casabe, Europeans are not capable of eating, and wanted
to supply with the roasted plantains they are accustomed to
eating. . . .

The givaro men are mulatto-like, and the women properly
gypsy-like; they wear no clothes but shirts and long skirts as
they are barefoot, using their shoes only to dance the zapateado [rhythmic shoe dancing] that is their style, and they do
it bizarrely. I noted the great devotion they have for the souls
[in purgatory], proof of being good Christians, manifesting it
in that they pleaded and tenaciously gave the missionary fathers
that came in the ship their few goods as alms so they could
say mass for them, which caused me considerable admiration.
Their rooms are of four sides, and boards they have dispersed
in the woods.

This was the earliest account of Puerto Rico I found that mentions the Jíbaro population. They eat casabe, dance "bizarrely,"
and sleep in what are probably *bohíos*—all of which current
Taíno/Boricua activists claim are Indigenous practices. Other
eighteenth-century travel accounts also mention this peasantry, which according to Francisco A. Scarano (1999) was
probably already commonly known as Jíbaros. These reports
focus on the perceived indomitability, generosity, humility, and
laziness of the Jíbaros, which are enabled by the richness of
nature in Puerto Rico.[4] Their day-to-day customs are ascribed
to an Indigenous heritage, and depending on the writer, their
"racial" composition is depicted as either White, Indigenous,
or mulatto (Abbad y Lasierra 1959 [1778]; Ledru 2013 [1797]).[5]
In 1778, Benedictine monk Fray Iñigo Abbad y Lasierra published what is widely considered the earliest and most com-
prehensive history of Puerto Rico since 1493. He describes the

rural inhabitants of Puerto Rico—their homes, practices, and morality—extensively:

> Así como los [campesinos] habitantes de Puerto Rico han adquirido de los antiguos moradores de esta Isla la indolencia, frugalidad, desinterés, hospitalidad y otras circunstancias características de los Indios, han conservado igualmente mucho de sus usos y costumbres. La construcción e ideas de sus casas, su establecimiento y morada en los bosques, la vida sedentaria, la afición a las bebidas fuertes y espiritosas, la propensión a los bayles y otras inclinaciones, son comunes y propias a estos pueblos, sean contrahídas por el trato y unión mutua o por efectos propios del clima, o consecuencias naturales de ambas causas. (Fernández Méndez 1995a, 316)

> Just as the [rural] inhabitants of Puerto Rico have acquired from the former residents of this island their indolence, frugality, disinterest, hospitality, and other characteristic circumstances of the Indians, they have equally conserved many of their uses and customs. The construction and idea of their homes, their establishment and dwelling in the forests, the sedentary lifestyle, the inclination for strong and spirited drinks, the tendency toward dances and other inclinations, are common and proper to these people, be they contracted through their contacts or mutual union or by proper effect of the climate, or as natural consequences of both.

After describing the practices of the rural inhabitants of Puerto Rico, which had been adopted from the Indigenous *former* residents of the island, Abbad y Lasierra continues,

> Las casas que tiene hoy en la isla son generalmente de una misma construcción que la que usaban los Indios, ideadas según las circunstancias del país lo exigen, por el excesivo calor y abundancia de lluvias. . . . Su comodidad es muy poca; una sala que llaman soberado, y otra que sirve de dormitorio. . . . Por lo

común duermen en Amacas, colgadas entre los postes o vigas que sostienen el techo. Las camas, que llaman barbacoas son pocas e incomodas. . . . Algunos tures o silletes de cuero, y a falta de estos algún banquillo tosco, componen todos sus muebles. El menage de cocina no es muy ostentoso: una olla y algunas cazuela de barro basta para cocer la comida de qualquiera familia; los platos, cucharas, vasos, escudillas, y demas utensilios, los hacen de Higuera o fruta que da el árbol totumo. . . . Acostumbrados desde luego a conformarse con este uso de los indios, no han cuidado de utilizar el excelente barro que hay en muchas partes de la isla. (316–317)

The houses that they have today on the island are generally of the same construction that was used by the Indians, designed as the circumstances of the country called for, because of the excessive heat and the abundance of rains. . . . Their comforts are very little; a living room they call soberado, and another that serves as a bedroom. . . . Commonly they sleep in Amacas, hung between the posts or beams that support the roof. The beds, which they call barbacoas, are few and uncomfortable. . . . Some tures or leather chairs, and lacking these some rustic stool, compose all of their furniture. Their kitchen items are not very ostentatious: a pot and a clay casserole is enough to cook food for any family; the plates, spoons, cups, bowls, and other utensils, they make from gourds or the fruit the calabash tree gives. . . . Accustomed of course to be satisfied with this use by the Indians, they have not cared to use the excellent clay in many parts of the island.

The terms Abbad y Lasierra uses to describe the homes of Puerto Rican peasants—*soberado, amaca, barbacoa, ture*—are all widely considered to be derived from the Taíno language and are still currently in use in Puerto Rico. While Abbad y Lasierra does not use the term *jíbaro*, his description of the country folk fits with descriptions of jíbaros when it became a relatively common term in the late 1800s. In this excerpt, there is some ambiguity with respect to the source of such Indigenous knowledge, but it seems to indicate Abbad y Lasierra's understanding that the rural jíbaros adopted such practices from contact with the Taíno in the past. For example, in 1887, Dr. Francisco del Valle Atiles—renowned for his roles as a medical doctor, sociologist, and mayor of San Juan—wrote an extensive description of the jíbaro in "El campesino puertorriqueño: Condiciones intelectuales y morales," echoing themes in Abbad y Lasierra's earlier work:

> Ya el indio borincano construía más o menos como hoy construye el jíbaro; lo cual basta para hacernos evidente el pobre adelanto de éste, quien después de tres siglos, en nada ha mejorado las condiciones de la morada que servía a una raza incivil. . . . Podríamos añadir que quizá no fue la mejor de las casa borinqueñas la copiada por los conquistadores y sus descendientes . . . podemos deducir que los aborígenes construían mejores casas de las que pueden darnos idea la generalidad de los bohíos primitivos, aun imitados por el campesino de nuestros días (Valle Atiles 1995 [1887], 516).

> The borincano Indian already constructed [homes] more or less how the jíbaro builds today; which is enough to make evident their poor development, who after three centuries, have not at all improved the living conditions that served an uncivil race. . . . We could add that maybe it was not the best of the borinqueño homes that was copied by the conquerors and their descendants . . . we can deduce that the aboriginals built better homes than would be evident in the primitive bohíos, that are still imitated by the country folk of our day.

Del Valle Atiles discursively erases the possibility of Taíno survival by ascribing their ongoing practices to contact with jíbaros, who are understood as a separate "race." The jíbaro, here framed as the descendants of conquerors who adopted inferior home-building practices from the Taíno, is not understood as the descendant of the Taíno. The doctor continues,

Lo defectuoso de la casa del jíbaro coincide con un ornamento también pobrísimo del interior de ella. La hamaca, usada por el indio, y mueble indispensable al jíbaro, acaso algún lecho de tablas, y en raras ocasiones algo donde sentarse, es casi todo lo que en un bohío se encuentra. (516)

What is defective with the jíbaro house coincides with an also extremely impoverished ornamentation in its interior. The hammock, used by the Indian, and indispensable furnishing for the jíbaro, maybe some bed of boards, and in rare occasions something on which to sit, is almost all that you find in a bohío.

He continues to describe the defectiveness of the jíbaro in terms of their speech with a broad description of their phonetic patterns, their poor intellectual and moral development, and their musical proclivities (517), positioning the jíbaro within the trope of the noble savage. Racially, he describes the jíbaro as being descended from (sun-tanned) Europeans, Africans, or both. He does not mention the possibility that the Indigenous practices he observes among the people he calls jíbaro could indicate that they are, in fact, Indigenous Taíno peoples.

The description of the jíbaro or general rural folk as mixed, White, Black, pardo, or partially Indigenous varies depending on the authors and their goals. The groundwork for the term's racial ambiguity and later debates about who it designates was laid as early as the 1700s. Scarano notes the ambiguities inherent in the term *jíbaro*:

Para algunos, los jíbaros son pequeños y enjutos, pero fuertes; para otros, endebles y anémicos, palabra esta última que adquiere un significado central en los debates finiseculares . . . son de una vivereza singular, pero comprometida por la alimentación; son blancos, negros, mulatos, o mestizos, dependiendo de quién los describe . . . si bien de un autor a otro la inconsistencia es notoria, no faltan casos en los que la contradicciones son vertidas en un mismo texto. (1999, 66)

For some, the jíbaros are small and gaunt, but strong; for others, frail and anemic, this last word acquiring a central meaning in turn of the century debates . . . they are of a singular liveliness, but compromised by their eating habits; they are White, Black, mulatto, or mestizo, depending on who describes them . . . if the inconsistency is apparent from one author to another, there is no lack of cases in which the contradictions are dispersed within the same text.

One thing eighteenth-century observers could agree on was that the jíbaro had distinct speech, habits, and living environments from the elite populations of the city. Their way of speaking was marked as uneducated, their habits were considered rustic, and their dress was understood to consist of a wide-brimmed hat (often called a *pava*), a machete, and comfortable, loose, cotton clothing called *indianas*. Figure 3.3 illustrates what Scarano argues would become a popular nineteenth-century practice, though it was already occurring during the late eighteenth century—namely, elites donning the dress and voice of the Jíbaro to critique the colonial government.

During the nineteenth century, the term *jíbaro* (alternately spelled *xivaro, jivaro, givaro,* or *gíbaro*) became commonplace. In 1849, *El Gíbaro* by Manuel A. Alonso, often described as the father of Puerto Rican literature, was published and widely circulated, eventually becoming part of the canon of literature currently taught in high school Spanish classes in Puerto Rico. Alonso uses poetry and prose to offer a detailed account of local customs and rustic practices. These often take the form of descriptive prose in Alonso's voice alongside verse written in an imagined jíbaro voice:

Los bailes de garabato son, como he dicho, varios, y traen su origen de los nacionales españoles y de los indígenas, de cuya mezcla ha resultado un conjunto que revela claramente el gusto de unos y otros. (Alonso 1970 [1849], 37)

The garabato dances are, as I have said, many, and they originate from the Spanish nationals and the indigenes, from whose

FIGURE 3.3. Luis Paret y Alcazar, *Autorretrato*, oil on wood, 1776. Museo de San Juan Collection. Museo de Arte de Puerto Rico.

mixture an ensemble has resulted that clearly reveals the tastes of one and the other.

The following poem is emblematic of how Alonso represents the jíbaro voice. His choice of spelling serves to iconically represent the jíbaro as uneducated:

Original (in jíbaro style):	In conventional standard Spanish:
Ey jueves a eso e la una,	El jueves a eso de la una;
Poquito menos o más;	Poquito menos o más;
Cuando yegó primo Sico,	Cuando llegó primo Sico,
Que me diba a combial	Que me iba a convidar
Pa un baile, que aqueya noche	Para un baile, que aquella noche
Jasian en la besinda,	Hacían en la vecindad,
En caje de una comae	En casa de una comadre (41)

Thursday around one
Little less or more;
When cousin Sico arrived,
That he was going to invite me
To a dance, that that night
They were going to have in the neighborhood
In the house of a neighborhood friend

The jíbaro in this text is considered to be "native"—referring probably, however, to a natively produced ethnicity resulting from the mixing of Taíno, Spanish, and African populations and traditions rather than exclusively to a pre-Columbian Taíno Indigenous one. However, the everyday practices of the jíbaro—linguistic, cultural, and domestic—are described as traceable to the Indigenous Taíno, though these practices are distinctly understood as remnants from a people who existed long ago. With *El Gíbaro*, Alonso established the contours of what would become the mythologized Jíbaro, the key figure in national folklore, a metaphor for a Puerto Ricanness that was distinct from Spain and, later, the United States.

As scholars have argued elsewhere, the mythologized Jíbaro embodied notions of stubborn resistance, which became useful for local elites when expressing discontent with Spanish rule (Córdova 2005; Scarano 1999; Torres-Robles 1999); as early as 1814, local elites would voice this mythologized Jíbaro figure when critiquing the government in public forums (Anonymous 1814).[6] Puerto Rican historian Luis E. González Vales (1988) notes that an 1814 letter to the *Diario Económico de Puerto Rico* was one of the first instances of the term in popular print. In the letter, the "patient Gívaro" is an ex-government functionary who is critical of dishonest officials profiting from taxpayer contributions.

This deployment of the mythologized Jíbaro figure to ground Puerto Rican nationalism and colonial dissent fixed the forms and practices that became characteristic of jibaridad. Jibaridad itself can be understood as the bundle of jíbaro identity characteristics that could be claimed by Puerto Ricans. In spite or perhaps because of the fascination with the Jíbaro archetype and the celebration of jibaridad, which by the mid–twentieth century had become synonymous with the essence of Puerto Rican nationality, tensions with the population who actually identified as jíbaros began to emerge. Antonio Salvador Pedreira, a canonical Puerto Rican intellectual, critiqued the extension of jibaridad to the entire Puerto Rican population:

> De acuerdo con el último censo un 73 por ciento de nuestra población vive en el campo, y no podemos aceptar que tres cuartas partes de nuestra población esté compuesta de jíbaros genuinos. (1935, 16)

> In accordance with the last census, 73 percent of our population lives in the countryside, and we cannot accept that three quarters of our population is composed of genuine jíbaros.

Pedreira proposes to break down what he considers to be the various categories or types of jíbaro, including the "jíbaro citizen," a status that belongs to any and all Puerto Ricans, and the "jíbaro-jíbaro," who was born in the mountains and "conserva casi intacta, mejor que nadie, la herencia psicológica de sus antepasados" (1935, 17; conserves almost intact, better than anyone, the psychological inheritance of their ancestors).

Jibaridad, as embodied in the Jíbaro and as a metaphor for the shared essence of Puerto Ricanness, proved to be a fruitful national icon in the political campaign of Luis Muñoz Marín and the PPD (Partido Popular Democrático; Popular Democratic Party) in Puerto Rico's transition to electoral politics in the early 1950s (Córdova 2005). In fact, the iconic pava-wearing profile of a Jíbaro, flanked by the words "Pan-Tierra-Libertad" (Bread-Land-Liberty), became the symbol of the PPD and is still in use to this day.

As Córdova argues, "The PPD's emblem boldly asserted a 'people.' It directly addressed jíbaros while also inviting Puerto Ricans from all walks of life to identify with the cultural myth it mediated" (2005, 175). In highlighting the "Jíbaro" as a subject of the PPD campaign, Muñoz Marín secured the vote of the peasant rural class while inviting the rest of the population to claim this symbol of essential Puerto Ricanness as their own.

By the time the Jíbaro came to represent the essence of the Puerto Rican nation, the Jíbaro was consistently represented as White—a native peasant with Spanish heritage who had acquired some rustic Indigenous practices—and there was rare, if any, mention of the island's Black population. In several instances, even contemporary authors define the Jíbaro as White. For example, psychologist and Latino studies scholar Irene López describes jíbaros as "White rural peasants living in the interior region or 'the heart' of the Island, who were considered 'authentic' Puerto Ricans" (2008, 174; see also Duany 2002b; Torres-Robles 1999).

Written in 1965, though still required reading for me as a student in 1993, *Bienvenido Don Goyito* is the fictional, satirical chronicle of the adventures of Don Goyito, a jíbaro, as he moves from the rural countryside to his daughter's home in the wealthy Condado area of San Juan. Don Goyito is an everyman bumpkin, a Puerto Rican Beverly Hillbilly, and notably, he is described and illustrated on the cover as White. His Whiteness, a pointed avoidance of the African and/or Indigenous backgrounds that many Puerto Ricans have, mirrors the contemporaneous political-cultural projects that were encouraging Don Goyito's real-life counterparts to mold themselves in the image of the modern Puerto Rican citizen, fit for the island's emerging industrial future.

From the '40s through the '60s, the Division of Community Education (DIVEDCO) used films, pamphlets, books, posters, and presentations in local communities to educate the island's jíbaros about hygiene, nutrition, and the technological advances brought on by industrialization (Lloréns 2014; Thompson 2005). While this propaganda celebrated the spirit of the Jíbaro, it also portrayed many everyday elements of jibaridad—from food and hygiene habits to family relationships—as barriers to modernization and progress and even unhealthy. These "educational" materials served to justify the continued governmental intervention in jíbaro daily routines while further extending the metaphor to all Puerto Ricans.

And so while the spirit of the Jíbaro was increasingly honored as an icon of the national essence, the rural peasants who were identified as jíbaros were increasingly looked down upon. Esmeralda Santiago summarizes the ambivalence in her memoir, *When I Was a Puerto Rican*:

> If we were not jíbaros, then why did we live like them? Our house, a box squatting on low stilts, was shaped like a bohío, the kind of house jíbaros lived in. . . . Our neighbor Doña Lola was a jíbara, although Mami had warned us never to call her that. Poems and stories about the hardships and joys of the Puerto Rican jíbaro were required reading at every grade level in school. My own grandparents, whom I was to respect as well as love, were said to be jíbaros. But I couldn't be one, nor I was to call anyone a jíbaro, lest they be offended . . . I was puzzled by the hypocrisy of celebrating a people everyone looked down on. (1993, 12–13)

For Santiago, the jíbaro was both an everyday fact and a historical icon, a celebrated figure and a lowly, shameful status. My own fourth-grade confusion about what exactly it meant to be a jíbaro and whether the word was a grave insult (implying poverty and backwardness) or a noble designation (implying purity and authenticity) was not the naive befuddlement of a transplant but, in fact, the essence of the ambiguity surrounding jibaridad. This ambiguity, which is woven into the very fabric of Puerto Rico and Puerto Ricanness, is the backdrop against which Taíno/Boricua counternarratives are told.

The Spaces That Remain

Among Taíno/Boricua activists, the jíbaro is an everyday figure and a source of Indigenous continuity. Tito, the self-proclaimed Jíbaro-Boricua Indigenous organizer, argued that Indigenous practices have survived and continued through the rural jíbaro population and that jíbaro Spanish varieties reflect Indigenous language influence. Tito was adamant about this understanding of Puerto Rican history. He was equally adamant about how history as written and promoted by Puerto Rico's elites, who were ignorant about the island as a whole and arrogant in thinking they could represent its history as a shared and united one. They had erased Indigenous continuity in part by elevating and circulating an archetypal White Jíbaro myth that excluded actual jíbaros and their experiences.

When I traveled with Tito, he often ended up driving me over narrow hillside roads in his beat-up jeep. The paved main roads, surrounded by lush, verdant vegetation, led to unmarked paths, which we followed to the homes of elder jíbaros. Some of their houses were concrete, some were wood with zinc roofs, but they all felt curated to illustrate the rural populations that Tito felt were often skipped over in representations of the island. Tito's project was to acquire information from those elder jíbaros, whom he called "true representatives of the native culture," in order to buttress his own activist agenda with greater "authenticity." He also hoped that these elders would become active in his movement and lend it further legitimacy. Most of the elders we visited were over seventy, and some were in their nineties—people who could remember their childhoods in the early twentieth century. Few of them actually said they were Taíno, but many of them said they were indios and jíbaros.

In her book about a Mexican street peddler named Esperanza Hernández, *Translated Woman*, anthropologist Ruth Behar describes how Esperanza experiences her "Indianness" less as an ethnic identity and more as a reflection of Mexican class/race distinctions. Her "Indianness" is about "her social standing and her historical past" as well as "her color and physical features" (1993, 8), but the rest of her has been "de-Indianized," her Tlaxcalan identity "displaced, though not forgotten, in the long process of colonial and post colonial domination" (9). It is in this sense that many Puerto Rican Taíno activists understand rural people who identify as indios—they see themselves as apart from a whitened elite class as well as connected to certain practices and forms of talk associated with being indio, but they did not necessarily embrace being Taíno/Boricua as a distinct political identity.

The primary goal, then, for activists such as Tito is to instill an Indigenous Taíno/Boricua political subjectivity in those who identify as indios and jíbaros in rural Puerto Rico. This was Tito's agenda as he listened to the jíbaro elders as they described their childhoods—how they ate, cleaned clothes, grew food, and organized their daily activities. Whenever an elder used a word with an Indigenous origin, Tito would look over at me with a face that said, "You see?" On one of our visits, during Tito's conversation with Doña Justa and Don Álvaro, who were both in their seventies, we sat in the living room of their small concrete house. Tito and I sat on the couch facing Justa in a rocking chair and Álvaro in an armchair, with other family members moving in and out of the room. Tito's management of the conversation was subtle but insistent—using strategic questions to keep Justa and Álvaro focused on topics like the grinding of cornmeal, which he regarded as relevant to the Jíbaro Boricua Indigenous Movement's (MIJB) project and related to what he considered genuine Jíbaro Boricua Indigenous knowledge. Yet when an elder recalled anything that did not fit with Tito's very specific ideas about jíbaro Indigeneity, he attempted to shift their attention toward topics and objects that better suited his vision of Indigenous jíbaro life—moving, for example, away from plantains, a staple of the island's diet associated with Puerto Rico's African heritage, to corn products, which are associated with the pre-Columbian Indigenous population. In spite of Tito's efforts to control the content of these interviews, to skew them toward the Indigenous jíbaro identity he wanted these elders to represent, they often ignored or disregarded his interventions and persisted in relating the versions of their lives that they wanted to share. Toward the end of our conversation, his goal for the interview became explicit. He wanted to ensure that I would hear from who he considered the "real Boricuas" rather than the San Juan "Spaniards."

Throughout these kinds of exchanges, Tito wanted to evidence to me as an anthropologist that Jíbaro Boricua Indigenous knowledge was maintained by elder rural populations. One of the ways he seemed to align with these elders in order to elicit the ways of speaking and the practices he was interested in was by adopting a register of speech that reflected the elders' rural style of Puerto Rican Spanish. In fact, it was during the conversation with Justa and Álvaro that I first witnessed Tito switch his speech register from his usual Puerto Rican Spanish variety to include the more salient aspects of a rural jíbaro Puerto Rican Spanish characterized, for example, by its pronunciation of the final /e/ as [i] and the fricativization of /r/ to [x], reflective of how he perceived Justa and Álvaro to speak.

About a week later, Tito took me to visit Don Luis and Doña Mariana. Their house was at the end of a small road on the top of a hill, surrounded by fruit trees, with several banana and plantain stems in the driveway. Luis greeted us, offered me a mango, and showed us to his living room, where he introduced me to his wife, Mariana. I sat alone on the couch, Luis sat in an armchair, and

Tito sat in a folding chair next to him. I could see Mariana in the kitchen preparing a snack. Rodrigo, a neighbor, soon joined us. Once the conversation was underway, Tito attempted to set up a scenario for Luis and Rodrigo that would lead them to consider how they would survive if the government could no longer provide them with economic subsidies. Luis explained why he would be fine if the government took away his welfare, but Tito's real goal was for them to discuss survival strategies prior to the existence of governmental welfare subsidies, so he attempted to redirect the conversation: "Pero vamos a preguntarle a tu mujer que va hacer si no hay cupones" (But let's ask your wife what she will do if there is no welfare). But instead of following where Tito was trying to lead him, Luis focused on what he was reading into Tito's question—a presumption that he would be worried if his welfare disappeared. Luis explained, "No hay justo desamparado ni aunque mendige pan. Dios le da el pan de cada día" (There is no just man forsaken even if he is begging for bread. God gives the bread of each day). Luis illustrated his point with a story about finding a twenty-dollar bill that helped feed his family in a time of need, but Tito interrupted him to ask what would happen if someone came along and took the providential twenty away. That line of questioning led Luis, Rodrigo, and Mariana to reminisce about how they got by after the last hurricane left them stranded with no water or electricity, and Tito again attempted to redirect the conversation to Indigenous survival strategies.

As in the prior conversation with Justa and Álvaro, though Tito rarely used nonstandard Spanish or colloquial speech forms, in attempting to refocus and regain control of the conversation with Luis, Rodrigo, and Mariana, he relied on a colloquial and rural variety of Puerto Rican Spanish. I observed as he deleted the intervocalic d in demasiado to instead say demasiao and aspirated the final s in dispuestos to instead say dispuestoh. While these are both common features of colloquial Puerto Rican Spanish and also conventionally associated with rural speakers, in general, Tito's speech was characterized by how he always pronounced the intervocalic d and the final s, so in these contexts, his pronunciation was marked. Though this might have been a momentary idiosyncrasy or reflective of Tito speaking to someone other than me, these shifts often happened when he was asking a question repeatedly but still not getting the responses he was looking for. He did this again in our conversation with Luis and Mariana as he tried to insert himself in their overlapping (yet distinct) conversations about dealing with adversity, where they used many colloquial Puerto Rican Spanish speech forms, such as the apocopation of *para* to *pa-* and the use of *n* rather than *m* in words ending in *-mos* (i.e., *cocinábanos* rather than *cocinábamos*). Tito's use of what might be called jíbaro rural speech patterns in his conversation with Luis, Mariana, and Rodrigo suggests an effort to achieve his ends by establishing a connection with his interviewees—a sense of familiarity or comradeship.

Tito's conversation with Luis, Mariana, and Rodrigo was not anomalous. When he attempted to steer elders into discussion of traditional Indigenous practices, his agenda, as I saw it, was complicated and multilayered. First, there was me. He wanted me to understand what he believed to be the true version of the Puerto Rican rural Indigenous jíbaro past so that I would not replicate what he saw as problematic narratives that minimized and trivialized the continuity of Indigenous presence in Puerto Rico. While I initially understood these interviews as opportunities for Tito to build an activist movement, to recruit new members of the MIJB, I came to see that Tito was less interested in trying to organize these elders than he was in trying to learn from them, to receive and document their stories and knowledge, to collect and publicize what seemed to him irrefutable evidence of Indigenous continuity, and to promote Indigenous lifestyles and communities as an alternative to what he considered to be unsustainable capitalist structures. And here again, my arrival fit into Tito's larger project: I had access, as he understood it, to a different and potentially much larger scale for the circulation of these narratives of continuity.

On one occasion, we stayed in Tito's house so that I could meet Willy, a farmer in his fifties who lived in the rural northwest foothills of Puerto Rico. When Willy arrived, Tito and I were sitting on the floor of his house as he searched for manuscripts based on the work of Oki Lamourt Valentín, whom Tito described as the intellectual progenitor of the Jíbaro Indigenous movement. As we sorted through manuscripts, I asked Tito and Willy why they thought that most people in Puerto Rico have been skeptical of the possibility of Indigenous continuity and why they might not agree that jíbaros are Indigenous. In response, Tito talked about the educational system in Puerto Rico and its role in erasing Indigenous histories and practices and in denigrating jíbaro ways of speaking:

OK "¡Ah! No me hables en español, y mucho menos la lengua indígena." Ya la lengua indígena había sido proscrita por los españoles, luego los ingleses gringos, eh proscriben el español. Eh, pero la lengua indígena y el acento indígena, (?) es atacado vilmente; si tu hablabas jíbaro, tú venía, "Mihter, mihter, aquí le traji al neni pa' que me le de clasi, que yo quiero que el aprendah." "Está bien, señora, váyase tranquila que yo se lo educo."

OK. "Ah! And don't speak to me in Spanish, and much less in the Indigenous language." The Indigenous language had already been proscribed by the Spanish, and then the English gringos, eh, proscribed Spanish. Eh, but the Indigenous language and the Indigenous accent, they are attacked vilely; if you spoke Jíbaro, you came, [in stereotypical jíbaro rural Puerto Rican Spanish] "Mister, mister (Mihter, mihter), here I brought (traji) the kid (neni) for (pa'){me} you to give classes (clasi), because I want him to learn (aprendah)." "It is all right, ma'am, go calmly, for I will educate him (for you)."

Tito's imagined exchange between a mother and teacher draws from salient linguistic stereotypes of rural jíbaro Puerto Rican talk, particularly the raising of word final /e/ to /i/, to voice the mother as a jíbara, contrasting her speech with the teacher's. Tito connects the Indigenous to the jíbaro, where the jíbaro is understood as the figuration of Indigeneity threatened through schooling under U.S. colonial rule. This interpretation stands as an alternative (and for Tito, it is the only acceptable alternative) to the more widely circulating archetype of the mythologized Puerto Rican Jíbaro. For Tito, the story of the double colonization of Puerto Rico is reflected in the everyday speech of the island.[7] He argues that the Spanish forbade speaking the Indigenous language and that later, the U.S. schooling system scorned jíbaro speech, which Tito considers to be the remnant of an Indigenous way of speaking. This discussion of education, which comes to stand for a broader set of colonial tensions, is the backdrop to my discussion with Willy, who continued by describing how some jíbaros came to understand themselves not as Indigenous but as U.S. Americans:

Porque aun eso mismos jíbaros, aunque tú no lo creas, decían que eran americanos porque eso eran lo que habían escuchado y eso era lo que le habían enseñado . . . cuando tu ibas a la escuela el primer grado . . . siempre nos enseñaban el lao contrario de la verdad. O sea, el bueno era Cristóbal Colón y los indios eran los malos. . . . Mi abuela . . . era una india, pero india india, pero india completa. Esto no es india de decir que "Yo tengo unos ideales, que soy indio porque tengo esos ideales." Aquella era india de verdad. Y ella era una persona bien humanitaria. Si tú pasabas por la casa de ella, tenías que entrar a tomar café . . . en lo que era el fogón . . . ella tenía el fogón todo el tiempo prendido, o sea tenía comida todo el tiempo en ese fogón, y antes era mucho los ñames, yautías, batata y guineo.[8] Se comía todos los días allí, no podía faltar eso.

Because those very jíbaros, even if you don't believe it, said that they were American because that is what they had heard and that is what they had been taught. . . . When you went to school in the first grade . . . they always taught us the side contrary to the truth. That is, the good guy was Christopher Columbus, and Indians were the bad guys. My grandmother . . . was Indian, but Indian Indian, but completely Indian. This is not Indian to say that "I have some ideals, that I am Indian because I have those ideals." She was Indian for real. And she was a very humanitarian person. If you passed by her house, you had to go in to drink coffee . . . and there was the custom of the outside cooking fire. . . . She had one on all the time, that is, she had food all the time on that stove, and before it was a lot of yams, taro, sweet potato, and banana. It was eaten every day there, that could not be missed.

Willy describes his grandmother the way people often describe the island's jíbaros: cooking in a *fogón*, eating food that might have been grown in their home garden, and being hospitable. By drawing on common descriptions of the jíbaro to describe his Indian grandmother, Willy folds the category of Indigenous onto the jíbaro, effectively defining jíbaros as the Indigenous population of the island. In fact, many Taíno/Boricua trace their Indigenous ancestry through their jíbaro family members, and many people in the broader Taíno/Boricua Indigenous movement define jíbaros as an Indigenous population.

Tito's and Willy's recollections of their jíbaro background as the anchor of their Indigenous self-identification is not unique. Likewise, Mukaro, the leader of the United Confederation of Taíno People (UCTP) based in New York City, grounded his Taínoness in his family's jíbaro background. I had heard of Mukaro and his organization, including their work at the United Nations representing the Taíno at the Indigenous Forum, from a few groups in Puerto Rico. As soon as I arrived in New York in the summer of 2008, I got in touch. Mukaro worked at the Museum of Natural History, where I met him in a conference room. He was warm and open to discussing his own Indigenous heritage, which was also anchored by his jíbaro ancestors. In the following excerpt from our discussion, he argues implicitly against the institutionally sanctioned image of the Jíbaros as White peasants and explicitly against the claim that although Indigenous practices remain, Indigenous people do not:

My family is jíbaros, you know what I'm saying? From Guayanilla . . . and being that jíbaro, we know that that's also the native, you know for us. . . . Yes, we have . . . all kinds of traditions . . . everything from hammock making to basket making to—there's things in our language, there's things in our religion, the Catholic religion that's practiced in the island . . . it all retains these Indigenous elements, but yet, even biologically, there's some . . . continuity, right? But they're not Indians. In other words, they can do all this Indian stuff, they even have some . . . biological connection, but they're not Indians, you know? So, and I was like, "How can that be, you know? How could you . . . have a biological connection, and a cultural connection, but not be those people?"

Mukaro's sense of the Indigenous traditions that survived through the jíbaro, where the jíbaro is explicitly cast as the island's native population, overlap with Tito's interest in certain preindustrial practices, such as basket and hammock making, but is also inclusive of the forms of Catholicism practiced on the island. Whereas Tito's exchange with the two groups of elders seemed to eschew any mention of practices of non-Taíno origin, suggesting a more purist stance toward contemporary forms of Indigeneity in Puerto Rico, Mukaro was inclusive of jíbaro practices with Spanish origins, seeing elements of Indigenous Taíno belief and practice as having been woven into Puerto Rican jíbaro Catholicism. For Mukaro, there did not seem to be a conflict between Catholicism and Taíno identity, since his jíbaro ancestors had adopted the religion and thus made it Taíno.

Moving from practices to biology, Mukaro was visibly frustrated as he described Puerto Rican biologist Juan Martínez-Cruzado's mitochondrial DNA (mtDNA) research, which revealed that more Puerto Ricans (about 52.6 percent) had some native Taíno ancestry than would be expected if the Taíno had been completely exterminated during the Spanish colonial genocide in the sixteenth century. Mukaro argued that mtDNA research supported his family's oral histories of survival, which for him were the primary sources of his Indigenous identity, and all of which—mtDNA data and oral histories alike—were disregarded by many scholars and educated Puerto Ricans. Mukaro and other Taíno who look at mtDNA evidence acknowledge that race cannot be subsumed to the biological but are also sensitive to the ways that their physical traits have been historically bundled and indexicalized as socially meaningful and productive of racial categories such as indio. This awareness, in turn, means that while Taíno/Boricua may highlight their bodily indices, including DNA, as signs of Indigenous survival, they also acknowledge the different experiences and positionalities structurally imposed upon different racialized bodies and are inclusive of people who may not necessarily *look* Taíno/Boricua on the basis of their family oral histories (González 2015). These kinds of arguments linking the Taíno and jíbaro circulate broadly among Taíno/Boricua activists and are mutually understood as not requiring justification or clarification. A 2008 book, self-published by a local Indigenous group, argues,

> A los habitantes de Borikén se les conoce como Boricuas, que significa, Hijo del Sol, pero entre nosotros nos decimos Jíbaros. . . .
>
> Es tan obvio que no han podido eliminar nuestra cultura básica, la indígena. Y que aunque practicamos tradiciones africanas y españolas, y la lengua que hablamos hoy sea una mezcla y no una pura, aún somos, en mayoría, étnicamente un pueblo indígena jíbaro Boricua. (Báez Santiago and Martínez Prieto 2008, 32, 125)

> The inhabitants of Borikén [Indigenous word for Puerto Rico] are known as Boricuas, which means Son of the Sun, but among ourselves we call each other Jíbaros. . . .
>
> It is so obvious that they have not been able to eliminate our basic culture, the Indigenous culture. And that though we practice African and Spanish traditions, and the tongue we speak today is a mix and not pure, we are, in our majority, ethnically an Indigenous jíbaro Boricua [Indigenous word for Puerto Rican] people.

In Puerto Rico, there are at least two distinct concepts and images of the jíbaro—one constructed through personal and familial memories and another built through larger institutional and national narratives. Both Indigenous Taíno/Boricua and non-Indigenous-identifying Puerto Ricans lay claim to the jíbaro as a defining figure, but each group promotes a different version of the icon—one White, nostalgic, patriotic, mythic; the other Indigenous, authentic, and continuous, existing from the past to the present and on into the future. These jíbaros are like uncanny twins—seemingly the same but utterly different. The tension between these different versions of the jíbaro contributes to the continuing ambiguity of the term and to current struggles over the right to define and claim it.

Conclusion

On May 1, 2019, several Jíbaro-Boricua joined in May Day protests against governmental austerity measures. The activists posited the recognition, visibility, and agency of their Indigeneity as a pathway that might offer solutions to Puerto Rico's economic and political crises. By sharing stories and traditions that reconfigure and interrupt mainstream categories of national identity, like the one contained within the figure of the jíbaro, Taíno/Boricua activists make plain the incongruities between widely circulating official discourses of Puerto Ricanness and their own understanding of what it means to be from the island. These struggles over meaning reveal how the semiotic associations among terms, historical tropes, ways of speaking, and sociocultural alignments also affect broader political orders (Goebel 2010; Pagliai 2009; Rampton 2011; Roth-Gordon 2009). Attention to the contestations surrounding the multiple referents contained within jibaridad and how the term became referentially grounded throughout a variety of interactions make clear that debates about the jíbaro are not only about its referent but about "struggles to define the indexical values" (Newell 2009, 157; see also Gallie 1969 [1956]) of Indigenous continuity and survival that underlie Taíno/Boricua political action.

In this way, Mukaro, Tito, and Willy maintain that the Taíno/Boricua were never extinct and that current Taíno/Boricua practices are attached to current Taíno/Boricua peoples through the jíbaro. Within the Taíno/Boricua controversy, unwritten memories and recollections take on immense value because they do not conform to what is understood as a colonial project of imprinting and creating a national sentiment on the island at the expense of local Indigenous narratives. The Jíbaro from my schoolbooks can exist only if the jíbaro of today remains a schoolyard taunt and nothing more. If the jíbaro of today are not just so-called backwater rural folk but, as some claim, descendants of the Taíno, maintaining Indigenous traditions in a straight line from their Indigenous ancestors, then a century-long project of defining what it means to be Puerto Rican begins to unravel.

4

Impossible Identities

There are two images that bothered many Taíno activists during my fieldwork. The first is a cartoon printed in the national newspaper *El Nuevo Día* alongside an opinion piece by journalist Mayra Montero. The piece, titled "Espejitos" ("Little mirrors") was a response to the 2005 demonstrations at the Caguana Ceremonial Indigenous Heritage Center in Utuado, where Taíno groups came together to protest the attempt to charge Taíno an entrance fee to access the site for their ceremonies. The cartoon depicts a small group of protesters. A tall, fair man with sporty sunglasses, sneakers, and a barcode *nagua* (cotton loincloth) stands alongside two women in traditional ceremonial gear and braids—one with a feather on her head and a *guanin* (a gold-and-bronze disc worn around the neck of Taíno leaders) indicating her leadership position, the other holding her fingers to her lips like an ingenue. All three carry cell phones on the waist strings of their naguas. Next to the depiction of the ingenue is a sign that reads "Taino Pauer" (notably, in Hispanicized English instead of Spanish or Taíno). In the context of the cartoon, I interpret the sign as connecting the protest to other ethnic movements, such as Black Power, or contemporary slogans, such as "girl power," in order to undermine the movement's locality and authenticity.

Abuela Shashira of the Consejo General de Taínos (CGT), who called herself "una taína moderna" (a modern Taíno woman), laughed at the stereotypes represented in the cartoon, but she was troubled by the suggestion that modernity and a genuine Taíno identity were incompatible. She often said, "¿Por qué me haría la vida más díficil, cuando se puede hacer más fácil? Claro que llevo cellular y miniván y computadora también. ¿El mundo cambia y yo no voy a cambiar? ¡Ay bendito!" (Why would I make my life more difficult when you can make it easier? Of course, I have a cell phone and a minivan and a computer too. The world changes and I am not going to change? Oh please!). She was bothered that the expectation was that the Taíno could not exist in a modern form, that they have not adapted to the current era. The barcode on the man's nagua especially irked her, along with the caption that accompanied it: "The authentic Taínos must be turning over in their tombs, feeling as if someone wanted to beguile them with little mirrors. Because that is what it is about, mediating little mirrors and bells in exchange for gold" (Montero 2005). For the abuela, her concern that the celebration of important Taíno ceremonies could be monetized was at the root of her protest, so the claim that she was pretending to be Taíno for some sort of monetary gain was a grave insult.

A 2007 piece in the University of Puerto Rico newspaper *Diálogo* titled "¿Somos indígenas?" (Are we Indigenous?) was accompanied by another cartoon, this one an image of a tree whose trunk is engraved with faces that represent the racial triad, Puerto Rico's democratic myth of Spanish, African, and Taíno heritages. The tree's leaves form the shape of Puerto Rico's main island, with different shades of what are ostensibly skin-colored fruits corresponding to the island's diverse and often mixed population. The Taíno face on the trunk dominates the tree, gazing proudly into the distance, overshadowing the helmeted Spanish face, whose eyes appear to be hooded and/or downcast. The African section of the trunk, along with its roots, has been cut away and cast to the side, a saw lying beside it. Leader of Liga Guakía Taína-ké (LGTK) Yarey's exasperated response to this tree of Puerto Rico was, "Sí, somos una mezcla, eso se sabe!" (Yes, we are a mix, that is known!). She was frustrated that claims of Indigeneity were seen as a rejection of what most Puerto Ricans, including the Taíno, understood to be their mixed-race heritage and that critics pointed in particular to a potential loss of the island's African heritage through Taíno activism instead of seeing a critique of White Spanish Europeanness.

These cartoons represent two major criticisms of Taíno/Boricua identification and mobilization. The first image speaks to the assumed impossibility of Taíno/Boricua survival beyond the Spanish genocide during the conquest and colonization of Puerto Rico. The second image reveals the racial dynamics that complicate claims to being Taíno/Boricua. In Puerto Rico, where the hegemonic myth of racial democracy has trivialized its African roots while simultaneously extinguishing and celebrating its Indigenous heritage, what does it mean to claim to be Taíno?

Racial Imaginaries in Puerto Rico

The Puerto Rican racial triad, where the heritage of all Puerto Ricans is represented as the composite of three distinct ancestral cultural legacies—the Spanish, the African, and the Taíno—became especially mobilized in the mid–twentieth century through state institutions, including the Instituto de Cultura Puertorriqueña (ICP; Puerto Rican Institute of Culture), the Division of Community Education (DIVEDCO), and the Department of Public Instruction. As the first director of the ICP, Ricardo Alegría was a major figure both within Puerto Rican archaeology and in the diffusion of the racial triad's ideology throughout the island. Puerto Rican archaeologists Jaime R. Pagán Jiménez and Reniel Rodríguez Ramos (2008) argue that Alegría's archaeological work on and institutionalization of Taíno ceremonial sites, coupled with the ICP's explicit celebration of Puerto Rico's Indigenous heritage, shaped many Puerto Ricans' historical memory and the contemporary understanding of the Taíno.

The post-1950s cultural nationalism espoused by the Estado Libre Asociado (ELA; Free Associated State Commonwealth of Puerto Rico) and government-sponsored cultural institutions such as the ICP both scripted and celebrated a narrative of Puerto Rican history that included the Taíno as an important, laudable, yet extinct population that left valuable legacies to which all Puerto Ricans can claim, but they did not include Taíno as a current category of belonging. Cultural anthropologist Arlene Dávila (2001) explains that the racial triad was, in part, a response to a need to define Puerto Rico against a commercial U.S. other as Puerto Rico's subordination to the United States as a commonwealth was formalized in the 1952 constitution. In response, the island's cultural, intellectual, and governmental elites constructed a national myth of homogenized diversity, emphasizing Puerto Rico's unique cultural heritage as the shared essence of all Puerto Ricans. In bureaucratic discourses, the Taíno became mythologized as Puerto Rico's ancestral legacy, to which any non-Spanish cultural practices were attributed. As a supposedly extinct group, no one could assert to be Taíno or declare authority over how to best represent the Taíno, but all Puerto Ricans could claim to have traces of Taíno heritage. The island's African roots were dismissed as not having made significant contributions to the Puerto Rican essential character. The island's African heritage was also folklorized and relegated to a second-tier status—the racial triad acknowledged the contributions of Africans only to delimited domains of practice (namely, music and dance). This midcentury legacy persists today; Taíno and racial triad symbolism continue to be used as enduring icons of Puerto Rico and its inhabitants (Martínez-San Miguel 2011).

Though the racial blending myth was designed to espouse an ideal of racial equality contained within the ancestry of every Puerto Rican, in effect, it delineated a hierarchy of racialized heritages that projects different levels of desirability and inhabitability. Such contradictions have resulted in a disjuncture between idealized discourses of racial harmony and lived realities of racialization and racism in Puerto Rico (Hernández Hiraldo 2006; Lloréns, García-Quijano, and Godreau 2017; Torres 1998). Racial blending ideologies on the island can be understood as "color blind" (Bonilla-Silva 2006) and discursively negating the experiences of many non-White Puerto Ricans.

As argued by cultural anthropologist Isar P. Godreau (2008), racializing terms in Puerto Rico are not strictly fixed by any physical characteristics. Rather, terms related to physical criteria are often used in ways that may be meant as an insult or courtesy based on a hierarchical framework of assumed preferences (Suárez-Findlay 2000). These assessments are often delineated by socialized practices of looking at a person, breaking down his or her physical characteristics, and mapping them on to a specific racialized color-type (Gravlee 2005). Such rituals have been entextualized in school social studies textbooks, where each heritage is described in terms of physical traits that students are encouraged to identify in themselves and others (Godreau et al. 2008).

Cultural anthropologist Hilda Lloréns (2018a) looks at the racial continuum in Puerto Rico, which is represented on one axis by "pure White" and on the other by "pure Black," and "indio" is understood as an intermediate, mixed category. Notions of racial belonging do not depend on genealogical claims but are instead subject to external evaluations of hair texture, skin color, nose shape, and so on. Quoting Mintz's concept of "socially relevant distinctions" (2005, 39), Lloréns considers how these evaluations may point to "specific perceptual distinctions, processes of assignation, and wider cultural tropes about racial and social standing vis-à-vis other individuals and the society at large" (2018b, 34). These racial ideologies, discourses, and practices impact the very possibility of imagining a tenable Taíno/Boricua genealogy. Within a discourse that figures looking indio as a product of and an intermediate point on the continuum between White and Black, claims to being Taíno/Boricua might be understood as an erasure of Blackness. And in a system that divorces racial assessments from ethnicity and genealogy, making claims to being Taíno/Boricua—especially for those that don't even *look indio*—seems like a ridiculous proposition.

As noted in the ethnographic works of Godreau (2015), Rivera-Rideau (2013), and Dinzey-Flores (2013), among others, place and race are often connected in Puerto Rico. Many Taíno expressed the feeling that rural areas were Indigenous, nonwhitened jíbaro spaces (in contrast to the more dominant discourses that whitened the jíbaros understood to inhabit rural Puerto Rico); that coastal areas were Afro-Indigenous spaces; and that each town's pueblo, or town center—as well as the general San Juan metropolitan area—were Spanish or White spaces, from which they often felt excluded. One pattern I observed in some Jíbaro-Boricua narratives about their Indigeneity was a felt marginalization based on their status as rural, working-class Puerto Ricans who are physically marked as neither White nor Black. In the Puerto Rican racial continuum, looking indio is understood as an acceptable identification for someone who is in between Black and White and has straight dark hair—insofar as it is claimed as a physical description rather than as an actual ethnic or genealogical assertion. Similarly, Puerto Ricans are often racialized as either Black or White based on phenotype rather than genealogy. To claim the *ethnicity* that is associated with the physical racialization would be understood as suspect. It is acceptable to claim to be indio, *negro*, or *blanco* based on appearance, but claiming to be Taíno, African, or Spanish would require further proof of this genealogical link. Therefore, in this context, claiming to be Taíno and organizing movements around the ethnicity are seen by some Puerto Ricans as inauthentic and dishonest.

Narratives of Identity and Belonging

Narratives about identity and belonging, such as the kind used by the Taíno/Boricua as they work to establish Taíno/Boricua as an acknowledged category of identification in Puerto Rico, play a key role in constructing potential futures, in forming personal and group identities, and in social mobilization (Basso 1996; Green, Strange, and Brock 2003; Redman 2005; Steinmetz 1992).[1] To analyze how Taíno activists work to form a recognizable identity category for themselves in the midst of a cultural and racial understanding that explicitly relies on their supposed extinction, I draw on a framework suggested by Mary Bucholtz and Kira Hall, who argue that identity "is inherently relational"—that "it will always be partial, produced through contextually situated and ideologically informed configurations of the self and other" (2009, 25). From this perspective, we can observe how people respond to others' configurations of identity by playing up similarities or differences and by pointing out the authenticity or artifice of others' identity performances and then authorizing or delegitimizing them. Building on this framework, I focus on the delegitimizing evaluations the Taíno encounter as they present themselves to non-Taíno.

I understand the conflicts over claims to Taíno/Boricua identity as endeavors toward the right to define what it means to be Taíno/Boricua in contemporary Puerto Rico and the Caribbean. I draw on Tianna Paschel's work on struggles over rights to representation within Black political mobilization in Brazil and Colombia. Paschel adapts Bourdieu's notion of fields to consider "the power of representation, who defines the language of the debate, and who legitimizes categories" (2016, 18). As Paschel and other scholars argue, most Latin American countries adopted a *mestizaje* racial discourse in the twentieth century, which marginalized nonelites in favor of highlighting national affiliation and denying ethnoracial difference as a source of group identity (Golash-Boza and Bonilla-Silva 2013). This had the further effect of trivializing the experienced racism and material marginalization of Black and Indigenous populations in the Americas. Taíno mobilization in Puerto Rico occurs in the context of a similar racial discourse.

Recognizing Taíno

When I started my full-time research with Yarey during the spring semester of 2007, she was taking her undergraduate classes on fieldwork in towns throughout the center and southeast of the island. I would meet Yarey and twenty to thirty of her students on Saturday mornings at the University of Puerto Rico–Río Piedras parking lot, where we would wait for the yellow school bus that would take us all to the rural—and ostensibly more jíbaro-populated—sites Yarey had identified for the day. When we arrived at our first stop, we traveled in groups of two or three to knock on doors and ask people if they were willing to answer a few questions about their neighborhood and family history. More often than not, they would invite us in to their homes and offer us coffee and candid responses. Yarey was especially interested in finding elders with stories of Puerto Rico in the early 1900s. Speaking to these elders was like unlocking a treasure trove for Yarey. She would ask questions about their parents—whether they had been blancos, negros, or indios—the work they did, what their houses looked like, the vocabulary they used to describe those houses, how the neighborhood had changed, and what they thought had caused those changes. She would ask about the plants and fruits people ate, how they got their food, and their sense of the local environment. The interviews were rich and would typically reinforce Yarey's feeling that elders often identified as indios, that the Taíno language had an extensive influence on their vocabularies, and that their everyday acts of washing clothes, cooking, and other domestic tasks often drew on what she understood to be an articulation of Taíno vocabulary and cosmology. These interviews propelled Yarey to work full time on Taíno Indigenous advocacy in the southeastern towns where her family was originally from, Maunabo and Yabucoa, and where she had spent her childhood summers with her grandparents and extended family.

During the summer of 2007, Yarey's advocacy goals began to solidify in the form of a cultural immersion program that she designed and implemented in elementary and middle schools as a part of her work with the Liga Guakía Taína-ké (LGTK), a group whose mission is to educate communities about Taíno heritage through the public school system. She initially funded the program with her own adjunct teaching salary and later by securing small contributions from private and municipal organizations. By teaching students and their parents about the Taíno roots of many Puerto Rican practices and traditions, LGTK hoped to inspire them to recognize their own practices and traditions as Taíno. Yarey believed that this would help students and parents eventually recognize themselves as Taíno. I often drove with Yarey to small rural schools in Yabucoa and Maunabo to meet school principals, to whom Yarey would promote her program, to be delivered at no cost to the school. If the principal approved the program, Yarey would offer the teachers an orientation. If Yarey

FIGURE 4.1. Classroom setting including Yarey and teachers. Photography by Sherina Feliciano-Santos.

was successful in recruiting the teachers, she would meet with parents.

After Yarey had been at work promoting her program for about a month and a half, at one relatively large school, the teacher liaison was very invested in the program and arranged for the parents to meet Yarey. Tables were arranged in a *U* shape, with parents sitting around the projector screen, where Yarey and another member of the LGTK stood. Yarey initiated her talk by making explicit reference to the ideology of the three ancestral roots of Puerto Ricanness.

Entonces me dedique a formar un programa llamado programa de inmersión cultural lingüística. ¿Y qué pretendemos con este programa? Acercar a su hijo a su cultura indígena. Pa' que conozcan su raíz indígena, que no somos solamente españoles y africanos. Que tenemos también una raíz indígena. Qué somos tres razas, ¿no? Pero siempre hablan de la raíz española y la africana. ¿Y la indígena? Siempre está olvidada. Este programa es para engrandecer este componente de nuestra cultura, la parte indígena, sin olvidarnos que somos qué: una mezcla, ¿no? De tres razas. Qué somos africanos, y somos europeos pero también somos indígenas, ¿no? (pause) "Pero eso es un disparate, profesora, a los taínos los exterminaron; en Puerto Rico no hay taínos" (pausa) [Apuntando hacia una persona que se ve estereotípicamente indígena] ¡Mira un taíno allí!

And then I dedicated myself to forming a program called program of cultural linguistic immersion. And what do we expect with this program? To get your child closer to their/your Indigenous culture. So they know their Indigenous root, that we are not only Spanish and African, that we also have an Indigenous root. That we are three races, no? But they always talk about the Spanish and African root. And the Indigenous one? It is always forgotten. This program is to enlarge this component of our culture, the Indigenous part, without forgetting that we are a mix, no? of three races. That we are African, and we are European, but we are also Indigenous, no? (pause) "But that is nonsense, professor (fem), the Taíno were exterminated; in Puerto Rico there are no Taíno!" (pause) [Pointing to a stereotypically Indigenous-looking person] Look at a Taíno there!

Yarey managed potential tensions between her audience's understanding of Puerto Rican history and the material she was presenting by making all three roots of the Puerto Rican racial triad claimable and inhabitable and by voicing Taíno-aligned expressions as well as what she presumed to be non-Taíno-aligned parents' concerns about her program and point of view—"But that is nonsense, professor . . . in Puerto Rico there are no Taíno!" Yarey responded to this anticipated argument by pointing to a stereotypically Indigenous-looking person: "Look at a Taíno there!" By refocusing the audience's attention on what she considered to be visible markers of contemporary Indigenous heritage, she hoped to interrupt her audience's notion that the Taíno had been exterminated.

She then extended and complicated this argument by drawing on her understanding of recent, controversial mitochondrial DNA (mtDNA) findings among the Taíno, pointing to people in the audience who did not look stereotypically Indigenous and arguing that they too could be Indigenous.[2]

> Mira un taíno aquí, viendo un taíno! (pause) Pues sí, pues si somo-somos indígenas, y los estudios genéticos han demostrado en la UPR Mayagüez confirman que el puertorriqueño, el puertorriqueño igual que el cubano tenemos una liga indígena, tenemos una liga indígena que no importa el color de tu piel no importa la textura de tu pelo, eso no importa, tu puedes ser un negrito-negrito-negrito y tener mas sangre indígena que este nene [points to stereotypically Indigenous-looking boy]. Ella es blanquita [points to a stereotypically White-looking woman], parece una gringa, ¿no? Y puede tener más sangre indígena que el nene. Que no son los rasgos físicos, este estudio dice que somos un 61 por ciento ADN materia genética indígena. Que la sangre indígena predomina en nuestra sangre y la sangre no miente.

> Look at a Taíno here, seeing a Taíno! (pause) Well yes, well yes we ar-are Indigenous peoples, and the genetic studies in the UPR Mayaguez confirm that the Puerto Rican, the Puerto Rican the same as the Cuban we have an Indigenous mixture that the color of your skin doesn't matter, the texture of your hair that does not matter, that does not matter, you can be Black-Black-Black and have more Indigenous blood than that boy [points to stereotypically Indigenous-looking boy]. She is White [points to a stereotypically White-looking woman], looks like a gringa, no? And she could have more Indigenous blood than the boy. That it is not physical characteristics; this study says that we are of 61 percent DNA Indigenous genetic material. That the Indigenous blood predominates in our blood, and blood does not lie.

Yarey bolstered her argument, that we must study and understand the often neglected Indigenous aspect of our Puerto Rican culture, and her intellectual bonafides by making claims to an unseen yet scientifically "provable" index of Indigeneity, mtDNA, using the popular notion of "blood" as a compelling metaphor. The school became a successful site for her program.

Not all schools proved as welcoming. At a smaller, more rural school in the same region, Yarey's attempts at teacher recruitment encountered much more resistance.

1	TEACHER A:	DIGAME, yo sé <u>mucho</u> de los *indios*, a mi me encanta la historia.
2	YAREY:	<u>Excelente.</u>
3	TA:	Yo parezco una española de ojos verdes yo no sé, yo no tengo nada de los in-=
4	Y:	=No pero, estas equivocada=
5	TEACHER B:	=¿Pero el pelo? Es lacio.
6	Y:	<u>Estas equivocada</u>=
7	TA:	=No, este pelo no es lacio.
8	Y:	Puedes tener el=
9	TA:	=No, mentira, mi hermano tiene el pelo kinky, uno.
10	Y:	¿Pues kinky? Puedes tener el pelo kinky=
11	TA:	=No, yo-yo me di un-un tratamiento=
12	Y:	=Pero eso no importa, el pelo kinky no importa, lo que importa es el espíritu=
13	TA:	= Los ojos verdes son de mi mamá y mi papá. Mi mamá-mi papá tiene los ojos azules. Mi mamá tiene ojos verdes.

1	TEACHER A:	TELL ME, I know <u>a lot</u> about the Indians, I love history.
2	YAREY:	<u>Excellent.</u>
3	TA:	I look like a Spanish woman with green eyes I don't know, I don't have anything from the in=
4	Y:	=No but, you are mistaken=
5	TEACHER B:	=But the hair? It's straight.

FIGURE 4.2. After-school presentation in the library with parents. Photograph by Sherina Feliciano-Santos.

6	Y:	<u>You are mistaken</u>=
7	TA:	=No, this hair is not straight.
8	Y:	You can have the=
9	TA:	=No, a lie, my brother has kinky hair, one.
10	Y:	Well kinky? You can have kinky hair=
11	TA:	=No, I-I gave myself a treatment=
12	Y:	=But that doesn't matter, the kinky hair doesn't matter, what matters is the spirit=
13	TA:	=The green eyes are from my mom and my dad. My mom-my dad has blue eyes. My mom has green eyes.

Teacher A constructed herself as *not* potentially Taíno by focusing on her physical appearance as an index of her ethnoracial heritage, claiming to look like a Spanish woman because of her green eyes. Additionally, the tone of Teacher A's response indicates that being labeled as potentially india was insulting to her. Whether this resulted from a racist sense that being india was beneath her or a sense that Yarey was reaching too far in claiming her as potentially Taíno, the teacher rejected Yarey's continued attempts to include her. Since the LGTK aims to be inclusive of persons of any physical appearance—not just those who look stereotypically Indigenous—Yarey did not consider Teacher A's "Spanish look" as an impediment to her potential Taínoness. For Yarey and LGTK, and many other Indigenous groups on the island, Puerto Rico's discourse of racial blending and claims to Indigeneity were not mutually exclusive—one could be a product of the racial triad and *also* be Taíno. While Teacher B attempted to read a stereotypical Indigenous trait in Teacher A's straight-looking hair, Yarey repeatedly attempted to interrupt Teacher A and disrupt her argument by locating Indigeneity within a person's spirit rather than his or her physical traits. But Teacher A ultimately dismissed Yarey by returning to her initial statement about her curly hair, her brother's kinky hair, and her green eyes. This interaction reveals several processes. First, in turn 1, Teacher A positions the Taíno as a historical rather than contemporary category. Second, while Yarey is not focused on highlighting physical criteria in this exchange, in turns 7, 11, and 13, Teacher A uses physical criteria to reject any identification with Indigeneity, perhaps informed by stereotypes embedded within the racial triad or by media imagery of Taíno and Indigenous peoples.

In the following excerpt, I consider Yarey's further attempt to disrupt Teacher A's reasoning. Drawing on literature suggesting that the term *jíbaro* may have been an appropriation from the Taíno language, Yarey tried to discursively bring together the concept of the Jíbaro and the contemporary Indigenous population of the island.

1	YAREY:	¿La palabra jíbaro, de donde viene? ¿Jíbaro?
2	TEACHER B:	¿De los-de los indios no es?
3	Y:	¿Jíbaro?
4	TB:	¿De los indios no es?
5	Y:	Muy bien, un aplauso para ella.
6	ALL TEACHERS:	((aplauso))

1	YAREY:	The word jíbaro, where does it come from?
		Jíbaro?
2	TEACHER B:	From the-from the Indians, isn't it?
3	Y:	Jíbaro?
4	TB:	From the Indians, isn't it?
5	Y:	Very good, an applause for her.
6	ALL TEACHERS:	((applause))

In other presentations, the embedding of the Jíbaro within an Indigenous Taíno framework had been a crucial step in convincing teachers of the significance of Yarey's program and the value of updating students' concept of the Indigenous presence in Puerto Rico. Since the Jíbaro is often correlated with rural Puerto Rico and the schools were in a rural area, discussions of the Jíbaro also served to create a shared identification between Yarey and the teachers.

In the excerpt above, to begin her argument, Yarey asks the teachers to help her reconstruct the lexical origin of the word *Jíbaro*. Teacher B responds that the word originates from "the Indians." Yarey hears Teacher B's response (in the video, she nods in agreement) but has Teacher B respond a second time to make sure that everyone hears. For Yarey, the Indigenousness of the term *Jíbaro* served as evidence of the continuity of the Indigenous people. In asking and receiving applause for Teacher B, she secures a moment of alignment between herself and the teachers. Yarey then attempts to share other evidence of the contemporary Indigenous presence in Puerto Rico. However, Teacher A interrupts again:

1	TEACHER A:	pero esa historia de los *indios* también, este,
		le voy a decir, {?} a mí me encanta la historia,
		PERO lo que estoy dando yo en mi clase
		de estudios sociales, la estoy dando de las
		TRADICIONES, y los niños no saben nada
		de las tradiciones.
2	YAREY:	¿Y cuáles son las tradiciones?
3	TA:	Porque, ya se perdieron esas tradiciones.

4	Y:	¿Pero cuáles?
5	TA:	Ah, pues las de {?} que se daba antes, el Día de Reyes, ya se olvidó ese Día de Reyes que es tan importante pa' los niños, ahora es *Santa Clos.* ¿Cuántos de los estudiantes que hay en segunda unidad y en *high school* escuchan música típica Jíbara de [nosotros?
6	Y:	[Qué bien]
7	TA:	una] música tan bonita.

1	TEACHER A:	but that history of the Indians as well, um, I will tell you, {?} I love history, BUT what I am giving in my social studies class, I am giving it about the TRADITIONS and the kids they know nothing about traditions.
2	YAREY:	And which are the traditions?
3	TA:	Because, they have already been lost those traditions.
4	Y:	But which?
5	TA:	Ah, well of the {?} that were given before, the Three Kings Day, it has already been forgotten that Three Kings Day that was so important for the kids, now it is Santa Claus. How many of the students that are in middle school and in high school listen to typical Jíbaro music of [us?
6	Y:	[Very well]
7	TA:	Such] a pretty music.

Here, Teacher A's assertion that though she loves history, she is teaching her students about traditions establishes a distinction between Indigenous history (which could connote a past that has not been maintained in practice) and Puerto Rican traditions (which could imply the past as maintained in practice). When Yarey presses Teacher A to name specific traditions, she responds with two examples: Three Kings Day and Jíbaro music, which is typical of *nosotros* (us), she says. Teacher A's use of *nosotros* was ambiguous with regard to whether she was reclaiming these Jíbaro traditions from the Taíno origin Yarey reveals or whether she had potentially acceded to Yarey's framework. Yarey uses the ambiguity of the teacher's use of *us* as a point of departure in her argumentative thread:

1	YAREY:	Ok. [y el reggaeton
2	TEACHER A:	[NADIE ni esto, el reggaeton
3	Y:	¿Y el reggaeton? ¿De dónde viene el reggaeton? (4 s) ¿La raíz del reggaeton?
4	TEACHER B:	Ah, el deso de los indios porque eso es más o menos=
5	Y:	=¿El rosario cantao? [¿Católicos aquí? ¿Católicos? ¿Cuántos a ver? ¿Católicos?]
6	TEACHERS:	[{talking}]
7	TA:	Yo.
8	Y:	¿Católicos?
9	TEACHER C:	Yo.
10	Y:	¿Católica? ¿Católica?
11	TB:	Yo también.
12	Y:	Ok. ¿El baquiné?
13	TA:	El baquiné ya eso no se ve ...
14	Y:	Muy bien. ¿Rosario Cantao?
15	TC:	De los, de=
16	Y:	=¿Pero de dónde viene?
17	TC:	De los de antes
18	Y:	¿Pero de dónde?
19	TEACHER D:	De los indios
20	TA:	De los Africanos.
21	Y:	El rosario cantao=
22	TA:	=Es PREcioso.
23	Y:	es un areito. Es un areito. ¿No?
24	T:	mmhmm
25	Y:	¿Nos cuentan qué? De los tiempos de Cristo, ¿no? ¿De la muerte de Cristo, ¿no? ¿Un areito

cuenta qué? Las tradiciones de los Taínos, no
tenían escritura. Entonces, ¿dependen de qué?
De tradición oral.

26 TA: Oral.
27 Y: Las narraciones. {silence}
28 TA: Eso es de los tiempos de las trad- de los épicos
por allá-
29 Y: de los Taínos.
30 TA: de Roma.
31 Y: TENEMOS TRES MESES de inmersión,
tres meses de inmersión cultural . . .

1 YAREY: Ok. [and reggaeton
2 TEACHER A: [NOBODY not even this, el reggaeton
3 Y: And the reggaeton? Where does reggaeton
come from? (4s) The root of reggaeton?
4 TEACHER B: Ah, the thing of the Indians, because that is
more or less=
5 Y: =The sung rosary? {Catholics here? Catholics?
How many let's see? Catholics?]
6 T: [{talking}]
7 TA: Me.
8 Y: Catholics?
9 TEACHER C: Me.
10 Y: Catholic? Catholic?
11 TB: Me too.
12 Y: Ok. The baquiné?
13 TA: The baquiné you don't see that anymore . . .
14 Y: Very well. Sung rosary?
15 TC: Of the, of
16 Y: But where does it come from?
17 TC: Of those from before
18 Y: But where from?
19 TEACHER D: From the Indians?
20 TA: From the Africans.

21	Y:	The sung rosary=
22	TA:	=Is PREcious.
23	Y:	is an areito. It's an areito. No?
24	T:	mmhmm
25	Y:	They tell us what? Of the times of Christ, no? Of the death of Christ, no? An areito tells what? The traditions of the Taínos, they did not have writing. Then they depend on what? On oral tradition.
26	TA:	Oral.
27	Y:	The narrations. {silence}
28	TA:	That is the time of the trad-Of the epics over there-
29	Y:	Of the Taínos.
30	TA:	of Rome.
31	Y:	WE HAVE THREE MONTHS of immersion, three months of cultural immersion.

In this excerpt, Yarey lists some of the most iconic traditional practices in Puerto Rico, including reggaeton,[3] the sung rosary, and the *baquiné*,[4] which are often generally understood as having been primarily influenced by the island's African heritage, as Teacher A asserts (Bofill Calero 2014; Nazario 1961). But Yarey, in keeping with the work of some recent Indigenous scholars, including Castanha (2011), argues that these practices have also been influenced by Taíno spiritual practices and cosmologies and, in the case of reggaeton, indirectly refutes Teacher A's claim that younger people do not listen to traditional music. Yarey's reasoning on reggaeton parallels her belief that Indigenous peoples are still present in Puerto Rico, though they may be creolized.[5]

Yarey later shared with me her frustration with Teacher A, whose response was representative of how many people react to claims of Indigeneity in Puerto Rico. These reactions are often the result of challenging people's expectations concerning the

Indigenous extinction in Puerto Rico and about who has the institutional and narrative authority to make claims about national historical trajectories.

Conclusion

Drawing on a framework that pairs the interactional negotiation of identity with the role of narrative in the production of culture and identity, the Taíno/Boricua navigate the construction of boundaries around a Taíno/Boricua identity category. They counter challenges from those who question their right to claim a Taíno/Boricua identity with alternative founts of authority—in some cases, their narrated familial memories; in others, their educational expertise. They respond to arguments that their claims to Indigeneity erase their African heritage by asserting racial mixture but positioning that mixture on Indigenous terms. That is, they rejected any assertions that racial mixture has obviated claims to Taíno/Boricua *or*, more recently, Afro-Taíno heritage and cultural identity, which tends to get outright denied. Since these responses are emergent, dynamic, and interactionally built, ideas about what it means to be Taíno/Boricua and how best to anchor and justify such an identity differ, sometimes wildly, from person to person.

Yarey's interactions with parents and teachers reveal the challenges encountered by many Taíno/Boricua. The lack of recognition and potential ridicule that accompanies their presumably "impossible" identification presents a vexing interactional challenge: How do you speak on behalf of what might be interpreted as an untenable subject position? As many Taíno/Boricua do, Yarey managed this by highlighting widely held Puerto Rican historical assumptions about Taíno/Boricua discontinuity and contrasting this to Taíno/Boricua practices, words, genetics, histories, and oral narratives. In her conversations with teachers and parents, Yarey attempted to construct an interactional realignment that could lead to a broader recognition of Taíno continuity and an acknowledgment of her Taíno ancestry.

Although critics of Taíno/Boricua often accuse them of being inauthentic and seeking recognition out of financial self-interest, in my observations, what actual Taíno/Boricua most often sought was an acknowledgment of their Indigenous subjectivity—of their identifications, practices, preferences, memories, and family histories. They were not claiming an absolute difference from other Puerto Ricans; they accepted their own mixed genealogies and sought recognition for the Indigenous heritage of other Puerto Ricans. For many, being Taíno/Boricua was a matter of identifying as and seeing the world as a member of this group. Anyone from the Caribbean whose family may have indicated that they were indios, or whose practices and worldview might indicate Taíno/Boricua heritage or spirituality, might be able claim Taíno/Boricua heritage. Once someone became a member of a Taíno or Jíbaro-Boricua group, the reinterpretation of their trajectory through an Indigenous narrative is what most often demarcated belonging.

This chapter, along with the previous two chapters, highlights the ways in which Taíno/Boricua challenge conceptualizations of Puerto Rican history, national figures, and racial ideologies. In the following chapter, I explore how these challenges impact projects of language reconstruction among different Taíno/Boricua organizations.

PART 3

Taíno Heritage and Political Mobilization

5

(Re)Constructing Heritage

Narratives of Linguistic Belonging among Taíno Activists

The Taíno/Boricua language as a separate code has not been spoken, according to recorded history, in centuries. Each Taíno/Boricua person and organization I met through the course of my research had different ideas about whether the Taíno/Boricua language was truly gone and, if it was, how they should go about reconstructing it. Each Taíno/Boricua language project embodied its group's different ideologies of language and notions of how to imagine, configure, preserve, enact, and promote their heritage, which were implicitly and explicitly compared and contrasted with other groups' beliefs and approaches to reclaiming Indigenous identity.

Some groups, such as Taíno Nation (TN) and Movimiento Indígena Jíbaro Boricua (MIJB), attempt long-term comparative reconstruction of what TN calls the Taíno and MIJB calls the Jíbaro language. Each of these reconstructions relies on different understandings of the language's genealogy. Others, such as Guaka-Kú (GK) and Liga Guakía Taína-ké (LGTK), seek to mobilize tokens of Taíno vocabulary in their speech and focus on creating discrete writing systems to encode what counts as Taíno language. The debates surrounding these efforts generate distinct, sometimes incompatible notions of how to competently speak as a Taíno/Boricua social actor and how to define the boundaries of broader categories of "authentic" or "legitimate" Taíno/Boricua belonging. Studies of language ideology have noted the interactional effects of debates grounded in different beliefs regarding language and social meaning (Irvine and Gal 2000; Jaffe 1999; Silverstein 1979; Woolard 2002). The Taíno/Boricua activists I spoke to identified different motivations for engaging in projects of language revival and cultural reclamation—some sought a better understanding of meaning making among their ancestors, for example, while others mobilized to gain recognition from the Puerto Rican government in order to obtain rights to speak for the care of sacred grounds.

Many Indigenous groups and scholars see language revival projects as important phenomena through which to reclaim and mobilize Indigenous cultures. The Taíno/Boricua case presents particular challenges because there are very limited linguistic resources to draw from. Scholars believe that Taíno was last spoken at some point in the sixteenth century (Arrom 2000 [1980]; Alvarez Nazario 1996). Unlike other Indigenous or minority languages—such as Manx (Ó hIfearnáin 2014), Wôpanâak (Makepeace 2010), Kaurna (Amery 2016), and Miami (Leonard 2008)— no Bible translations, legal documents, word lists, or speakers have been recorded that might aid the reconstruction process. The available documentation for Taíno is limited to a few sentences transcribed in early chronicles of the Americas (Pané 1999 [c. 1496]; de las Casas 1974 [1552]), place names throughout the Greater Antilles, and words that have been adopted by Spanish (and other languages, such as English). The meanings and genealogy of some Taíno words are known due to their continuous usage since the conquest, when the terms were incorporated to name Caribbean plants, objects, and practices that were new to the Spanish invaders. Most linguists who study Taíno agree that it was an Arawakan language, so Arawakan languages have been used to comparatively reconstruct aspects of the Taíno language (Granberry and Vescelius 2004). Debates about the vitality of Taíno based on beliefs about related languages from which to reconstruct it, or whether reconstructing it is even necessary, bring to mind linguist Wesley Y. Leonard's discussion of myaamia and how its linguistic and cultural awakening was facilitated by recognizing "the fallacy of extinction" (2008, 32). Instead, by rejecting the forms of linguistic purism that deny legitimacy to reclaimed languages as representing "historically spoken language," language reclaimers are able to move forward in their projects of reclamation (2008, 29).

Studies of language and cultural revival have shown how the restoration of a minority language is often understood as emblematic of the associated community's resilience, growth, and public visibility (Zenker 2014; Urla 1988; Urla 1993; Macdonald 1997). Recently, Zenker has demonstrated that in the context of the Irish language revival in Northern Ireland, many social actors possess "a strong conviction that the Irish language contains a different worldview from the one embodied in English" (2014, 63). Reclamations of Taíno language practices are not anchored in any one set of expectations or ideals about what speaking Taíno should sound like. In fact, many Taíno/Boricua do not consider language as a significant marker of cultural continuity. Linguistic anthropologist Jenny Davis examines the importance of discussing language reclamation movements in the context of "the personal lives, communicative practices, and embodied experiences in which they are inherently embedded" (2017, 37). By looking at the impact of colonial structures upon Indigenous languages, Davis draws on historian Jean O'Brien's notion of lasting, to look at the discursive conflation of Indigenous peoples with specific characteristics, which are then understood to be lost if those characteristics are lost too. This technology of erasure serves to deny the existence of the groups who are understood as having lost, for example, their languages as the singular index of their survival. Instead, Taíno/Boricua discuss and debate the role of language in relation to the movement, including inter- and intragroup debates about which linguistic codes to speak both among themselves and to the larger Puerto Rican public—Spanish? A reconstructed Taíno? Yucatec Mayan? They also investigate more general reconstruction questions regarding orthography, the purpose of the language and its contexts of use, who is authorized to speak it and correct others, and what language varieties are privileged. Arguably, there is an inverse relationship between the amount of documentation available to anchor the Taíno language reclamation project and the heterogeneity of Taíno concepts of what it means to speak Taíno. This chapter considers how language ideologies materialize in practice to present an overview of how various groups are actively seeking to reclaim a Taíno/Boricua Indigenous identity through language.

Jíbaro Spanish

Many Puerto Rican–based Taíno/Boricua groups favor the rural Jíbaro Spanish language varieties often spoken by the elders who maintained traditional Indigenous practices in their daily lives—even when they may not have claimed to be Taíno/Boricua themselves. As a model of Puerto Ricanness, the Jíbaro represents the normative values of a moral, proud, agricultural, Spanish-speaking, practical, and authentic Puerto Rican. In practice, the term could also be used to insult a person as poor, backward, unfashionable, and uneducated. The tension in this duality is reflected in evaluations of Jíbaro Spanish—at once authentic and backward, legitimate and institutionally deauthorized. It is a reliable index of the past, understood as less touched by contemporary educational pressure to move toward more supposedly "correct" varieties of Spanish.

The most salient phonological features of Jíbaro Spanish are the realization of the final /e/ as high /i/ and final /o/ as high /u/ in multisyllabic words (and in some other contexts as well), the null initial *h* as /h/, and the velarization of the *rr* when not followed by a vowel in careful speech (in comparison to the more highly salient /r/ as /l/ in the same contexts for other varieties of casual Puerto Rican Spanish; Holmquist 2005; Navarro Tomás 1966). Grammatically, people broadly recognize Jíbaro differences in verb conjugation, with particular salience for the use of *haiga* rather than *haya*, *-istes* rather than *-iste* for informal second-person singular preterit indicative verb forms (e.g., *fuistes*), and *-nos* rather than *-mos* for some first-person plural imperfect indicative verb forms (e.g., *estabanos*). The prosody of Jíbaro Spanish is also salient, often proceeding at a slower tempo than more urban varieties and with a recognizable cadence. The Jíbaro vocabulary is also understood to draw on more archaic forms of Spanish and to include a larger Taíno-derived component.

In my observations, Taíno leaders would use elements of Jíbaro Spanish to underscore the authenticity and legitimacy of their positions as Taíno/Boricua. Additionally, they would seek out rural Puerto Ricans who spoke jíbaro varieties to include them in their organizations and recover information about traditional practices. In these cases, the image of jibaridad, promoted by the cultural arms of the Puerto Rican government as the most authentic realization of Puerto Ricanness, became reframed as not a multirooted Puerto Rican but as the repository and current realization of Taíno heritage.

While no one during my fieldwork was recognized as speaking ancestral Taíno, Jíbaro varieties of Spanish are understood by many Puerto Rico–based Taíno as being most Taíno, and any variety of the Spanish language is preferred to the English language. Groups like the General Council of Taíno (CGT), with members from a number of towns in the northern region of Puerto Rico, would negatively evaluate United States–based Taíno who did not speak Spanish. At the 2018 Smithsonian symposium on Taíno in New York City, Abuela Shashira from the LGTK complained that she felt excluded by the last group of panelists' choice to speak English rather than Spanish. She explained how Spanish, in a way, was the language closest to their ancestors, since it was spoken to them and made theirs, while English was a foreign language in every sense. Spanish, for the abuela, held a more intimate connection to her spoken expression of Taínoness. Linguistic anthropologist Anthony Webster (2010, 2015) has shown how language intimacies, deeply felt connections to linguistic forms, serve to create "bonds of sociality." In the context of Indigenous groups, these intimacies are not necessarily delimited to the Indigenous languages often associated with the group but also to any number of colonial languages, such as Spanish in the case of the Taíno, that may reflect the deep histories and connections among those who share a history of speaking in and making community through them. These connections, too, can create and mark generational, spatial, and ideological boundaries by reifying those linguistic intimacies and the bonds they have made or failed to make. Jíbaro Spanish emerges, then, as a Taíno linguistic heritage, but like the figure of the jíbaro itself, it is a fraught heritage that may be evaluated as uneducated, ignorant, and unauthoritative even as it may also be understood as authentic and genuine.

Taíno Tokens

As the LGTK's cultural immersion program, spearheaded by Yarey, became established throughout schools in southeast Puerto Rico, their language project took form in the construction of orthographic boundaries around Taíno vocabulary to demarcate it as different from Spanish. LGTK activists developed a script based on Taíno pictographs—Taíno imagery found inscribed throughout Puerto Rico's natural landscape (see figure 5.1)—that corresponded to letters in the Latin script. The pictographs were selected for their iconic similarity to a letter in the Latin script. While not circulated widely on the island, this script was used in some of the schools in which LGTK implemented their Taíno Indigenous heritage program for an hour a week during students' social studies classes.

A few months after the script was first introduced, I went with Yarey to a middle school where she was planning to pitch the LGTK program. Walking through the halls, I was surprised to spot a student writing in the script, which had not been introduced in that particular school. He explained that he had learned it from his younger sibling who was in the LGTK program and that he and his friends (regardless of whether they identified as Taíno) found the script useful for communicating secret messages. This fulfilled, at least in part, the LGTK's expectation that the circulation of the script might serve as a material index of Taíno survival. Furthermore, they hoped that some children and their families would come to see Taíno as an extant identification category, one that they might eventually adopt. Yarey's visits to students' families

FIGURE 5.1. "Abecedario Taíno" worksheet. Photograph by Sherina Feliciano-Santos.

and LGTK-organized public events often did prompt parents and their children to identify as Taíno, and over the next year, further participation in LGTK events led to some parents and children becoming active members of the organization.

The LGTK's Taíno script is a form of textual symbolic boundary making with respect to Spanish. These processes recall Margaret Bender's work on Cherokee scripts, in which she shows that "for many Cherokees, . . . syllabary signs express (and enact!) the community's recent cultural revitalization and index the physical spaces of the reservation as authentically Indian spaces" (2008, 96). Choices made in a script's production and use can semiotically underscore linguistic differentiation or alignments and reflect attempts to create, break, or solidify different kinds of sociocultural identifications (Jaffe et al. 2012; Choksi 2015). In this way, token uses of a language serve as "indices of identity" that intertextually link past uses of language and "sociocultural knowledge" of those uses (Ahlers 2017, 40). Iconically representing the Taíno difference from the Puerto Rican mainstream through the use of a special script also served to demarcate Taíno modes of expression and spaces, such as the classrooms and homes of children who employ the script.

Partly due to the attraction of the newly developed script, which may have been interpreted as material evidence of the reconstruction of the Taíno language, LGTK's Taíno heritage appeared in a major local newspaper, *Primera Hora*. The newspaper reported,

En el programa piloto Inmersión Cultural-Lingüística de la Liga Guakía Taína-ké cerca de 120 menores, principalmente de cuarto a sexto grado, de dos escuelas de Maunabo aprenden sobre el vocabulario taíno y se basan en una codificación escrita inventada, utilizando los símbolos de los petroglifos indígenas, para escribir las palabras. Cabe destacar que otras tribus han hecho ejercicios parecidos ante la ausencia de una codificación escrita. (Rodríguez-Burns 2007)

In the Cultural-Linguistic Immersion pilot program of the Liga Guakía Taína-ké, close to 120 minors, principally from fourth to sixth grade, from two Maunabo schools learn about Taíno vocabulary, and they base themselves on an invented codification, using the symbols of the Indigenous petroglyphs, to write the words. It is important to emphasize that other tribes have done similar exercises when confronted with the absence of a written codification.

The LGTK saw *Primera Hora*'s coverage of their school program as a sign of great success, which served to further legitimize their efforts at linguistic recovery.[1] This media exposure helped the LGTK obtain resources for the program and allowed them to recruit linguists to help reconstruct the Taíno language. Linguistic anthropologist Jocelyn Ahlers notes that when languages cease to be spoken, the indexical links between language and community are also disrupted. However, teaching programs that have the goal of reawakening a language through its use in the community may have the alternative effect of "erecting barriers" due to the perception that it is creating a barrier to community cohesion (Ahlers 2014, 33). Since the Taíno script was developed and used by LGTK membership in LGTK classes, other groups became concerned that this script might circulate as a unique emblem of being Taíno and serve to further separate Taíno groups by limiting, rather than extending, intelligibility.

Awakening Taíno

Tuján, the leader of GK, was known in his town in southeastern Puerto Rico for often walking barefoot, sleeping in a cave full of Taíno petroglyphs, and teaching a class on Taíno cultural heritage at a local private Christian school. Though he was widely seen as an eccentric character whose livelihood depended on the kindness of others, due to his teaching, his involvement in the municipal cultural center, and a local radio show he hosted, he was also quite influential in representing Taíno people in regional political and cultural debates. He considered himself, and was considered by others, to be clairvoyant. He was careful to write down his thoughts, visions, and perceptions of events and people, some of which he compiled in a self-published book. In the following excerpt, Tuján describes how certain words influenced his path as a Taíno. Some of the terms in Tuján's list (which were all capitalized in the original text) are still widely used in Puerto Rican Spanish, others are place names, others name plants and animals, and yet others are archaisms still spoken within rural Spanish varieties.

I also include an excerpt from his introduction to the terms and his instructions on how to read them:

Unas voces con las cuales se dio forma a la razón de ser pueblo taíno. Aquí colocaremos algunas [palabras] que afectaron mi trama y mi sentido de usarlas . . .

AREYTO, BAGUA, TEY, BAIRA, BAJAREQUE, BOHIO [sic], BAJARIS, BATEY, BATU, BEHIQUE, BIBIJAGUA, BIJANI, BOGUEY, BURENES, BURENQUEN, BRU-CAYO, CABAO, CACIQUE, CANEY, CANOA, CAO-BANA, CAONA, CASABE, CEMI, COAIBAI, CIAS, COJOBA, COROZO, DUJO, GUAILI, GUATIAO, GUAJEY, GUAMIQUINA, GUAMO, GUANARA, GUANIN, GUARICHE, GUATAUBA, GUAYACAN, SIBA. HIGUERA, JAGUEY, JAYUYA, JURACAN [sic], JUTIAS, MACANA, MACAO, MAQUETAURIE, MARACA, MOCA, NACAN, NITAÍNO, SAROBEI, COINI, TUREY, YARAGAUA, YUCA, YABOA

El hecho de leerlas en voz alta y con sentido de lograr un acto de reconciliación de pensamiento se crea un ambiente digno de lectura (T. Dávila 2001, 24).

Some voices with which the Taíno people's reason of being was given form. Here we will bring together some [words] that affected my trajectory and my sense of using them . . .

AREYTO, BAGUA, TEY, BAIRA, BAJAREQUE, BOHIO, BAJARIS, BATEY, BATU, BEHIQUE, BIBIJAGUA, BIJANI, BOGUEY, BURENES, BURENQUEN, BRUCAYO, CABAO, CACIQUE, CANEY, CANOA, CAOBANA, CAONA, CASABE, CEMI, COAIBAI, CIAS, COJOBA, COROZO, DUJO, GUAILI, GUATIAO, GUAJEY, GUAMIQUINA, GUAMO, GUANARA, GUANIN, GUARICHE, GUATAUBA, GUAYACAN, SIBA. HIGUERA,

JAGUEY, JAYUYA, JURACAN, JUTIAS, MACANA,
MACAO, MAQUETAURIE, MARACA, MOCA, NACAN,
NITAÍNO, SAROBEI, COINI, TUREY, YARAGAUA,
YUCA, YABO

The act of reading them out loud and with a sense of accom-
plishing an act of reconciliation of the mind creates a dignified
reading environment (T. Dávila 2001, 24).

Because of their relationship to Taíno heritage, these words are
performative in philosopher of language John Austin's (1975) sense;
as such, they are capable of producing transformations in people
and space. For Tuján, saying them aloud is like an incantation,
not a referential act. The power of these words resides in the intent
of the speaker and in the acoustics of the symbols themselves to
create a Taíno meditative space. Tuján's book was one of many self-
published works circulating among Taíno and local Indigenous
circles in Puerto Rico. He envisioned his book as a guide to awakening "sleeping consciousnesses"—Indigenous self-awareness. It
was through an engagement with Taíno vocabulary, with words
that created Taíno meditative spaces, that Tuján strove to inspire a
Taíno worldview in his readers.

Like LGTK members, GK organizers also used a script to
semiotically demarcate Taíno as separate from Spanish. GK used
a Latin script as its base, but the letters were subverted by joining
them with their mirror image at their sides (a sort of palindrome)
or by superimposing the letter's respective mirror image over its
center axis in the case of the letters that correspond to $M, N, O, Q,$
$V, W,$ and X (see figure 5.2).

GK argued that this subversion undermined Puerto Rico's
colonial relationship with Spain as represented by Spanish and its
writing system. According to Tuján, the letters in the GK script
"hide their meaning in plain sight," which served as an allegory
for the Taíno people, who are often hidden in plain sight. Though
the letters themselves were meant to allow those who were liter-
ate in Spanish and English to easily decipher the phoneme they

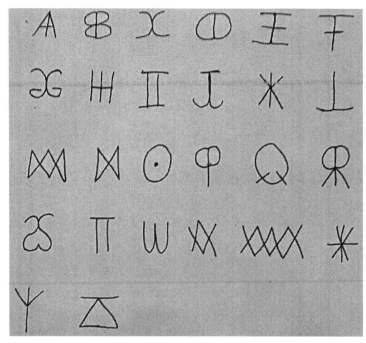

FIGURE 5.2. The Guaka-Kú script. Photograph by Sherina Feliciano-Santos.

represent, the meanings contained within would not be readily apprehended. Not only were the letters themselves proposed as challenges to the Latin script, but words were to be spelled from top to bottom instead of from left to right, and proper names were only spelled with consonants. GK intended for their script to reveal something essential about people through the spelling of their names. For example, the group named me Anajuke, which means "white flower of the Earth," because I arrived when the higuerillo tree was in bloom with many small white flowers. By studying the shapes and forms that were created by the rendering of my name in GK script, the group attempted to gain insight into who I was and whether they could trust me (see figure 5.3). Two group members took up this task and initially disagreed in their interpretations. One saw a beetle, the other saw an owl. They ultimately settled on the owl, given that I was there as an observer. It

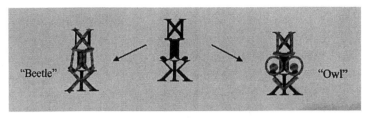

FIGURE 5.3. The spelling of Anajuke according to the Guaka-Kú script and writing conventions. Photograph by Sherina Feliciano-Santos.

was not clear to me what it would have meant if they had instead settled on the beetle.

This naming practice also depended on my acceptance of the name (I did not know that then). When I finally called myself Anajuke one day, Tuján said that because I had claimed my name, he would tie some twine around my ankle to officially tie me to my name. He advised me to not remove the tie until it fell off on its own, which would complete the process. Such procedures, he explained, helped communicate to the spirits that I had accepted my new name and my connection to the Taíno people. I left the twine around my ankle for the duration of my research with Tuján. In doing so, I also opened myself up to being "read" by Tuján on other levels. I asked Tuján what he meant the first time he attempted to read my *cuadro espiritual* (spiritual frame). Though initially he withheld an explanation, Tuján eventually described the spiritual frame as the compilation of spiritual traits and ancestral relationships that surround any person, which were decipherable to those with the gift of clairvoyance. Readability and decipherability in this spiritual realm were akin to issues of authorship/authority in academia. The ability to successfully conduct readings is not only about being able to communicate with the spiritual realm but also about strategically positioning oneself as someone with specialized knowledge and skills. For social actors in LGTK and GK, the use of Taíno words created a discursive space where Taíno ways of understanding and communicating—even if morphosyntactically framed by Spanish—were privileged. This exemplifies what Jocelyn Ahlers calls a "Native Language as Identity Marker" (NLIM) style, which serves "to perform not only the identity of the speaker, but to create a discourse space in a larger sense, as a Native American discourse space, and to pull the audience into that creation" (2006, 73). In this way, nonfluent heritage speakers of Native American languages foreground an ideology where "the metacommunicative/pragmatic function of such language use over referential function serves to highlight a broader Native American identity shared by speaker and audience" (58). Additionally, the use of a Taíno script further demarcated Taíno discourse in writing, objectifying its difference from Spanish, and served as an emblem of Taíno reclamation and heritage.

Finding and Reconstructing Taíno/Boricua

During the period of my research, two organizations were actively pursuing long-term projects to reconstruct and restore an Indigenous Puerto Rican language. Such endeavors are inherently fraught with complications at various levels. In the case of the Taíno language, the process entails gathering information from the remaining vocabulary and related languages of Taíno, performing both comparative and historical reconstruction work, deciding how to incorporate such resources and which resources to incorporate, creating teaching materials and spaces, training teachers, setting attainable goals, implementing Taíno teaching programs, and instituting mechanisms to appraise the success of such programs in order to secure their sustainability.[2] Each step of this process is interrelated and carries the potential for disagreement between members within each particular group and among different groups. Such disagreements, in turn, are bound up with claims to authority (who gets to make choices), claims to knowledge (who is understood to have the training and experience to make such calls), sociopolitical alignments (what sorts of cultural-genealogical associations inform / result from making claims about linguistic-genealogical associations and vice versa), and acts of marking or erasing boundaries among groups (what sorts of dividing lines result from choices about language genealogies and restoration outcomes).[3]

I first encountered the TN on a research trip to New York City.[4] They had been involved in language reconstruction since the '70s and were drawing heavily from other Arawakan languages to remake and construct the Taíno language, which they referred to as Taíney. I met with members of the MIJB in the later stages of my research. They were focused on efforts to disassociate from Arawakan languages and instead use Yucatec Mayan to reconstruct an Indigenous language in Puerto Rico. They referred to themselves and their language as Jíbaro-Boricua instead of Taíno, since they argued that *Taíno* was a colonial misnomer. The rejection of *Taíno* in the group's name was also a rejection of the claim that their language was Arawakan. The TN, mainly organized within New York City, was taking advantage of the resources available at the New York Public Library and at the Center for Puerto Rican Studies at Hunter College, CUNY. The MIJB, based in rural northwestern Puerto Rico, was gathering data through interviews with rural Jíbaro speakers and drawing from dictionaries in Yucatec Mayan. Though, at the time of my research, neither had completely reconstructed an Indigenous language, TN's efforts were understood by its members as ongoing, while MIJB's were understood to be complete.

While both groups consider their Jíbaro ancestry to be their link to Indigeneity, they conceptualize Indigeneity differently. For the MIJB, it is linked to a Mayan genealogy; for the TN, it is linked to an Arawakan ancestry. This genealogical divide is informed by distinct ontologies, mythologies, and histories that affect the processes and outcomes of their respective language reconstruction projects, which are the source of a serious division among Indigenous groups in Puerto Rico. That division impacts other major points of contention among different Indigenous groups, including debates about political action, relevant audiences for their work, and the goals for the Indigenous resurgence on the island. Issues and beliefs surrounding Indigenous language projects are related to larger expectations of what Indigeneity looks like as much as they reflect concerns about heritage.

Debates about Origins

Tito Guajataca, a member of MIJB, had a very radical concept of what it meant to be Indigenous Boricua. Though I had heard about him and his politics, I had not yet met him in person when he first called me. He told me that my contact information had been given to him by someone who thought that I should speak to the "genuine native population" of the island. When I asked him what he meant by *genuine*, he replied that Taíno was the name given to island's population by the colonizers, and while *Taíno* is an Indigenous word (like they claim *Jíbaro* and *Boricua* are), it is not the name of the group. He explained that *Taíno* just meant something like "we are good people," and the Spanish had understood the term as the island population's group name. Instead, Tito said he was a Jíbaro-Boricua, one of Puerto Rico's genuine natives. He then set about convincing me of the importance of the work he was doing while arguing that my work with the so-called Taíno was a waste of time. To him, they were not Indigenous but merely performing being Indigenous.

The first time I met Tito in person, I sat in one of the many hammocks inside his living room. He offered me some local black coffee. Tito asked if my recorder was on and then proceeded to give me his version of the history of northwestern Puerto Rico, his region of the island. He stopped, left for a moment, and came back with a number of manila envelopes, which he handed to me as though they held treasures. Within each envelope was a photocopied, typewritten, unpublished manuscript by Oscar Lamourt Valentín, also known as Oki.[5] I had read about Oki (Castanha 2004) but had been unable to find any of his work in the library, so I was surprised to actually see his writings. Tito had been a student of Oki's, and before Oki passed away, he named Tito as the custodian of his work. Tito told me which manuscripts I could copy and distribute and which I could cite but not circulate. He was concerned that another group would find the writings and take credit for them, distributing and teaching the knowledge they contained without truly understanding them. I was allowed to see many of the manuscripts, but Tito never gave them to me all at once; new manuscripts appeared at each visit. For Tito, Oki's work was essential in defining his movement's approach to thinking about Indigeneity on the island, since he understood Oki to have been a pioneer in revealing the Mayan origins of the island's Indigenous language. As I continued my research, I found that people who shared Tito's vision of Indigenous resurgence on the island often cited Oki's writings as having helped them define their own expressions of Indigeneity.

Oki's manuscripts focus on revealing the Jíbaro as Puerto Rico's true native peoples, arguing that the Indigenous presence in Puerto Rico has been continuous, de-authorized, and misunderstood. Oki also insists that the pre-Columbian language spoken on the island was not Arawakan but more closely related to Mayan. Oki labels the Indigenous population as *Jíbaro* or *Boricua* rather than *Taíno*, which he explains in his introduction to an unpublished yet moderately circulated manuscript written in English, "The Extrapolation and the Limits of Language":

> For being retrospectively extinct and being disauthorized from having an identity of one's own on the basis of someone else' [*sic*] identity, and ascribed as belonging to a colonial demographic inventory . . . we refer to ourselves as the "Jíbaro," and within the context of our own geography "Boricuas," The word we employ to designate our own compatriots is "pana" while our island is named by us "Borinquen." One can observe of course that these are native language terms "as if they were spanish," [*sic*] but then that only means that morphemologically [*sic*] they are denied any significance on their own, so that they can only be defined as someone else' [*sic*] language, and then what we could find is that they are in fact epistemologically disauthorized. (Lamourt Valentín n.d., 1)[6]

This understanding of Indigenous languages on the island as de-authorized by their absorption into Spanish is shared by many groups, though how such languages are genealogically traced may vary. The evidence Oki provides for a Mayan origin depends on a series of steps whereby he takes the Hispanicized spellings of the remaining Indigenous words in Puerto Rican Spanish and renders them into what he claims are the Mayan morphemes that form the non-Hispanicized word, which he then defines in Mayan and translates/glosses back into Spanish. Here is an example from the same unpublished manuscript:

> Since our identification is an eponymous term "Jíbaro" or "can.ch'íb-al.o'" in the native language, referring to "caste, gener-ation, lineage in the direct Male line" . . . the "male" in question is the ancestral hero and demi-urge "Iguana Lord" or "Itzamnah" called Kukulcan by the Quiché and Quetzacoatl by the Toltec . . . But as the present work has been pointing out from the start, the native language we have been talking about is a maya-thantik . . . mayanese [sic] speech, albeit, with a certain number of charac-teristics qualified as quite archaic, such as the retention of "ng"; otherwise it grammatically approaches with minor alterations the Yucatec-Lacandón (Mopan? Itzae?) group of Maya-thantik. (9)

Such arguments about the island's Indigenous language being a Mayan language are not only about language but also about specific lineages and alignments with respect to Indigenous populations in the Americas more broadly. In a book based on Oki's work, the authors, Uahtibili Báez Santiago and Huana Naboli Martínez Prieto of the Movimiento Indígena Chib'al'o [Jíbaro]-Boricua (MOVIJIBO)—another Indigenous group that, like the MIJB, rejects the Taíno name and any claim of Arawakan genealogy—explain,

> Nuestra isla era la cabeza o isla principal del conglomerado de islas que comprenden el área desde Isla Margarita hasta la Penín-sula de la Florida, en lo que hoy se conoce como las Antillas. Al igual que toda el área antillana fue, y todavía es, habitada por

aborígenes de la etnia Can'Chib'al'o, con una cultura y sistema de creencias que caracterizan una historiografía Maya. (2008)

Our island was the head or principal island of the conglomerate of islands that comprise the area from Margarita Island to the Florida Peninsula, in what is known as the Antilles today. The same as all the Antillean area it was, and still is, inhabited by aboriginal peoples of the Can'Chib'al'o ethnicity, with a culture and belief system that characterize a Mayan historiography.

This orientation draws from Yucatec Mayan and presumes that the morphological items found in dictionaries of Taíno roughly correspond both to the Indigenous words that are preserved and still used on the island today (most often in the form of place names and in the realm of domestic practices) and to instances of the island's Indigenous language found in the chronicles of Friar Ramon Pané, Bartolomé de las Casas, and a few others.[7] The logic in this argument is that each native word can be broken down into its component morphemes, which in turn can be read and interpreted through the Mayan language, and that the ability to do this reveals a genetic language connection that is due to an ancestral ethnic relatedness. Oki credits his success in deciphering the composition of Indigenous words on the island to methods learned in a course on medical etymology. That the purported Mayan origin of Indigenous Puerto Rican language was uncovered by what appeared to members of the MIJB to be an academic and objective method further served to legitimize this thesis.[8] Those members of the group, like Tito, who demonstrate the ability to deploy Oki's methods to use Mayan to decipher Jíbaro Boricua are well respected and seen as authoritative.

Mayan versus Arawakan

The distinct interpretations of terms that emerge from the understanding of Indigenous expressions as either Mayan or Arawakan influence the interpretation of the island's Indigenous past as well as the reconstruction of the Taíno and Jíbaro-Boricua language. Table 5.1 shows the significant interpretive differences for some of the most central terms in contemporary Indigenous culture in Puerto Rico. The first column includes words that are currently used or recognizable in Puerto Rican Spanish, and the second column contains the most conventional glosses for their meanings. The third column consists of Oki's Mayan-based reconstruction of the corresponding word with the morphemic correspondences he has identified. For example, for *Borinquen*, alternately spelled *Borikén*, Oki reconstructed the word to have been *Bohlikin* based on Mayan morphology. The fourth column shows how Oki has glossed the meaning of the word—in this case, "Island of the Dawn." The fifth and sixth columns show the Arawakan analyses of the same words. The fifth column reconstructs the meaning of *Borinquen/Borikén* based on other Arawakan languages, and the sixth column includes a gloss of the word's meaning based on an Arawakan comparison.

Once, when we were driving through an area in the northwestern region of the island called Cibao, Tito asked me if I knew what the word *Cibao* meant. I said, "Rocks," which is the Arawakan-derived gloss for the term. "Well, that's if you subscribe to the Arawak version," he responded. "However, if you read Oki and realize the Mayan origins of the language, *Cibao*, or in its correct pronunciation, *Shibao*, means 'place of departure.'" Though I was admittedly skeptical of Tito's etymology, his explanation resonated with other members of his group, who interpreted the Cibao region as the place where the Jíbaro-Boricua movement would depart/begin rather than linking the name to the area's physical landscape—its rocky surface. I attributed this specific interpretation to this region being where many of the group members and their families were from. For those who understood the area to be linked to the departure/beginning of the true Indigenous movement in Puerto Rico, the region's inhabitants were seen as the "genuine native descendants," the Chib'al'o, also known as the Jíbaro.

TABLE 5.1.

TERM	CURRENT GLOSS	OKI MAYAN VERSION	OKI MAYAN GLOSS	ARAWAKAN VERSION	ARAWAKAN GLOSS
Borinquen/ Borikén	Indigenous term for the island	boh→to scrutinize li→in the east cardinal direction kin→sun	"island of the dawn"	bori→noble ke→island or buren→ instrument where yucca is prepared ke→island	"island of the noble" / "island where yucca is prepared"
nigua	bothersome / small bug that bites	nich→to take bites uah→life	"bug that bites"	nigua→small thing	"small thing"
guaitiao	friend/ally	u-ah→of theirs ti'→with hau→classifier of divided things / half	"exchange"	wa→land or wã→ocean tiyawo→friend or wa→our tiaho→friend	"our friend"
Agüeybaná	name of a cacique	ah→lord uay→lodging bana→marine iguana	"lord of the land of the marine iguana"	a→noun designator guey→sol ba→big/great -na→verb designator	"great sun leader"
cacique	leader	c→our ah→ master tzich-eh→ very reverenced	"our reverenced master"	ca→the ci→head ke→land	"the head of the land"
Oubao Moin	land of blood	hau→turn around ba→as such o→class marker mu→brother-in-law in→my/mine	"like my brothers-in-law / the people we marry with"	oubao→island moin→blood	"island of blood"
cemí	three-point spiritual artifact	dzem→to alleviate / calm a wrong/damage in→my/mine	"my fixer of damages"	ce→god/ supernatural mi→spirit	"ancestor spirit"

SOURCES: Oki Mayanized terms from Lamourt Valentín (n.d.); Arawakan terms from Alvarez Nazario (1996); Arrom (2000 [1980]); Granberry and Vescelius (2004).

Taíney

During the summer of 2008, I traveled to New York City to meet with the various Taíno groups based there. One of the groups, the TN, invited me to interview them about their language reconstruction efforts. I met JBL, David, and Wakonax at Wakonax's home in Brooklyn.[9] We sat in the living room. JBL, who appeared to be in his late sixties, sat in an armchair to my right. Wakonax, probably in his late forties or early fifties, sat to my left. On the other side of the coffee table directly in front of me sat David, who seemed to be about my age, in his late twenties or early thirties. The apparent ages of these three men coincided with the authoritative hierarchies that emerged in my conversation with them—especially in relation to decision-making in the language reconstruction process. JBL told me that he had been working on reconstructing the Taíno language since the '70s. He explained that the impetus for the project developed out of a recognition of his own Taíno ancestry, an ancestry contained within his Jíbaro family background. He told me that it was controversial to claim to be Taíno then, as it is now, but having grown up a Jíbaro, he knew that was who he was. Wakonax and David listened as JBL elaborated on the origins of the language reconstruction project.

Throughout our conversation, all three men were careful to call the language Taíney instead of Taíno. JBL explained, "*Tain-* is 'good,' *-ney* is—comes from *igney*, o *ine*, which is 'man' . . . and the *no* in *Taíno* is the plural, the plural 'human.' When you wanna say *people*, you use the *-no*. So 'the good people,' *Taíno*. And since *tain-* is 'good,' the *-no*, being an *n*, there is no need for the other *n*, so you put *Taíno*. That's the plural . . . and when you identify a language, you don't identify with it as a plural but as singular." For JBL, *Taíno* is the appropriate term for the people, and *Taíney* is the correct designation for the language. This reflects Taíno grammatical norms and practices as reconstructed by his group.

My conversation with JBL, David, and Wakonax began in English—I suspect due to David and Wakonax's greater fluency in English—but JBL consistently switched to Spanish throughout,

often while speaking about Indigenous and Jíbaro topics, a possible insight into how he was conceptualizing the indexical connections among Spanish, jibaridad, and Taíno identifications. In the
excerpt below, where JBL discusses the sources he has used in his
language reconstruction work, he speaks entirely in Spanish:

Oh, yendo al idioma, yo estudié muchas fuentes, pero las fuentes
primordiales, las más importantes son el Eyeri o el que llaman
mal nombrado Caribe insular, y el Lokono. Y tenemos más
fuerzas con el Lokono que el mismo Caribe insular o el Eyeri.
Compartimos de las dos tenemos de las dos, pero el Ta-el Taíney,
como yo le digo, o el Taíno como dicen corrientemente, está más
relacionado para mi entender con el Lokono que con el Eyeri
porque el Eyeri es una lengua, lo que llaman una lengua *n*, pert-
enece a *n* . . . ¿qué qué queremos decir con eso? Los pronombres
comienzan, el primer pronombre comienza con la *n* mientras que
el Taíney comienza con la *d* . . . exactamente como el Lokono, yo
fui estudiando tanto el Eyeri tanto como el Lokono, y también
el Guajiro, porque hay cosas del Guajiro, y me puse a hacer
listas de palabras y a compararlas y los significados, y fue muy
deslumbrante y a la misma vez muy bueno para mí encontrar
que habían paralelos. Definitivamente, eh, por ejemplo, te voy a
dar un ejemplo: en República Dominicana todavía se le dice a la
calabaza, *auyama*, y la-la palabra exactamente igual la encuentras
en el Lokono y significa lo mismo.

Oh, going to the language, I studied many sources, but the
primary sources, the most important, are the Eyeri, or what they
wrongly call Insular Carib, and the Lokono. And we have more
strength with the Lokono than with the very Insular Carib or
Eyeri. We share from both, we have from both, but the Ta—the
Taíney, how I call it, or the Taíno, as they say commonly, is
more related to, in my understanding, with the Lokono than
with Eyeri because the Eyeri is a language, what they call an
n language, it belongs to *n* . . . what do we mean by that? The
pronouns begin, the first pronoun begins with the *n*, while Taíney

begins with the *d* . . . exactly like the Lokono, I studied both the Eyeri as well as the Lokono, and also the Guajiro, because there are things from the Guajiro, and I made myself make word lists and to compare them and the meanings, and it was enlightening and at the same time very good for me to find that there were parallels. Definitely, eh, for example, I will give you an example: in the Dominican Republic, they still call the pumpkin *auyama*, and the-the word exactly the same you find it on Lokono, and it means the same thing.

For the TN, choices about what languages to use for comparative reconstruction are based on the overlap and convergence of lexical and morphological forms. In the above excerpt, JBL mentions three Arawakan languages that he has studied to build current forms of Taíney: Eyeri, Lokono, and Guajiro. JBL draws on the morphological characteristics of the languages to explain why Lokono is the best fit. He also illustrates similarities between Lokono and Taíney with respect to particular words that are still used in Lokono and in the Spanish of the Dominican Republic. In part, decisions about language reconstruction are made with word lists, which are studied to find overlaps (or differences) that are significant and numerous enough to justify using (or not using) a particular language as a source. The word lists are based on Taíney-derived words still in use throughout Puerto Rico and the Dominican Republic and also draw from words found in the sixteenth-century Caribbean travel chronicles of Ramón Pané and Bartolomé de las Casas, who wrote about their encounters with the Taíno. Though interested in existing Taíno-derived words in Spanish, the TN was primarily focused on agglutination in Taíney, which is the linguistic process whereby complex words are formed by joining morphemes without changing them phonetically. Because of this, the TN invested significant effort in analyzing the morphemes that compose Taíney words to gather information about the structure of the language.

JBL has spent close to forty years looking through the surviving Taíney vocabulary, Eyeri, and Lokono for patterns of difference and similarity in spelling and morphology. Through the identification of certain patterns, JBL feels that he is able to extrapolate from these languages to interpret and reconstruct Taíney. For example, in the next excerpt, JBL explains that he found a pattern of correspondence between Loko and Taíney, where he concluded that /a/ in Loko corresponded to /e/ in Taíney, /l/ corresponded to /n/, and /h/ becomes omitted. With this pattern, he was able to take the Loko word *jalika* (why) and manufacture the word *aneke*, which is now used in Taíney to mean "why." He explains,

Las fuentes que usó fueron los hermanos Moreau que estuvieron de misioneros con los Lokono, y de allí yo estudie eso y vi mucho, mucho, muchas las fuentes. Incluso, a base de eso yo decidí que muchas de las palabras que no tenemos pues simplemente hay que ir a la hermana lengua, tomarlas y acomodarlas a la forma Taína a la estructura Taína—Taíney. Cuál es la diferencia? Como en otras, otros pueblos indígenas de aquí de las Américas, grandes, pueblos grandes muchas veces se dividen la misma etnia se dividen diferentes dialectos y eso lo vemos entre los Iroquíes, y lo vemos entre los Lakota, están los Lakota, los Dakota y los Nakota, ¿cuál es la diferencia? Que en su, por ejemplo los pronombre, usan, unos usan la *d*, otros usan la *n* y otros usan la *l* ¿entiendes? Entonces yo encontré que lo mismo sucede con el Eyeri, con el Loko, y con el Taíney, eh, el Eyeri por ejemplo usa la *r* intervocálica y la usa también al principio. El Taíney usa la *r* intervocálica pero la *d* como afijo, prefijo al principio, y a veces usa la *d* intervocálica también, aunque es menos común te voy a dar un ejemplo, en el loko, eh, existe la palabra *jalika* que significa {?} Y el equivalente en Taíney, encontré es *aneke*, o sea que la *a* de *jalika* se convierte en *e*, la *l* en *n*, y la *h* {j} no se usa en Taíney, y pos allí con esa misma palabra, en la forma que lo escribas, te da el porqué quien qué y así si yo fui he ido reestructurando todo eso acomodándolo a la forma en que el Taíno se expresaba y claro en muchos casos tuve que volver a investigar lo mismo, reflexionar, y buscar. Estábamos hablando de la palabra *guanábana*, ¿verdad? en Taíney se dice *wanábana*, y el español lo escribió *guanábana*, en el eyeri se dice *walápana*, ¿ves la relación? y en el loko *warápana*, o sea que la *l* en un caso se vuelve *r*, en el Taíney se vuelve *n*, y la *p* se trastoca en *b* en el Taíney, mientras que en Eyeri y en Loko se mantiene la *p*, ¿entiendes? Entonces en el mismo significado, *guayaba* que en realidad debe ser *wayaba*, allí los eyeris dicen *coyaba*, y los loko *malyaba*, ¿eh? que a pesar de las diferencias que hay en ciertas consonantes se le sale el sentido de la palabra; sale lo que significa.

The sources that (he) used were the brothers Moreau that were missionaries with the Lokono, and from there I studied that and saw a lot, a lot, a lot the sources. Additionally, based on that I decided that many of the words that we don't have, well, simply, we just have to go to the sister language, take them, and accommodate to the Taíno form to the Taíno structure—Taíney. What is the difference? Like in others, other Indigenous peoples from here of the Americas, large peoples many times the same ethnicity are divided in different dialects, and we see that among the Iroquois, and we see that among the Lakota, there are the Lakota, the Dakota, and the Nakota, what is the difference? That in their, for example, the pronouns, they use, some use the *d*, other use the *n*, and others use the *l*, understand? Then I found that the same happens with the Eyeri, and with the Loko, and with Tainé, eh, the Eyeri, for example, uses the intervocalic *r*, and it also uses it at the beginning. The Taíney uses the intervocalic *r* but the *d* as an affix, prefix at the beginning, and sometimes uses the intervocalic *d* too, although it is less common. In the Loko, eh, the word *jalika* exists that means {?} And the equivalent in Taíney, I found, is *aneke*, that is that the *a* of *jalika* is converted in *e*, the *l* in *n*, and the *h* {j} is not used in Taíney, and well with that same word, in the way that you write it, it gives you the why, who, what, and in that way I have gone restructuring everything, accommodating it to the form in which the Taíno expressed themselves, and clearly in many cases I had to go back and investigate the same, reflect, and look. We were talking about the word *guanábana*, right? In

Taíney you say *wanábana*, and the Spanish wrote *guanábana*, and in Eyeri you say *walápana*, see the relationship? And in Loko *warápana*—that is, the *l* in one case becomes *r*, and in the Taíney it becomes *n*, and the *p* is converted to *b* in Taíney, while in Eyeri and in Loko, the *p* is maintained, understand? Then in the same meaning, which in reality should be *wayaba*, there the Eyeris say *coyaba*, and the Loko, *malyaba*, eh? That in spite of the differences that there are in certain consonants, the sense of the words comes out, the meaning comes out.

In addition to the comparative reconstruction work, the group uses their membership application process to obtain new information about the words and practices of the Taíno, compiling information about the potential remnants of Taíno that are still in circulation so that the TN can continue to build their argument that the Taíno language and culture are still present in the Caribbean. In the excerpt below, Wakonax explains how they acquired an important piece of information about the Taíno language, one that he argues told them something new about Taíney agglutination and greeting practices.

1	WAKONAX:	We created a registry, and in the registry, people needed to write an essay, "How Do You Know You're Taíno?" Not to prove that they were. No. It is really—really, it's like a misnomer. "How is it that you are aware that you are Taíno?" . . . is what it meant, and then, what happens? People tell stories. "My grandmother used to tell me this, tell me that," and a little piece comes out . . . "Oh, there's a word we never heard before." "There's a little one." "That's the biggest one." That's the one that told us about the agglutination of the language.
2	SHERINA:	Oh, which word was that?
3	JBL:	Haiakapashke . . .

w: This guy, he signed up. Wrote in his thing, and he says, "Every time that we have a family gathering, you know, everybody greets each other with the phrase *haiakapashke*," and so, he says, uh, "But we don't know what it means," you know? "We lost the meaning." And this guy goes, and he starts taking it apart and comes out with a whole phrase, an introductory phrase, like when you travel to another village, you introduce yourself using that phrase, and within the phrase is enough information—who you are, where you're from, and who your family was.

While I remained unclear on the exact meaning of the word *haiakapashke*, this anecdote lends insight into how the membership application process served to aid language reconstruction by extending the scope and use of Taíney vocabulary, expanding knowledge of traditional practices as a whole, and demonstrating the continuity of these words within particular pockets of Indigenous networks. Wakonax explained how even though the man explicitly said that he didn't know the meaning of the word *haiakapashke*, his description of its use was sufficient to aid the TN in recovering its significance. This information-gathering practice was not limited to the application process. In another instance, Wakonax described how a chance encounter with a workman who explained the origins and significance of his Taíno name led to the recovery of a Taíno conflict-resolution practice known as the "ceremony of the seven stones." The TN can use the individual stories of family-based practices to reconstruct the social life of the Taíno.

David, JBL, and Wakonax recognized that Taíney in use as a spoken language may belong to a distant future, but they noted how elements of the language were creeping into their everyday speech. David explained that he and other Taíno youth have coined new uses for a few Taíney words. They use *guanajo*, Taíney for "turkey," as a friendly insult—as in, "What's up, guanajo?"—and *turey*, the Taíney word for "sky," to mean "gay" via an index-ical association with *pato* "duck," a term for gay in Spanish (LaFountain-Stokes 2007). A sort of slang, these words seemed to enable particular kinds of closeness between David and his friends by giving them a shared code. Both David and JBL discussed this integration of Taíney vocabulary into either Spanish or English, which JBL described as a kind of Creole—as a way to begin the process of restoring Taíney to regular use. It is through regular and repeated use that terms like *guanajo* and *turey* become attached to particular pragmatic meanings. These processes of lamination (Eisenlohr 2004a, 2006; Silverstein 1993), such as those described by David, illustrate how the emergence of novel uses of language incorporate, from their formation, the specific prejudices—the taken-for-granted particular understandings of how the world is organized—held by speakers.

Teaching Taíney

The TN's website indicated that they had offered classes in Taíney, and I was curious about the process of teaching a language that was still being reconstructed. For JBL, the issues with teaching Taíney had nothing to do with the language itself and everything to do with what he saw as the corrupting, colonizing influence of U.S. culture on Taíno people. He talked about his interest in starting a cultural immersion program for youth to counteract the pernicious effects of living in the United States; adults, he felt, were a lost cause.

Wakonax, however, described how the rapid pace of change in Taíney posed challenges in the classroom:

One of the problems of this has been that, um, a lot of the real heavy work that these two guys [David and JBL] did in terms of the grammar happened in the last five or six years . . . and we kept saying, you know, "Wait." They didn't wanna wait. They learned. So there were all these songs that . . . we had to change the words because the grammar didn't fit, and there [were] phrases and stuff that people were learning that, you know, then you had to say, "Excuse me, but you have to change that," and to teach an adult is one thing, to unteach him. . . .

Each new development in Taíney was accompanied by having to "unteach" adults who had already learned specific linguistic forms. Given that the reconstruction of Taíney is a constant process of recovery of ostensibly formerly used forms along with the manufacture of terms for concepts that may not have existed in the past, many learners of Taíno were frustrated when they were told that a language form they had already mastered had been found to be wrong. This was understood by learners as an impediment to creating a community of speakers around the language. Wakonax expressed his own frustrations with the shifting nature of a language under (re)construction:

There are songs that are changed now that other people sing that I refuse to sing—changed because to me, it's the meaning of the song. But the words have changed, so I sing songs, and people go, "We don't do it like that" now. I say, "I don't care" because I—I am communicating something. So . . . that's one of the things, a big problem, and people want to speak right away, right away, but . . . the language was in process of evolving, and the grammar, and they didn't understand, you're gonna learn this today, and maybe next year or next week, you're gonna have to undo that and change this one, this pronoun.

Wakonax clarifies that he is less invested in keeping up to date with the changes in the language than he is in using the language to communicate. Whereas JBL evaluates linguistic production from the standpoint of its match with his ideal of an accurate and precise form of Taíney, Wakonax evaluates it in terms of what people can reasonably attain in practice and use to communicate in everyday life:

I marched in the Yonkers Puerto Rican Day parade yesterday, and so I was rehearsing in my head, "What am I gonna say to them," you know? Well, I said, like, "Welcome." Uh, I don't think we have the word yet for welcome, so I can't say that, so I can just say, uh, I can say *ketaurie*, but that's like "long live"—"Ketaurie Borikén!" I can't say that, so I say, "Ahh, daka [I am] Wakonax. Daka Taíno." And I had this whole thing rehearsed on the way up, but it's sort of like around it, like we can't say "Look, there's the sun in the sky." We can say *look*; we can say *sky, sun*, but we can't say where it is. We don't have that syntax.

The following interaction between Wakonax and JBL reveals some of the frustration that learners like Wakonax might feel when their Taíney performances do not match up with TN's expectations concerning language accuracy. Wakonax explains how the chief of their organization wrote a version of the Christian Our Father prayer that had been previously been translated into Taíno by Puerto Rican historian Cayetano Coll y Toste (2011) in the late nineteenth century. In the chief's version, he added additional words to capture more Taíno foods and landscapes:

1	WAKONAX:	Cibanacán, who's a chief, um, he um, wrote out the words to the equivalent of the Our Father, uhh, but it's got more words about sea and water, land and, uh, *batatas* [sweet potatoes], used *casabe* [yuca bread].
2	JBL:	It's one of the, the Padre Nuestro *que es que se ideó este el* Doctor Cayetano Coll y Toste, ok, and *incluso todavía muchos grupos lo usan, pero yo estoy trabajando en una versión propia del idioma* [the Our Father that this Doctor Cayetano Coll y Toste came up with, ok, and many groups still use it, but I am working on a version that is accurate in the language].

3	W:	But we started changing it already, and we replace *baba* as "father," so now, and for instance, would be proper word for father.
4	J:	Itini.
5	DAVID:	Itini.
6	W:	So I would say, *este* em, *guakia*, "our," *itini*, "father"=
7	J:	=*Waka, waka itini*,
8	W:	*Waka itini*=
9	J:	=*Waka itini*, para=
10	W:	=Together, *guaka itini, turey toca, guami, keni*, "land" and=
11	J:	=You are using the old version still.
12	W:	*Keni, Guami caraya guey*, "sun and moon"=
13	J:	=I would rather than say *keni*, I would say, right, *guama, que es "señor*," right? *Amona, que es la "tierra," oya de "tierra," y agua, kuniabo, ke-uniabo es—ke es "y." uniabo es "agua."* [*guama*, that is "lord," right? *Amona*, that is the "earth," *oya* of "earth," and water, *kuniabo, ke-uniabo* is—*ke* is "and," *uniabo* is "water."]

Wakonax begins by talking about the use of Taíney in ceremonial contexts, focusing on a prayer that was known and circulated by various Taíno groups. JBL quickly interrupts to point out that the prayer is not a "version proper to the language." Wakonax takes the redirection and talks about the rapid pace of change, where the word for "father" in the prayer has already changed, but JBL corrects Wakonax, telling him that the word for "father" is not *baba* but *itini*. Wakonax continues, correcting his use of *baba* to *itini* and using the word *guakia* for "our." Again, JBL corrects him—*waka*, not *guakia*. Wakonax again accepts the correction and continues his recitation of the prayer, but JBL interrupts—"You are using the old version still." Wakonax presses on, but JBL interrupts yet again, explaining what he feels is the correct vocabulary for the prayer by correcting *guami* to *guama* and continuing to explain the rest of the prayer.

Ultimately, Wakonax recognized that this exchange served as a kind of metaphor and pointed out that his back-and-forth with JBL reflected the difficulties inherent in teaching Taíney, which points to larger concerns regarding the teaching of Taíney, its ongoing reconstruction, and the question of whose responsibility it is to mediate between these two sometimes conflicting practices. While JBL frames the problem as people being "stuck to the old stuff," unwilling to adapt to correct vocabulary and usage as it is revealed through his reconstruction efforts, Wakonax sees the problem as people struggling to adjust to the relatively rapid pace of change:

1	WAKONAX:	You see now what I was talking about, about why it wasn't a good idea to teach the language?
2	JBL:	Right, because they're stuck to the old stuff that we were grappling with.
3	W:	It's not that we were stuck to the old stuff, it's that it changed, so I still know it in the old way, and so does everybody else, and people have picked it up from the book, and so a lot of other groups, also use—
4	J:	Use it that way—
5	W:	Yeah, use it that way. I mean, I'll change it, but it's gonna take time before it, you know, it comes out, so then it's like, guami caraya, busika guakia, um, ifta tau ti bo matum—
6	J:	And, you see, they still use the guakia, which is not really Taíno, which is Loko, see—
7	W:	If it's Loko, it's, you know, it's, uh—
8	J:	It's within the family, but—
9	W:	It's a grandfather language, you know—
10	J:	But, uh, you see, what, what people don't understand is that Coll y Toste, for lack of

		having information, he used those words, and
		he used, including, Carib words that don't
		belong there—
11	W:	Yes, Papa.

Wakonax closes another fraught exchange with an ironic "Yes, Papa," surrendering to JBL's status as an elder and leader in the reconstruction project, a status that ultimately thwarts Wakonax's efforts to fully explain his position. David, in many ways a buffer between Wakonax and JBL in such moments, pointed out that Taíno groups in Puerto Rico use "old" words and resist nudges to adopt the most current versions of Taíney. JBL agreed and provided an example—the word "guey" for "sun," when, JBL explained, "camuya" was the correct word, ultimately concluding that those who were unwilling to adapt to the new findings "have no understanding" of the structure of Taíney.

Talking Taíno

Questions of which linguistic practices are the most legitimate and which should be taken up by other Indigenous organizations are the subject of much heated debate in the Taíno/Boricua community. These distinct ideological positions on language and the associated differences in historical alignments and future orientations and goals pose obstacles to the consolidation of Taíno/Boricua language and social practices more generally, which, in turn, have impeded the political mobilization of the movement.

The MIJB's and the TN's approaches to language manufacture and implementation differ in significant ways. In addition to presuming different language genealogies and being based in different places, the key people in each movement have distinct relationships to the reconstruction project. Though Oki was active in researching and acquiring evidence for his Mayan proposal, he did not teach any courses. Instead, current MIJB activists scan through his manuscripts for words and word meanings. In fact, Tito's attempts to learn Yucatec Mayan are efforts to continue and keep Oki's project dynamic. Members of MOVIJIBO recently taught a class at the University of Puerto Rico (UPR) based on Oki's work. I have no indication that those who support Jíbaro-Boricua language efforts are updating the language at the same pace as the TN. The reconstruction work of the TN, on the other hand, has been quite dynamic in the last decades, which has made the language difficult to teach to general TN members, who must adjust to the constant changes.

The group divisions that emerge around differing practices of talking Taíno or Jíbaro Boricua construct Taíno social life and culture in particular ways, affecting internal alignments among members and external alignments with other Taíno and Native American organizations.[10] For example, MIJB's insistence on the Mayan origin of the Taíno language presupposes a distinct historical trajectory from the TN's conceptualization of Taíney as an Arawakan language. This in turn determines which groups the MIJB and TN are interested in visiting and learning from in Latin America. Unsurprisingly, the TN promotes exchanges with members of Arawakan Indigenous groups, while the MIJB rarely interacts with organizations that suppose an Arawakan genealogy, and they are uninterested in any Arawakan texts or exchanges with Arawakan Indigenous people unless those texts or exchanges might help them disprove the Arawakan origins of the Taíno language.

Conclusion

For the LGTK and GK, speaking as a Taíno was accomplished by collecting Taíno vocabulary and scripts that performatively, indexically, and iconically linked past Taíno to current Taíno social actors. The act of reclamation was performed by accessing Taíno language and demarcating the words from Spanish through the use of separate scripts. While the GK and LGTK drew on Taíno (as opposed to Spanish) terms to make Taíno discursive spaces, for them, what the words meant was not valued as much as what saying and writing the words could do—materially and symbolically. For the MIJB and the TN, speaking as a Taíno/Boricua involved reconstructing a linguistic code, including its grammatical system, that genealogically linked the Taíno/Boricua to other Indigenous groups in the Americas. Through this process, ethnic genealogies were claimed alongside linguistic ones. The different ideologies of language—as code, communicative resource, enactive force, and symbolic marker—that mediate Taíno/Boricua language reclamations affect the political consolidation of Taíno/Boricua activism by creating different attachments and boundaries that have contributed to a growing rift between different Taíno/Boricua groups.

The stakes for each group are not inconsequential. Since the Puerto Rican population at large is mostly either unaware or skeptical of present-day Taíno/Boricua identifications, the practices and beliefs of groups that obtain public visibility have the potential to define institutional and interpersonal expectations of how contemporary Taíno/Boricua should look, behave, and speak. While not every group seeks governmental recognition, all of them work toward the right to speak and be identified as a Taíno/Boricua social actor and to establish Taíno/Boricua as a recognizable identity category. Distinct approaches to the linguistic origins and communicative purposes of the native language spoken in Puerto Rico are couched within structures of authority, legitimacy, and power as much as they are about cultural assertion and self-determination.

Most of the people involved in the Taíno language reconstruction process have limited formal training in linguistics, so such boundaries between groups are further compounded by their ideas about how language works. Work in linguistic anthropology has shown how historical trajectories are embedded in language forms and practices (Das 2011). Additionally, the choices and debates involved in language reclamation show how languages do not have a one-to-one relationship to a culture (Swinehart and Graber 2012, 96) and are intimately tied to debates about the identities the reclaimed languages will come to index (Shulist 2016, 96). Among the Taíno/Boricua, we witness how the differences in meaning that emerge from the genealogies favored by each group are also projected into the mythologies, rituals, and histories each group favors, which in turn exacerbates the demarcation of differ-ence between Taíno/Boricua groups. Moreover, local regimes of authority and ideas of community both impact and are impacted by the different borders produced through these language efforts. These efforts, in turn, reflect the different investments being pro-moted and the linguistic intimacies being reflected in and through language reclamation (Meek 2014, 81; Webster 2010; 2012). Such conflicts over language have both broadly political and intimately interpersonal repercussions for how people may construct align-ments and futures (Davis 2020).

By analyzing the Taíno/Boricua work toward language recla-mation, we witness how choices in language reconstruction may generate different understandings of history itself, setting the stage for an epistemological schism among groups—that is, dif-fering opinions about which reference points to use for the his-torical, mythological, and linguistic sources of the language. These mythologies, rituals, and histories, made in and through the pro-cess of reconstruction, become a vehicle of cultural transmission and an instrument of social action. Here language is a form of recovery and representation and an investment in the future of the Taíno/Boricua people. At stake in each reconstruction project is the most existential work: proving that the Taíno are, will be, and have been here.

6

How Do You See the World as a Taíno?

Conceptualizing the Taíno Gaze

The first time I introduced my research on Taíno language and cultural survival to Abuela Shashira, elder and leader of the General Council of Taíno (CGT), she explained her belief that talking Taíno is grounded within the spirit of the Taíno people—that it is about feeling and knowing Taínoness, not about a particular code. Abuela was dedicated to socializing me into what she understood as the correct ways of speaking as a Taíno. Instead of answering my initial questions about Taíno language restoration, she showed me how to prepare a traditional Taíno dish and say a prayer. She told me that being or becoming indio was a matter of doing, not saying.

Almost a year later, I was staying over at Abuela's house quite often. She had become a key figure in my fieldwork, we enjoyed each other's company, and I was curious to learn more about life for a Taíno elder outside of meetings, ceremonies, and larger events. I woke up early one morning, and Abuela led me to her front porch. She told me to be quiet and just listen. I found myself enveloped by the sound of leaves rustling in the wind and birds chirping. After we listened for a while, Abuela told me that every morning, I should go outside and listen. Nature, she told me, speaks forth time and the weather, and through its various forces, it can also tell us of the wishes of the ancestral spirits. This, she said, is what I should include in my thesis about Taíno language.

Later, at a Taíno event with several other affiliates of CGT, I found myself walking across the river, stumbling over rocks to find the one I would use at a ceremony that night. Evaristo, the husband of the organization's secretary, stopped me. Less skeptical of me than he used to be, he held up a rock and asked me how many different colors I saw. I tried to anticipate the answer he was looking for. "Well, there are many different shades of the two main colors. I mean three main colors. I guess maybe hundreds if not thousands of colors." The way Evaristo smiled, I knew I hadn't gotten it right. He responded with a story: There once was a pair of siblings, twins—a boy and a girl—who fought because they were both competitive and different. They fought a lot over land and leadership, but one day, as they were fighting, they became trapped at the top of the mountain and had to stick together for warmth and protection. Once they were rescued, they were asked about the land they had been fighting over. They had come to realize that they were stronger, better together.

Evaristo asked me again, "How many colors do you see?" Getting the point, I answered that there was only one. "Now you are beginning to see," he said. "If you want to know how the Taíno know, you have to learn how to see things like a Taíno, how to understand things like a Taíno. That's Taíno communication for you, learning things in the way I just taught you now. No one will tell you it's like this, this, like that. They will show you how to understand it, not what to understand." He smiled at me, and just as I was going to ask him what he meant, he walked away.

For Evaristo, Abuela, and other members of the CGT, speaking Taíno was not limited to the use of tokens of the Taíno language. Instead, speaking Taíno was about seeing as a Taíno, interpreting as a Taíno, becoming and being Taíno (where being Taíno is, in part, about finding and expressing Taíno meaning in the world). As Abuela frequently reminded me, talking Taíno was less about access to scripts and more about knowing when and how to use Taíno vocabulary and how to express oneself in terms of a Taíno worldview. These included ways of talking about history and spirituality and the connection between self, group, spirit, and earth. Corrections of my speech in ceremonial, organizational, and even casual contexts—whether in straightforward Spanish or Spanish with Taino greetings or terms to cue the event as Taino—often focused on my interpretation of events and my interactional manner rather than on my word choices. In my observations, this was how novice members were corrected as well.

Camilla Rindstedt and Karin Aronsson argue that for older generations of Quichua speakers in San Antonio, Ecuador, "being Quichua is much more than speaking the language" (2002, 740). Instead, children are taught Quichua norms of behavior and are aware of the history of their ethnic identity. Though this case differs from the Taíno in many ways, there is a parallel with what Indigenous elders may focus on in socializing new generations. For the CGT, the attention to practices other than the production of language as sites of Taíno cultural survival and replication (such as the structuring of interactional routines, participation roles, and ideas about communication) can be linked to the ways in which "Indigenous patterns of interaction may be retained after the language used has shifted" (Field 2001, 249). This is because "aspects of a speech community's interaction that are most tacit are also the most resistant to change and are maintained through mundane routines and forms of everyday interaction" (2001, 249).

While the content of Abuela and Evaristo's interpretations might be idiosyncratic, their shared focus on how to communicate and see meaning in nature was a pattern in CGT speech practices. In fact, within the CGT, the ability to read such signals in the natural world often reinforced the authority of Taíno speakers. Ideas about appropriate communication often depended on the knowledge of shared trajectories as well as respecting what were considered Taíno patterns of interaction: attention to age, hierarchical structure, and participant roles in speech. Thus interactional expectations about how each participant's status, authority, and responsibility were interrelated, including who should speak to whom and how and when they were to do so, were guided by Taíno language ideologies.

Many of the CGT's meetings began with a ceremonial circle. Members would often share messages they had received from spirits through natural phenomena, dreams, and sometimes direct communication. When most members communicated these messages, the rest of the circle would typically respond, expressing interest and respect. In one of the first CGT meetings I attended, a man I will call Z, who had recently published a Taíno-themed novel and was a relative newcomer to the group, spoke up in the ceremonial circle, attempting to express what the spirits were telling him. No one responded. He was, essentially, ignored. I wondered why he did not get the same reception as others in the circle. I noticed that most members expressed the messages that they received in their own voices, with gestures that seemed to be their own. Though Z prefaced each message with *y dice* (it/they say) to clarify that he was not the author but the emissary, his voice still became creaky and breathy, unlike the way he usually spoke; his body language was also markedly different.

Later, in private conversations, CGT members told me they felt that Z had fabricated rather than received his message, so they did not see it as legitimate, authoritative, or respectful. As for what marked Z's performance as fabricated, the explanations I received were neither straightforward nor always obvious to me. Sara Trechter lends insight into what might have been at stake in Z's problematic performance. In her ethnographic work among Lakhota people in South Dakota, she argues that "practices such as exaggerated clothing, seeking of visions" (2001, 28) were marked as non-Lakhota and indexed Whiteness, a premise that could be analytically extended to outsider-ness more generally. In the Taíno context, Z's exaggerated manner may have indexed him as an outsider, which was compounded by his self-proclaimed authority to share a message from the spirits without having sufficiently established himself or his role in the group. Though some of the evaluations of the legitimacy of Z's message were based on his performance, they were also based on the logic and content of his messages.

Interpretation through a Magical-Metaphorical Gaze

A question I often asked Taíno people was how Taíno ways of interpreting natural phenomena, ceremonial objects, and events were different from any other way of interpreting them. One Taíno/Boricua elder and activist, Robinson Rosado, an archaeologist of Indigenous Caribbean material culture who associated with but was not exclusively a part of the CGT, felt that having what he called a *mirada mágica-metafórica*, a "magical-metaphorical gaze," was crucial to understanding the world as a Taíno. Such an outlook, he argued, allows the Taíno person to see metaphors and connections in nature—for example, the avian shape of markings in the bark of a tree may be understood as a bird seen flying earlier that day, a message that can be understood through its connection to significant birds in Taíno mythology. Markings in nature are not seen as random, incidental, or meaningless. Instead, they are understood as messages from the gods or ancestral spirits waiting to be deciphered and interpreted by those with a Taíno gaze. His work was sufficiently innovative to be profiled in Puerto Rico's major newspaper during the time of my initial fieldwork (Rivera-Lassén 2006).

During my research, many Taíno often remarked that archaeologists were unable to capture the significance of Taíno ceremonial grounds because the archaeologists' perspective was not that of the Taíno. Without a Taíno outlook to mediate the analyses of such sites, they argued, their ability to protect and administer their ancestral ceremonial grounds would be compromised. The Taíno also often criticized the way scholarly inferences about artifacts' meanings influenced how histories and mythologies about the Taíno were written—often without a space for Taíno people to question such inferences or the conclusions they inspired.

Understanding the concept of a Taíno magical-metaphorical gaze can provide insight into Taíno communication and worldview.

Robinson often spoke about the concept of the Taíno gaze in lectures he offered to other Taíno. I was present at one such lecture, which took place during the third anniversary of the successful protest of governmental attempts to charge everyone, including Taíno, to enter the ceremonial grounds of Caguana, located in Utuado, Puerto Rico. I was there with the abuela; with the chief of the CGT, Anaca; and other spiritual leaders and members. The protest had been successful in ensuring that Taíno wouldn't be charged to celebrate ceremonies on the sacred grounds. During this anniversary event, we camped near the site, carrying out ceremonies, going to lectures, cooking and sharing food, and singing and dancing together. Robinson, as a Taíno intellectual, gave a talk in which he drew on the idea of a magical-metaphorical Taíno gaze to reinterpret and shed light on the meaning of one of the most well-known artifacts at Caguana: the Woman of Caguana. In order to justify his broader argument regarding the magical-metaphorical gaze, Robinson began by explaining how seeing a particular shape in the clouds can be understood as a decipherable message from the gods.

1	ROBINSON:	También los indígenas veían todo en el aire, ves esto, yo, yo me he puesto a aislar en el cielo [algo] semejante a una tortuga, ¿no? y cuando ellos veían de acuerdo a su mirada mágica y metafórica una nube o una serpiente que está abajo, ves, los serpientes ellos lo veían como una designio de los dioses, de acuerdo a su, a su
2	ANACA:	Un mensaje
3	ROBINSON:	Un mensaje de los dioses, ves. ok. vamos a descifrar ahora aquí está, aquí es donde vamos a entrar al detalle de la mujer de Caguana, originalmente cuando hicieron, esto está en miles de libros pero nadie se ponía a, y decían que esto eran ancas de rana y todo el mundo lo creyó pero el que lo dijo no puso, no decía

porque eran "¡ah! porque se parece a ancas de
raya, de rana" tiene razón se parecen a ancas de
rana, es obvio, pero no explicó

1	ROBINSON:	Also Indigenous people saw everything in the air, see um, I, I have isolated in the sky [something] similar to a turtle, no? and when they saw according to the magical and metaphorical gaze a cloud, or a serpent that is underneath, see serpents, they saw it as the intent of their gods, in accordance with, with
2	ANACA:	A message
3	ROBINSON:	A message from the gods, see. Ok. Let's decipher now here this, here is where we will go into the details of the woman of Caguana, originally when they made, this is in thousands of books but no one was putting themselves to, and they said that these were frog legs and everyone believed it, but the one that said it didn't put, didn't say why they were, it was "ah! Because it looks like frog legs," he is right they look like frog legs, it's obvious, but he didn't explain

Drawing from an understanding of how the pre-Columbian Taíno interpreted the world around them by finding meaningful messages in natural phenomena, Robinson gives examples of how the Taíno might have understood and expressed these messages. He criticizes the typical interpretation of the legs on the Woman of Caguana as frog legs and instead proposes that they are iguana legs, which, for Robinson and others, makes more sense given that the ceremonial site features other iguana and turtle shapes; it also aligns with origin stories that include the iguana figure. Mythologically, this distinction matters, as one of Robinson's main claims is that the iguana was a key figure in the pre-Columbian Taíno worldview.

The magical-metaphorical gaze allows Robinson to identify essential similarities in different objects and events across time and space. These essential similarities—such as the shape of the iguana legs and iguana iconography across different ceremonial sites, myths, and human-made and naturally occurring object formations—gain iconic status, becoming meaningful and expressive in themselves. This interpretive mode is understood in part to be the communicative effort of nature, spirits, and Taíno ancestors. People like Robinson who are successful in identifying and interpreting these essential similarities are expected to share their insights.

In the excerpt that follows, Robinson continues to explain where he thinks this mode of understanding and making meaning in the world emerges from, and he contextualizes such practices within a larger frame of *cemí* worship and artistry. A cemí is a Taíno ancestral spirit as well as the name for the three-point sculptural object molded by Taíno artisans to house the spirit.

| 1 | ROBINSON: | Pero, ¿de dónde surge esa mirada mágica y metafórica? porque los indígenas dice Pané, volvemos a Pané, que un día, un indígena fue al monte y vio un árbol que se movía, ¿un árbol? y pues que es un árbol, para nosotros es un árbol, pero para él no era un árbol, era un árbol un ser vivo, y le dijo, y le habla con el árbol y le dice a la luz, "qué tú quieres?" y el árbol le dijo "llévame tráeme un bohique, un behique, un sacerdote," y se lo trajo, y entonces, el árbol, él le pido permiso para cortar el árbol y se lo llevó e hizo un un cemí, ¿qué pasa? de allí, vemos ese es el mejor ejemplo para ver que el taíno mira dos veces, mira el árbol, o mira una piedra, pero ves, después de que inicialmente ve el árbol y ve la piedra |
| 2 | ANACA: | ve el ser |

3	ROBINSON:	ve el ser que hay dentro. Así es que hay que mirar las cosas y ustedes están bien acercados en el camino, porque veo lo que me dijeron de eso, ustedes me lo dijeron que llegue que Anaca me dice del cemí, oke1.
1	ROBINSON:	But, where does that magical and metaphorical gaze come from? because the indígenas says Pané, we return to Pané, that one day, an indígena went to the woodland and saw a tree that moved, a tree? And well what is a tree, for us it is a tree, but for him it was not a tree, the tree was a live being, and he said to it, and he talks with the tree and he says in the light, "what do you want?" and the tree said "take me, bring me a bohique, a behique, a priest," and he brought it to him, and then, the tree, he asked permission to cut the tree and he took it and made a cemí, what happened? From there, we see this is the best example to see that the Taíno looks twice, sees the tree, or sees a rock, but sees, after initially seeing the tree and the rock
2	ANACA:	sees the being
3	R:	sees the being that is inside. So things have to be seen and you all are very close on the path, because I see that you told me of that, you told me when I arrived that, Anaca tells me about the cemí, ok.

Robinson explains that the magical-metaphorical gaze comes from the Taíno ability to see beyond the simple material facts of objects in nature—rocks, trees, flowers, and so on—to the beings that are housed inside those objects. This extrasensory gaze is essential to the Taíno spiritual world, where the expressive potential of trees and rocks produces spiritual artifacts like the cemí.[1] Rather than make a cemí object to house the ancestral spirit, in the excerpt above, Robinson proposes that the Taíno gaze allowed them to observe a naturally occurring tree or rock and see the ancestral spirit already within it. Upon seeing such a spirit, the Taíno could understand the spirit's message, which was a call for a behique, or Taíno spiritual leader, to ceremonially take the tree trunk or rock and carve it into a cemí artifact.

This is one of the reasons Robinson and other Taíno typically argue that archaeologists should not overlook the cultural worth of natural markings on rocks and trees found within ceremonial grounds. While not all of the markings may have been human made, they may be meaningful and communicate important information to the Taíno. In the following transcript, Robinson explains how these should be understood from the point of view of the magical-metaphorical gaze.

1	ROBINSON:	vamos a asumir lo que tú dices, vamos a asumir que eso es una cara que encontró, que hizo la naturaleza, que pasa, si asumimos eso, pues el indio la vio y pá' donde se la llevo <u>nada más y nada menos</u> para un contexto arqueológico, un contexto mítico, mítico, mágico, arqueológico, religioso todas esas cosas, ya tiene otro simbolismo no? okei, y si la mete en el centro de un batey ya implica más importancia
2	ANACA:	SI porque ellos asociaban los elementos [R: okei] con una, o sea, lo que narra el mensaje evolutivo mitológico [R: exacto] ese es el contexto del colectivo que forman
3	ROBINSON:	<u>Exacto</u>. Entonces vemos nuevamente la mirada metafórica del indígena, asumimos que fue una, que lo hizo la naturaleza pero, el indio dijo "no, esto lo hizo la naturaleza los dioses, porqué?" pues se parece un gato se parece un jaguar y nosotros conocemos el jaguar

por medio de la tradición oral de nuestros
ancestros que decían de Suramérica o Cen-
troamérica y yo dije pero acuérdate, cuando un
indígena coge un objeto hecho por la naturaleza y lo utiliza deja de ser un elemento natural y se le convierte en un elemento, que tu
sabes de eso, cultural. O sea ya esto no es un
elemento de la naturaleza, se convierte en un
jaguar, por la similitud que ellos vieron. Otra
cosa=

4   OTHER PERSON: =y es má::s adorado que el que ellos mismos
hagan{hayan}hecho

5   ROBINSON: exacto

6   A: porqué? porque se lo dio la naturaleza he allí el
poder de-de el

1   ROBINSON: let us assume what you say, let us assume that
it is a face that was found, what nature made,
what happens if we assume that, well the
Indian saw it and where did he take it well
nothing more and nothing less than to an
archaeological context, a mythical, mythical,
magical archaeological, religious context, all
these things, it already has another symbolism
no? Ok, and if they put it in the middle of a
batey {ceremonial ground} it already implies
more meaning, no?

2   ANACA: YES because they associated the elements
[R: ok] with a, or that is, what narrates the
evolutionary mythological message [R: exactly]
That is the context of the collective they form

3   ROBINSON: Exactly. Then we see again that the metaphori-
cal gaze of the indigena, we assume that it was,
that it was made by nature, but the Indian said
"no, this was made by nature the gods, why?"
well it looks like a cat it looks like a jaguar and

we know the jaguar through the oral tradition of our ancestors that said from South America or Central America <u>and I said</u> "but remember, when an Indigenous person takes an object made by nature and uses it, it ceases to be a natural element and becomes an element of, and you know about this, of culture. That is, this is no longer an element of culture, it becomes a jaguar, because of the similarity they saw" Another thing=

4   OTHER PERSON: =and it is mo::re adored than the one that they themselves could have made

5   ROBINSON: exactly

6   ANACA: <u>why?</u> Because it was given to them by nature, therein lies its-its power

Robinson and Anaca argue that identifying the essential similarity of a naturally occurring marking or design on a rock or a tree to an ancestral spirit or deity would have been understood as a divine message—even more so if that rock or tree was within a ceremonial space. And so while contemporary Taíno share their ancestors' orientation toward the natural world, non-Taíno who do not have a magical-metaphorical gaze would see these sites of divine intent as totally unremarkable. Taíno/Boricua activists instantiate their belonging as an ethnic group with a particular relationship to the land, cosmology, and material culture in part through their interpretation of the natural landscape of sacred ceremonial sites that are currently administered by Puerto Rican bureaucratic agencies. Since Taíno/Boricua have no official status or institutional recognition in Puerto Rico, they have no protected rights to ceremonial grounds and were not often consulted in archaeological interpretations of Taíno artifacts. In fact, many Taíno expressed their frustration that their ceremonial grounds were often called archaeological parks, which made them seem like folkloric sites rather than sacred locations. Many felt that in being relegated to archaeological study, which focuses on material culture, Taíno culture had been further objectified as a past culture that could only be analyzed by academics through its artifacts. Instead, Taíno intellectuals proposed that they were the ones who had the ability to interpret and understand Taíno artifacts as a form of living history.

Robinson's interpretations of signs in nature took into account the "pragmatic residue" (Silverstein 1979, 52) left by past readings of what he understood to be similar signs.[2] For example, a marking in the shape of a serpent on a rock may call to mind past contexts where he observed a serpent, saw a serpent marking or shape, and Taíno myths related to serpents. All of these instances and their related contexts together are understood to explicitly bear upon the interpretations of any novel instantiation of a serpent. For the CGT activists I observed, the ability to make meaning in the context of a sign's current instantiation with reference to the "elements of its history of use" (Bauman and Briggs 1990, 73) was a mode of communication where the right and appropriate meanings could be extracted from the world around them—both as it was in the present moment and as it had been in the past. In sharing these ways of making meaning, they were trying to get me to the appropriate episteme for understanding what it meant to communicate as a Taíno. Although the CGT were much more invested in seeing and interpreting the world as a Taíno than they were in any codified Taíno language, their attention to historical residues and derivation of meaning from signs is exactly how groups like the LGTK, GK, MIJB, and TN approach their language projects, deriving meaning from remnants of their Taíno/Boricua ancestors—pictographs, words, sister languages, and so on—in order to recover, protect, and reclaim Taíno/Boricua ways of interpreting and communicating.

Renewing/Reknowing the Self

Yuli, a member of the CGT who was widely respected even outside of that group, had a special relationship to the ancestral spirits and an ability to see many things that often go unnoticed. I was often surprised at how much Yuli seemed to know and understand about

FIGURE 6.1. *Trigonolito o piedra de tres puntas*, 1000–1500 D.C. Museo de América, Madrid, Spain. Dorieo, Wikimedia Commons (License CC-BY-SA 4.0).

me. An artisan, musician, and writer who was deeply involved in an artisanal cooperative in a small town located in the mountainous center of the island, Yuli was also largely responsible for the current circulation of the prophecy of Aura Surey mentioned in chapter 2.

I met Yuli on a trip to the artisanal cooperative she managed. On that first meeting, after explaining much of what she understood of the Taíno spiritual system, she told me that if I found my *cemí blanco*, I would find and reconcile with myself, bringing about my rebirth as a Taíno woman.

The cemí blanco, or the ancestral Taíno spirit within a human vessel—rather than one in rock or wood—was often referenced in CGT gatherings. Using a hand gesture, members could signal that they had acquired this Taíno spirit and consciousness. During the commemorative weekend gathering at Caguana, in addition to Robinson's talk, Yuli and other members also sang and danced to a number of songs, including one that Yuli wrote, which focused on the cemí blanco. Yuli introduced her song as follows:

Esta canción se hace en honor al cemí este es el cemí de la profecía. . . . Este es el cemí que vive dentro de cada ser, que se llama el sueño del cemí, así que si se quieren ir en el ensueñito pues que bueno.

This song is in honor of the cemí; this is the cemí of the prophecy. . . . This is the cemí that lives within each being, it is called the dream of the cemí, so if you want to go into a sleepy state, well, great.

Then she began to sing:

Soy cemí en la noche y del amanecer,
soy cemí en la noche y del amanecer,
y ahora y sin reproche también yo te diré,
que estaba esperando que tu despertaras otra vez,
también te contaré en la noche oscura encontré mi corazón
    latiendo
desde siempre para que estaba esperando
cuando el sol alumbrara mi fe
que mi pueblo lo ha vuelto está vivo y ahora lo sé
soy cemí en la noche y del amanecer
el mensaje que te traigo es para alumbrarte tu fe,
ya no duermo mas despierto estaré
para enseñarte el sendero ancestral otra vez

I am cemí in the night and of the dawn
I am cemí in the night and of the dawn
And now and without reproach I will tell you
That I was waiting for you to awaken again
I will also tell you that in the dark night I found my heart beating
Since always I have been waiting
For when the sun would enlighten my faith
That my people have returned and now I know it
I am cemí in the night and of the dawn
The message I bring is to enlighten your faith
I no longer sleep, more awake I will be
To teach you the ancestral path again

Materializing the inner self in terms of a fundamental symbol of Taíno religious beliefs and practices, the cemí, Yuli reminds listeners that people—like cemíes of rock and wood—can be vessels for ancestral spirits, which, after awakening a spiritual Taíno consciousness within individuals, will enable a collective Taíno awakening. The format of the song serves as a mechanism to awaken ancestral ways of knowing, an awareness of the Taíno spirit within themselves—which is, in a way, also an awakening of the Taíno gaze. When Yuli introduces the song, she encourages her audience to allow the lyrics to lull them to sleep, hoping that their physical awakening will prompt the awakening of their Taíno consciousness. For CGT members, the attainment of a cemí blanco goes hand in hand with the attainment of the Taíno ways of seeing and understanding the world that Abuela, Evaristo, Robinson, and others view as so essential to communicating as a Taíno. These achievements, in turn, concretize a CGT member's Taíno identity, confer more authority, and establish the member's role within the Taíno social field.

Conclusion

Tuján, of the GK, shared in Yuli's understanding of Taíno cosmology and spirituality, especially the idea of the cemí blanco. He was adamant about his belief that the people he referred to as "contemporary Spaniards"—Puerto Ricans who worked for certain governmental, cultural, and educational institutions, like the Instituto de Cultura Puertorriqueña (ICP; Puerto Rican Institute of Culture)—were preventing the public acknowledgment of Taíno traditions and perseverance. The way Tuján and quite a few others see things, a contemporary Spaniard not only has little potential to recognize their cemí blanco and claim their Taínoness, but the ICP and their ilk actively reproduce and perpetuate the colonial Spanish attitudes and policies that have been obscuring the Taíno presence in Puerto Rico since the fifteenth century. As Tuján and others understand things, the inhabitants of the island belong to one of two groups—contemporary Spaniards and everyone else—which includes the Taíno and Afro–Puerto Ricans. While this division creates an adversarial dynamic, the parallelism between contemporary Puerto Rico and the period of Spanish invasion and colonization also creates an opportunity for rewriting Taíno history as one of survival rather than extinction, a reimagining that offers new possibilities for understanding Taíno heritage and potential futures. The Taíno (and Afro-Puerto Rican) contemporary Spaniard dichotomy also presents another situation where those who have attained genuine Taíno understanding can assert their authority by using their insight to read others as either insiders or outsiders and serves to further underscore Taíno cultural values. Recognizing themselves as Taíno—as people who see as Taínos and speak as Taínos and understand as Taínos—allows Tuján, Yuli, Anaca, Robinson, Evaristo, Abuela Shashira, and others to find and interpret signs in the world around them, whether in the natural landscape or Taíno petroglyphs, in order to rewrite Taíno histories and posit Taíno presents and futures.

The CGT's way of interpreting and making sense of the world contrasts with other groups' more formal language reconstruction efforts. As I understood the abuela, which was then reflected across my interactions with other CGT members, they felt that Taíno communication is more than the words that are spoken; it is about ways of making meaning, interpreting situations and relationships, and participating in the world. In some ways, the CGT seemed to see projects of language reconstruction as obfuscating instead of revealing what it means to be—and see the world as—a Taíno.

7
Protest, Surveillance, and Ceremony

In the spring of 2008, the General Council of Taíno (CGT) was engaged in a campaign to protect the recently unearthed Jácanas burial and ceremonial grounds in Ponce, Puerto Rico. The CGT had organized a similar protest in 2005 over the Caguana Ceremonial Indigenous Heritage Center in Utuado (it was actually through the media coverage of that protest that I became aware of Taíno activism on the island). The Caguana protest was designed to bring attention to a number of concerns. First, the CGT argued that the Instituto de Cultura Puertorriqueña (ICP; Puerto Rican Institute of Culture), the governmental custodian for the site, and the archaeologists that informed their policies were ill-informed and ill-equipped to respectfully manage the grounds. Second, the CGT took issue with the site's entry fee, especially for the Taíno who wanted access for ceremonial purposes. Finally, they condemned the term *ceremonial park*, arguing that to call Caguana a park was to belittle the cultural value and historical importance of the grounds. Though the ICP eventually took legal actions against the leaders of the CGT for trespassing on the Caguana grounds during their protest, the CGT was successful insofar as they received extensive coverage in the media, which brought awareness to the Taíno movement in Puerto Rico and their other causes.

This chapter considers one weekend in the midst of the 2008 campaign, an event the CGT called the "Sacred Reclamation and Great Cleaning of Jácanas." This event, which the CGT envisioned to include different cultural, environmental, conservational, and community organizations, was meant to protest the building of a dam that had already harmed a Taíno ceremonial site that had been uncovered during the construction process. However, they ran into a number of difficulties, including struggles with government officials, which were complicated by the fraught relationship among the U.S. government, including federal agencies like the U.S. Army Corps of Engineers (USACE); the Puerto Rican government, including organizations such as the Departamento de Recursos Naturales y Ambientales (DRNA; Department of Natural and Environmental Resources), the Oficina de Estatal de Conservación Histórica (OECH; State Office of Historic Preservation), and the ICP; and Taíno groups, represented in this instance by the CGT. The CGT's interactions with the agents of these governmental organizations who were sent, ostensibly, to protect the Jácanas grounds were permeated by an expectation of surveillance, which created an environment of mutual suspicion and distrust. Here, surveillance refers to the heightened and directed monitoring of specific social actors with an aim of obtaining information and/ or delimiting acceptable actions, often couched in hierarchies of authority and power (Foucault 1995; Giddens 1977; Goffman 1962).

This expectation had a historical basis. A few of the CGT elders claimed to have experienced federal surveillance due to their involvement in Puerto Rico's proindependence movement in the '70s. In fact, between the 1930s and the 1990s, the U.S. and Puerto Rican governments systematically surveilled people who were suspected of proindependence activities.[1] This surveillance included the monitoring of organizations, meetings, and events with any rumored proindependence leanings. It also included the use of undercover local police to covertly watch and keep track of people thought to be affiliated with proindependence activities (Ayala 2000; Bosque Pérez and Colón Morera 1997; Martinez-Valentin 2003; Poitevin 2000). The information they collected was compiled into files called "carpetas [or listas] de subversivos" (files or lists of subversives), which often outlined even the ordinary daily activities of these individuals and organizations. The *carpetas* were compiled by Puerto Rican state authorities, but the information contained within them was managed by the Federal Bureau of Investigation (FBI). In 2000, the carpetas were publicly released, and many people became aware that they had been surveilled by the local and federal governments.

A number of the Taíno people I interviewed reported that they had carpetas. Many, though by no means all, had been active in proindependence activities between the 1960s and the 1990s. Many of them often told me to avoid giving any specific information over the phone for fears that their phones were tapped. Suspicion was rampant even within the Taíno community. After rumors that a Taíno group had sent members to spy on other groups, the CGT began video recording all official meetings and requiring all members present to sign their names in the record book.

The Archeological Findings

On October 19, 2007, the front-page headline of the popular newspaper *El Vocero* read, "They discover Taíno village." New South Associates, a private archaeological contract company based in Stone Mountain, Georgia, was hired by the USACE to conduct an archaeological survey, in accordance with Puerto Rico's Law 112 of 1988 (Asamblea Legislativa de Puerto Rico 1988) for protecting land patrimony, before constructing a dam meant to avoid flooding in the Jácanas sector of Ponce. While conducting the survey, New South found the remains of what may have been the largest Taíno ceremonial center in the Caribbean (Medina-Carrillo 2007).[2] In addition to obligating contract archaeologists to inform the ICP of any findings, Law 112 stipulates that all archaeological artifacts found in Puerto Rico belong to the Puerto Rican people and are to be held in custody by governmental agencies such as the ICP. This is not what happened. Instead, New South continued their dig without including local archaeologists or contacting the Land Archaeology Council of the ICP.

Puerto Rican archaeologists were outspoken in noting that these digs were not conducted according to protocol and that damage had been done to the rocks that compose the ceremonial court (Medina-Carrillo 2007). Moreover, some of the artifacts—most notably, sixty-six human skeletons—were sent for analysis to New South's offices in Georgia without consulting the ICP, which was in direct violation of local laws. This caused an uproar among local archaeologists—most of them affiliated with the University of Puerto Rico (UPR) and the ICP. Though both the UPR and the ICP are government-funded and affiliated institutions, they tend to be more autonomous in their politics than other bureaucratic branches. As journalist Norma Medina-Carrillo's investigation into the governmental procedures involved in approving the project continued, it became clear that two other government offices, the DRNA and the OECH, had bypassed the ICP's jurisdiction and colluded in allowing New South to ignore the stipulations of Law 112.

Planning for the federal dam project began in 1978 (Solórzano García 2007). After a two-decade hiatus, the project was restarted by the USACE in the 2000s with the help of two local agencies: the OECH, which is affiliated with the governor's office, and the DRNA, whose secretary is a member of the governor's constitutional cabinet. When local Puerto Rican archaeologists and Taíno confronted these agencies about their management of the project, especially concerning New South's handling of the dig, the organizations argued that because the dam was a federal project, the local Law 112 had no jurisdiction. Instead, they contended that the project was under the legal jurisdiction of the U.S. National Historic Preservation Act (NHPA) of 1966. In response, Norma Medina-Carrillo, a local archaeologist, argued that the NHPA includes a stipulation for the inclusion of local authorities in the management of "historical properties": "A representative of a local government with jurisdiction over the area in which the effects of and undertaking may occur is entitled to participate as a consulting party. Under the provisions of the Federal law, the local government may be authorized to act as the agency official for purposes of section 106" (quoted in Medina-Carrillo 2007).

She mocked the "third-rank functionaries of the Commonwealth of Puerto Rico" whose "'whimsical' interpretation" of the NHPA led them to ignore the provisions that would have entitled local officials to at least some control over the dam project and potentially given Law 112 some jurisdiction over the associated archaeological dig.[3] OECH and DRNA officials responded that since the dam project had been formulated before the creation and implementation of Law 112, they were not bound by it, regardless of any stipulations in the NHPA. Local archaeologists (both affiliated and not affiliated with the ICP) replied that since the archaeological dig began after the implementation of Law 112, the OECH, the DRNA, and New South all should be bound by its provisions.

As these events unfolded, mostly between October 2007 and February 2008, people in Puerto Rico—not just archaeologists and ICP officials—became alarmed at the collusion involved in the federal- and state-level dismissal of local laws and regulations and at the way local heritage was being so flagrantly mistreated and mismanaged. The local newspapers' extensive coverage of the controversy made it the topic of conversation in many of my interviews with both Taíno and non-Taíno people. A common concern raised by Taíno people was that the voice of the Taíno activists had been dismissed from the debate—perhaps because their rights to speak on behalf of the remains uncovered by New South were not institutionally sanctioned. Given their understanding of the U.S. Native American Graves Protection and Repatriation Act (NAGPRA) as well as what they saw as human rights concerns, they were somewhat shocked that the removal of human remains from the Jácanas site had not been more central to the argument between federal and state agencies. Because of concerns about looting, not even local archaeologists had been given permits to observe the site, much less the Taíno.

With growing concerns about the disturbance of the spiritual balance of the area and the disruption of their ancestors' burial sites, in 2008, three Taíno groups—despite their disagreements about how best to repair the damage that had already been done—along with many Jácanas community members united to occupy the areas surrounding the Jácanas site and held a series of ceremonies, protests, and interviews with the families still remaining in the area.

Though the Taíno activists struggled to gain a seat at the table in the ongoing discussions between local and federal agencies, with the cooperation of local archaeologists, they were finally able to secure an invitation to an important meeting on February 26, 2008, where governmental agencies, the media, and the Taíno assumed that a compromise would be reached regarding how best to manage the ceremonial site as the dam project moved forward. Leaders of the CGT who attended the gathering told me it was made clear to them that the administration of the site was seen as an issue for the agencies to decide, effectively excluding the Taíno from the discussion and discounting their ancestral investment.

The Taíno activists and community members began to organize a public protest at the site, hoping it would be as successful as the one they had organized in 2005. Initial planning went smoothly. Members of the CGT took on different responsibilities—contacting the media and different governmental agencies and actors, planning and organizing the actual event, getting supplies and arranging facilities. Given the media attention that Jácanas had received in the past three months, the CGT expected that the event would gain broad attendance and block the dam project.

However, the support they had expected from other environmental, political, and Taíno organizations did not come through. Community involvement in the protest waned as the planning stage continued. Though the protest was originally scheduled for March, it was postponed until April in order to try to secure new resources for the event; those resources never materialized. The day before the protest, the CGT received a letter from the DRNA informing them that any act of protest conducted near the site would be illegal and prosecutable by law. The CGT then reframed the protest as a cleanup of the nearby river, a public waterway from which they could not be legally barred, also hoping to attract a larger audience of people interested in environmental issues even if they did not identify as or explicitly support Taíno activism. Changes were made to all the schedules and handouts so that the protest's paper trail would reflect a cleanup of the river surrounding the sacred site.

Strategizing Encounters

On the morning of the protest/cleanup, Abuela Shashira and I were the first to arrive at the site. After we saluted the sun, we searched for dry wood and leaves for a fire. Two more CGT members, Anaca and Willy, arrived a little later. Together we held hands in a circle around the fire and said a prayer for strength and wisdom in the days ahead. Anaca and Willy went up to the abandoned house we had been using as our headquarters, and the abuela and I continued to tend the fire. A few moments later, a guard from the Cuerpo de Vigilantes (Guard Squadron) of the DRNA came over and asked what we were up to. The abuela answered, "We are just here to clean the river. We just want to make sure that the waters that feed the ground of this sacred site are clean. How are you?" The guard, respectful of an older woman, responded that he agreed with her that the contract archaeologists had not taken care of the site well enough. He offered to show her photos of the site on his cell phone and explained that he was just doing his job, just following orders. He warned her that he and the other guards had been told to be on the lookout for the Taíno and that she and her people should be careful because some guards would not be as sympathetic as he was. The elder smiled. We retrieved our belongings and returned to the abandoned house.

We had readied the house weeks before and prepared a batey, a ceremonial ground, in the yard. When we arrived, the house was just as we had left it except for some extra sheets left behind by people who had taken advantage of the clean shelter while we were gone. The batey was untouched. Rumors were, Chief Anaca told me, that the DRNA people were afraid that the batey was filled with *brujeria* (witchcraft), so they would not touch the rocks. Abuela had just begun to cook a *marota* (corn-based stew) for everyone who would attend and assist in the event when representatives of the DRNA stopped by the house. They were there, they said, to inform us that we were trespassing on "the government's private property" and that we needed to make plans to leave. Anaca immediately responded by asking what right the DRNA official had to tell us to leave. Abuela, however, took a different approach. Her eyes tearful, she offered them food and asked, "How would you feel if you found out that your ancestors were removed from their burial grounds and sent via FedEx to a foreign land?" The officials were silent. She continued, "All I am is an old woman, and soon I will be buried too. What will happen to me one day? In the future, when my people forget me, will I be removed from my resting place too? We know we cannot do anything now, except make sure that those that remain are respected. So, we will clean the river that feeds their lands tomorrow. That is all. We are cleaning the environment—is that not what you encourage us to do?" After some back-and-forth with the abuela, and after having all of us sign a notebook, which they verified against our IDs, the representatives said that they could make no promises and that we could stay there at our own risk. They left and did not show up again.

The ceremony that night was very intense and emotional. It was cool and the ground was rough under our bare feet. Abuela, who often led ceremonies, seemed physically, emotionally, and spiritually drained. She cried. She cried for the spirits of her disturbed ancestors. She cried because she had to keep fighting. She cried because she was tired. She cried because she had to put her own pride and rights aside in order to secure the protest. We all cried along with her. The elder asked us all to hug our mother, and everyone embraced the ground they stood on. I heard tears and sighs and deep breaths and, with them, the pain and fear of the people around me. When everyone stood again, we held hands and prayed that tomorrow, our goals would be accomplished.

Early in the morning the next day, we left our camp near the site and went out to the main road to wait for any other protestors who might join us. Soon after establishing a temporary camp on the side of the road, we watched as the guards blocked off the entrance to our camp with two DRNA vehicles. The CGT initially decided to avoid confronting the guards and continued to stage their protest at the side of the road. Attendance was meager, limited to the more active members of the organization. Few outsiders from non-Taíno organizations showed up. A little heartbroken and low spirited, the attendees continued cleaning alongside Highway 10, right alongside the Jácanas site. After cleaning all that we could clean, we ate a meal and sat by the side of the road while we waited to see who else, if anyone, would show up.

As the vehicle continued to block the entrance, Abuela, Anaca, and Willy became increasingly suspicious that the protest was being surveilled. The CGT reacted accordingly, including making a decision to record all interactions with the guards—a countersurveillance measure taken for their own protection but also a move that ensured these encounters with the Cuerpo de Vigilantes were framed as surveillance interactions regardless of the guards' original intent. When the DRNA representatives finally approached our group, Shashira and Anaca decided that they would be the only ones authorized to speak with them. The rest of the participants were to remain supportive yet silent. I was asked to record the exchange in case the interaction escalated.

Early on in the interaction, perhaps in a desire to align with the Taíno protestors and obtain their cooperation, one of the guards revealed that he considered himself Taíno—interrupting potential binaries between the Taíno as protestors and the guards as non-Taíno—though because of the CGT's assumption of surveillance, his assertion was not necessarily read as sincere. However, in the moment, Abuela Shashira and Anaca absorbed his realignment and responded by asking the guards to relay a message to their bosses—the absent non-Taíno adversary, for whom the guards were only relaying messages. The guards explained that they received their orders from elsewhere, pointing to the hierarchies that bound them and spatializing that hierarchy in terms of a linear chain of command, of which the governor of Puerto Rico was apparently at the top and the guards were at the bottom, establishing themselves as one-way mediators of the DRNA's decisions with little power to change or even negotiate directives.

1	ANACA:	Ehe, entonces, ¿cuál es el mal que estamos haciendo?
2	GUARD 1:	¿Cuál es el problema? Qué, que=
3	A:	=Eh, todo el mundo hiciera eso
4	G1:	Bueno, mira eso viene del secretario pa' bajo.
5	GUARD 2:	Del gobernador.
6	G1:	De arriba pa' bajo.

1	ANACA:	Ehe, then, what is wrong with what we're doing?
2	GUARD 1:	What is the problem? That, that=
3	A:	=Eh, if everyone did that
4	G1:	Well, look that comes down from the secretary.
5	GUARD 2:	From the governor.
6	G1:	From top down.

In trying to mediate and communicate their orders to the CGT, the guards opened the conversation to the Taíno activists' critiques of the DRNA. Shashira and Anaca focused on mailed correspondence that indicated that the Taíno should obtain permits from relevant federal agencies before their cleanup. Because Taíno activists do not consider federal agencies to have authority over Taíno affairs on the island, they found the idea of obtaining permits to clean a river to be ridiculous. Anaca was emphatic: "No, a *ningún* federal le voy a pedir permiso. Eso es un patrimonio *nuestro*" (No, I will not ask permission of *any* federal agent. This is *our* patrimony). Shashira and Anaca illustrated this absurdity by joking about needing federal permits to play the *fotuto* (traditional shell instrument): "Now I am going to tell you something. Now we have to ask the federals, eh, a permit to play the fotutos here?" In the following excerpt, they continue the joking by highlighting other tensions that become mapped onto the federal/U.S. and local / Puerto Rican binary, such as speaking "Engli::sh" or being "Taíno Indian."

1	SHASHIRA:	Te digo una cosa tú-tú te imaginas a mí, todo hablando en ingles
2	ANACA:	de Taíno Indian
3	S:	Si lo hablo solo porque si lo tengo que hablar, pero yo estoy en Puerto Rico que, en español, que aprendan español
4	A:	In Engli::sh

1	SHASHIRA:	I will tell you one thing, you-you imagine me, all speaking in English
2	ANACA:	Of Taíno Indian
3	S:	If I speak it only because I have to speak it, but I am in Puerto Rico, which is in Spanish, have them learn Spanish
4	A:	In Engli::sh

In the above exchange, Anaca and Abuela Shashira highlight what they perceive to be the absurdity of their current situation: asking federal permission to protect an ancestral Taíno site. This sense of ludicrousness is evident in how the abuela describes speaking English in Puerto Rico. The humor of this exchange relies on a discourse that understands English as foreign to Puerto Ricans, including Taíno. Anaca chimes in by jokingly speaking in an exaggerated American accent to parody the expectation that she is under the jurisdiction of the U.S. federal government.

After the guards left, the Taíno activists debriefed. Though the guards had attempted to distance themselves from the governmental orders they conveyed, the Taíno activists ultimately did not really trust them. The CGT agreed that the guards were there to gather information for their DRNA supervisors, all while lulling the activists into thinking that they were not being surveilled after all. And regardless of what the guards said or who they claimed to sympathize with, they still had the power to force the Taíno activists to leave. For the CGT members who stood by while Shashira and Anaca engaged the guards, self-suppression and silence were strategic techniques of (albeit limited) empowerment.

Shashira reminded the group that there were cameras around and that the Taíno should avoid any activities or areas that might get them arrested. Taínoness, she clarified, should not be invested in contesting this one instance of observation but should instead be focused on changing the laws that allowed for and enabled the surveillance of Taíno activists and the restriction and rejection of their rights to their ancestral remains. In addition to the admonitions, Shashira offered reassurance: "We have it all recorded—everything, *everything* that they said." Perhaps fearing that their protest would be misrepresented as having broken the law, Abuela felt a sense of security in recording the guards. She and the others saw this countersurveillance measure as insurance, another means of asserting what limited power they could in their asymmetrical interactions with the authorities.

It was not clear to me then, as a witness to everything that unfolded, and it remains unclear to me now, reviewing the recordings I made and the notes I took, to what extent the Taíno activists were actually being surveilled by the guards and to what extent the activists only assumed or imagined they were being watched. Regardless of the guards' intent, the Taíno expectation of surveillance was still relevant in how they prepared for, addressed, and later evaluated such interactions. We can understand surveillance not only in terms of hypervigilance but also in terms of hyperprotection from the hypervigilant—or potentially hypervigilant, as the case may be. As Ellen Basso states, "Suppression of voice is often one consequence of mutually perceived inequalities of power" (2009, 134). Such power inequalities become obvious in who and in what situation particular social actors feel a choice between "remain[ing] silent or . . . speak[ing] out" (129). Hyperprotection often takes on the very forms of monitoring that the surveilled hope to defend against. Though the Taíno avoided any direct challenge to the guards, in addition to their hyperprotective recording, they offered subtle challenges to the guards' authority and the hierarchies on which that authority rests. For example, in poking fun at the premise of federal authorization being required for Taíno events, they used the presumed surveilling and reporting gaze of the guards to relay their critique back to the officials who held the most meaningful power over the Taíno.

What Happened with Their Efforts?

We stayed at the side of the road for a while longer, disappointed with the low turnout and the guards' surveillance. Abuela asked me to turn my camera on. She said that since I was interested in how people talk about and understand things, she and Anaca would discuss "the ways of Taíno communication" for me. Abuela Shashira and Cacica Anaca share the responsibility of socializing and directing the group, and as their conversation unfolded, it became clear that they were also attempting to reframe the weekend's events, offering the group members a new interpretation with a distinctly Taíno perspective. Though they did not explicitly refer to the prophecy of Aura Surey, which predicted that the Taíno would politically reemerge five centuries after Spanish colonization, the interpretive frame of the prophecy cued a specific sense of causality and "mode of attention" to the world that allowed several different happenings to be woven into a coherent narrative—"what was supposed to happen"—that framed the event as a success despite the meager attendance and minimal media coverage (see Gumperz 1992 on contextualization cues).

The following exchange includes three speaking participants: Abuela Shashira, Cacica Anaca, and novice member Noemí (who at that point had been active in the group for approximately eight months). Willy (another member), Noemí's son, and I are also nearby. Abuela Shashira begins by drawing our attention to a rock across the road:

1   SHASHIRA: Ahora mismo, donde estoy yo senta', si tu
                miras aquella dos piedras que están de aquí,

		de de donde yo la estoy viendo, es un corazón, para mi [yo que veo
2	ANACA:	[aha
3	S:	es un corazón. {?} y el otro que esta al lao {¿no?} es un corazón. És una piedra cuadrada pero tiene una, como una raya, donde, si para muchos llamarían una cruz, que [y,
4	A:	[Sí
5	S:	para nosotros tiene otro [significado
6	A:	[Sí
7	S:	¿pero si tú ves es un corazón?
8	A:	Sí
9	NOEMÍ:	¿Está de lado verdad?
10	S:	Sí, [está de lado
11	N:	[Está de lado.] sí. [sí

1	SHASHIRA:	Right now, where I am sitting, if you look at those two stones that that are here, from from where I am looking, it is a heart, for me [what I see
2	ANACA:	[aha
3	S:	is a heart. {?} and the other one next to it {no? (as a confirmation)} is heart. It is a square stone, but it has a, like a dash, where, yes for many they would call a cross, that [and
4	A:	[Yes
5	S:	for us has another [meaning
6	A:	[yes
7	S:	but you see a heart?
8	A:	Yes.
9	NOEMÍ:	It's on its side, right?
10	S:	Yes, [it's on its side
11	N:	[it's on its side.] Yes. [yes

The elder describes a shape she wants us to notice on a rock as what "muchos llamarían una cruz" (many would call a cross), her serious tone and her frequent pauses keying us to the importance of what she is observing. She is careful not to say that the shape *is* a cross or that it looks like a cross. Instead, she distances herself and her audience from the more widespread Christian belief systems, explaining that this shape "para nosotros tiene otro significado" (for us has another meaning). Her use of *nosotros* (us) here establishes a difference between those who would call the shape a cross and those who would not, and by asserting that what some would call a cross has "another meaning," she alerts more novice members that the appropriate interpretation is *ours*, not *theirs*.

1	SHASHIRA:	Sí, sí te paras aquí, si te paras aquí y la puedes ver es un corazón. Dentro de esa piedra, dos corazones, dos corazones unidos allí . . . lo que yo decía es, si vamos a a lo que explicaba ella, el comunicarse para mí, eh, {?} como esta misma mañana como dice, aquí estaban los corazones de ustedes unidos, con nosotros, o sea, que ese fue el [el-
2	ANACA:	[el significado de las cosas que aparentemente que no son [casualidades
3	NOEMÍ:	[aha
4	A:	que son causalidades.

1	SHASHIRA:	If, if you stand here, if you stand here and can see it, it's a heart. Inside that stone, two hearts, two hearts united there . . . what I was saying is, if we go to what she was explaining, communicating for me, is {?} like this very morning like they said, here were your hearts united with ours, that is, that was the [the-
2	ANACA:	[the meaning of the things that apparently are not [casual
3	NOEMÍ:	[uhuh
4	A:	that are causal.

Abuela Shashira directs our attention to another rock, in which she identifies two united hearts, which she interprets as a symbol of the union of her audience's hearts with "ours." Whose hearts does she mean by "ours"? *Dice* is the third-person singular present indicative form of *decir* (it can also be the formal second-person present indicative form, but this makes much less sense in this context), indicating that the rock was a bearer of a message—"here were your hearts united with ours"—from the ancestral spirits in the area, perhaps the very spirits whose earthly remains the CGT sought to protect. Abuela's voicing of the ancestors serves to align the unspoken "us" of the spirits with the "you" of the Taíno people present, and it also conveys that she is attuned to and understands the ancestors' messages and that she has the authority to interpret the meaning of the stones for other Taíno. The ability to read signs of the prophecy in the world is a creative process, deeply connected to questions of authority, where Abuela's ability to read the spirits' message in nature authorizes her to make claims about the relevant and correct Taíno interpretation of the day's events.

After Abuela communicated the appropriate reading of the intertwined hearts, Cacica Anaca remarked that our sitting in this particular spot and seeing this particular rock was not a coincidence; we were all meant to be there; it was causal. From Abuela and Anaca's perspective, there was a causality—a deeper set of spiritual connections—involved in the message conveyed by the rocks. The conversation continued as Abuela Shashira explained how a shape revealed within a rock in the surrounding landscape could be interpreted as a sign that would help us make sense of how the event in Jácanas had turned out:

> E-Exacto, ver esas piedras en esa forma de corazón, la otra tratándola de proteger o eso, incluso como te dije, puede ser por lo menos lo que yo visualizo es como si fuera una, una cruz, que para nosotros pues tú sabes que tiene, tiene el signi- de la vida también, y, y entonces para mí yo pues mira este corazón de nosotros, aferrado dentro de esa piedra, de de esa roca, de esa piedra y esa montaña, aquí en Jácana. Sabes, que los corazones, te

acuerdas como te dije, salir es estrella en ese momento que hago así y veo esa estrella fugaz.

E-exactly, seeing those stones in that heart shape, the other trying to protect or that, moreover like I told you, it could be-at least like I visualize it's like it was, a, a cross that for us well you know well it has, has the meani- of life too, and, and then for me well look at that heart of ours embracing inside of that stone, of that rock, that stone and that mountain, here in Jacana. You know, that hearts, remember like I told you, that star coming out that moment I do like this and see that shooting star.

Eventually, Abuela returned to the cross shape in the stone and revealed that for "us," the shape signifies life—a life in connection with an ancestral Taíno embrace. As an elder and spiritual leader, Abuela is able to define the people around her as a collective, a group that shares her interpretation of a rock and its intersecting lines. The mode of attention afforded by the acquisition and recognition of the cemí blanco as well as being able to key in to what Anaca calls "the teachers . . . the true beings of light, spiritual ones," are essential to making a positive connection between what could be interpreted as a failed event and the larger framework of Taíno reappropriation as set forth in the prophecy. Before Abuela and Anaca began their discussion, the mood of the group was low, defeated. However, Abuela's read of the rock with the cross and the rock with the hearts, along with her description of a shooting star in the previous night's ceremony, shifted the group's understanding of the day.[4]

Twice Abuela Shashira repeated, "Estamos en lo correcto" (We are in the right). Anaca reiterated the statement. Although the events surrounding the CGT's protest may have fallen short of many participants' expectations, according to Abuela's analysis, the protest happened exactly as it was meant to happen. Abuela Shashira's ability to spot and read signs in nature and to understand the links between seemingly unrelated events (a rock bearing a cross shape and the previous night's shooting star)—what Anaca calls "otro idioma que nuestra gente conoce" (another language that our people know)—override the unmet expectations of the other members. Again, Shashira established, using the verb form *buscamos* (we search), that searching for signs from the ancestors is something that "we" (the Taíno) do, providing a model for how the group should interpret the events of the day. Anaca and Abuela's discussion reveals that nature serves as an important link between spiritual ancestors and present Taíno peoples. This, Anaca argued, is how one can recognize a Taíno—in a person's ability to read nature's messages, which are to be interpreted as spiritual messages, the way of seeing afforded by the cemí blanco.

After this exchange, we walked to the river, following Abuela's instructions. We were informed by a guard that we should not clean the river of debris as we had planned. Abuela's wisdom guided us to not defy the guard's instructions this time. Instead, Shashira asked that we ask the river for permission to take a few pebbles and ask the earth's consent to take some soil. We made our requests and then collected a few pebbles from the river and a few handfuls of dirt from the ground. Beside the river, the CGT conducted a water ceremony for their displaced ancestors. Later that night as we drove to Shashira's home on the other side of the island, she told me that she was planning to take the rocks and the dirt we had collected to the United Nations when she went later that month to participate in the seventh session of the Permanent Forum on Indigenous Issues in New York City. She hoped that the ancestral energy found within the rocks and dirt would ground her and lend her strength and wisdom as she left the island for a foreign (to her) land.

Conclusion

The bureaucratic encounters surrounding the Jácanas protest demonstrate another way in which the Taíno have sought to reposition the histories that erase them and reclaim their identity. The activists seem to understand surveillance in terms of "the supervisory control of subject populations, whether this control takes the form of 'visible' supervision in Foucault's sense, or the use of information to coordinate social activities" (Giddens 1977, 15). In coming to expect these forms of surveillance, the CGT has configured their own political strategies to respond to and protect themselves from governmental actions meant to subvert their endeavors.

After their efforts—both their initial plans for a protest and their revised plans for the river cleanup—were, in fact, subverted, the CGT's interpretive frame allowed participants to find connections and meaning in what otherwise could be seen as a random sequence of happenings. They could then understand the events in Jácanas as having unfolded in the way they were always meant to—replacing disappointment with purpose, hope, and unity in the form of a common Taíno identity rooted in Taíno ways of seeing and understanding the world.

Conclusion

Since I left the field in 2008, new alignments and alliances have formed among Taíno groups in Puerto Rico, novel projects have been put forward, different causes have been championed, and fresh faces have appeared among the activists. The Liga Guakía Taína-ké (LGTK; League of the Good Land/Earth) changed its name to Naguaké and has been active in several community projects. Some members of the LGTK's first class of students are already in college; many of them are now active in organizing Naguaké activities themselves. Tito from the Movimiento Indígena Jíbaro Boricua (MIJB; Jíbaro-Boricua Indigenous Movement) called one day to tell me that he had found an elderly person who still spoke Taíno and had been immersed in a project of learning the language from this elder for a year. I have not been able to contact him since he called me last. The Taíno Nation (TN) have stayed active with their language reconstruction project and continue adding new Taíney vocabulary to their website. Tuján from Guaka-Kú (GK) became sick for a period of time after my research. He then hosted a local radio show but passed away shortly after the municipal government of his town removed him from the cave with Taíno petroglyphs where he served as the custodian. The stress of travel and activism took its toll on Abuela Shashira. Abuela had a heart attack shortly after her return from representing the General Council of Taíno (CGT) at the United Nations in New York. After her recovery, she shared her frustrations about her experience there, where the Taíno delegation was never given a chance to speak. Though she appreciated meeting other Indigenous groups, she was angry that the Indigenous delegations—some with very pressing issues—were not given the floor. With what she calls a "quarter of a heart," the abuela is still indefatigable in her efforts. She and other CGT activists have actively sought to create connections with Indigenous groups from across Central America and the United States, hosting an encounter of elders to "promote Taíno identity in an exchange with other peoples with rich Indigenous roots."

I last saw the abuela, Anaca, and Yarey in September 2018. We had all been invited to speak at the historic National Museum of the American Indian symposium "Taíno: A Symposium in Conversation with the Movement," part of the *Taíno: Native Heritage and Identity in the Caribbean* exhibit designed to document and represent Taíno survival and perseverance into the contemporary era. The symposium was a daylong event with three panels: "Looking Back: Contextualizing the Taíno Movement," "Genetic Science and Genealogy: Recovering Native Ancestry," and "Looking Forward: A Shared Vision for the Taíno Movement."

I flew to New York City the Thursday before the symposium. The organizer at the Smithsonian asked me to come earlier and conduct an oral history of the Taíno leader of Naguaké, Carlalynne "Yarey" Meléndez, for them on Friday in addition to participating in the symposium panel on Saturday. I was nervous to see people I had not seen since I completed my fieldwork and apprehensive about encountering the arguments and tensions between different Taíno organizations. During my fieldwork, I had managed by compartmentalizing my relationships with different groups. But here they would all be in the same room for a whole long day.

When I arrived, I settled in and then caught up with the abuela and Anaca. While I was with them, I received a call that my grandmother was sick and hospitalized in Chicago, where she was living with my uncle. The next day, I caught up with Yarey over coffee, and we spent the rest of the morning recording her oral history. Afterward, I met the abuela and Anaca for a tour of the exhibit. The exhibit presented a cogent narrative of Taíno perseverance, though the abuela commented several times that it was a bit contradictory to display Taíno artifacts that should be in Puerto Rico. Indeed, the abuela's comments highlighted the irony of an exhibit meant to showcase Taíno continuities by displaying its pre-Columbian artifacts in an air-conditioned museum in New York and the tensions inherent in staging inclusion at a museum funded by a government that would never be able to recognize Taíno—the same government that had recently tightened its purse strings vis-à-vis Puerto Rico in the wake of the economic crisis and Hurricane Maria. When we left the exhibit, a few European tourists asked the abuela and Anaca if they were "real Indians" and proceeded to ask for a picture—they too were treated as an extension of the exhibit. We headed to a coffee shop, where I received another call. My grandmother had died. I cried in the abuela's arms.

On the day of the symposium, I woke up and headed to breakfast. Here were several Taíno that I knew from my research and some that I had read and heard about but had yet to encounter. All in one room. While I could sense the strain, I also sensed a commitment to the event and the importance of, at the very least, a performance of unity. After breakfast, we all headed to the first panel, which consisted of Jorge Estevez, Anaca, the abuela, and me. Jorge narrated the history of the different Taíno organizations and their mobilization from his perspective as a young Dominican Taíno navigating his own Indigeneity in New York City at the time when Taíno mobilization was becoming organized among the diaspora. Anaca explained her own motivations for organizing the first Taíno group in Puerto Rico in the '70s. The abuela spoke of her childhood and of the women in her life who taught her that she was india in spite of narratives that said otherwise and reminded everyone of the resilience and ancestral struggles that made Taíno organizations possible. Referencing Hurricane Maria, she told the audience that the island needed them, that there was still labor to do and unity to achieve. Then it was my turn. I spoke about memory and grandmothers, about all the stories never told. I wondered aloud what stories my own abuelas took with them, stories that I never thought to ask about, stories of the unspoken struggles they had survived so I would not have to. I talked about how current Taíno are testaments to the stories told, listened to, and made into the fabric of their identities. I discussed the importance of asking for those stories and of continuing to tell them. The audience's questions for our panel reflected a strong sense of searching for resources and opportunities to connect with other Taíno to share their own families' stories and to unite.

The second panel was dedicated to the controversial issue of Taíno DNA. Much of the public debate prior to the symposium had focused on mitochondrial DNA (mtDNA) studies conducted in Puerto Rico by J. C. Martínez-Cruzado and his colleagues (2001) of the University of Puerto Rico–Mayaguez Campus. His study found that 61.1 percent of his sample (n = 800) had Native American mtDNA, the majority of which corresponded with a probable Taíno origin. This study and others like it have been put to problematic use by members of some Taíno groups who, in trying to prove their claims in the face of skepticism, may overinterpret their significance and by scholars who anticipate a sort of eugenics project as an outcome of such studies. Some of the difficulty lies in the translation of genetic information into an exclusive notion of race, where people might claim "If I have Taíno mtDNA, I must be Taíno" rather than "If I have Taíno mtDNA, I must have had a Taíno ancestor." While mtDNA studies may indicate a longer period of contact between the colonizers and the Taíno than many present historical interpretations suggest, they do not on their own serve as evidence of Taíno cultural survival, especially as many self-identified Taíno may not have Taíno mtDNA, and many who do not self-identify as Taíno may have Taíno mtDNA. More than a few Taíno do not believe that these genetic studies are a validation of their survival. They argue instead that Taíno oral histories and presence authenticate the mtDNA findings. Responding to the DNA evidence, Taíno activist Jorge Estevez argues, "While recognizing the importance of genetic studies, I feel that we Taíno, as a people, validate the DNA evidence, not the other way around. This journey of self-discovery that I and many others are undertaking is about culture, not genes, for genes say little about us as a people" (Guitar, Ferbel-Azcarate, and Estevez 2006, 62). While some Taíno were eager to be tested, others rejected the testing altogether because they did not need a test to tell them who they already knew they were.

While the speakers on the genetic science panel—the only panel made up almost entirely of scholars (mostly biological anthropologists with expertise in genomic and mtDNA analysis)—talked about how cultural survival could not be extrapolated from mtDNA or genomic evidence and urged the audience to instead focus on oral histories and family narratives, the questions from the largely nonscholarly audience focused on how to reconcile genetic survival with a larger narrative of extinction. For them, the genetic evidence could serve to confirm their stories to a broader public that has continued to be skeptical of their claims.

Such skepticism often stems from concerns about why the Taíno highlight only the survival of Indigeneity, potentially downplaying other aspects of their heritage, but many current members of the movement identify as Afro-Taíno. In eschewing identification with the "third" Puerto Rican root, Spain, Taíno and Afro-Taíno also seem to align with de- and anticolonial political mobilization that seeks to act on behalf of politically, economically, and socially marginalized groups and encourage pride in being a member of a group that has been historically trivialized and erased. Claims to be Taíno, Afro-Taíno, or Afro-descended more broadly in Puerto Rico emerged as rejections of national projects based on erasures of rights, trivializations of identity, and denials of lived inequalities, all under the banner of racial blending.

Throughout the book, I have focused on the insights that have come about through my research with a few select groups. However, as I was made aware as soon as my dissertation was made available online, there are even more narratives, sometimes contested and other times aligned with the ones shared with me, that I have attempted to convey, circulating and informing Taíno/Boricua forms of subjectivity and social action. Researchers such as sociocultural anthropologist Christina M. González are producing vital work on transnational Taíno subjectivities and peoplehood, particularly among Puerto Ricans in the diaspora. Indigenous Caribbean Boricua activist-scholar Liliana Taboas

Cruz's trailblazing work applies Indigenous Boricua perspectives and decolonizing methodologies to the analysis of Caribbean archaeology and Indigenous Caribbean languages. She is committed to public education on these issues as well by launching a self-education platform (http://www.boricuacanibalclan.org) to assist others who may be revisiting their family stories, rethinking their pasts, and questioning the myth of extinction.

On October 10, 2010, Puerto Rico's main newspaper, *El Nuevo Día*, published a special online video article, "El Taíno vive," by photojournalist Rubén Urrutía. Viewers were greeted by a picture of a young Taíno woman and asked to "press the petroglyphs to see the videos"; there were seven, which together presented a short documentary of Taíno activism and practice in Puerto Rico. Though such increased visibility may indicate more acceptance of Taíno identity, the online comments reveal that some skepticism remains. For example, one commenter, SuperSuperMAN, wrote, "The modern taíno, who communicates with blackberry and eats breakfast at burger king," echoing the 2005 cartoon in *El Nuevo Día* that depicted Taíno protesters sporting sunglasses and cell phones. What constitutes being Taíno/Boricua in Puerto Rico depends on who you ask. Throughout the book, I have considered the discourses in and through which some Taíno/Boricua make their claims—some ambivalent, others ambiguous, and a few resistant, but altogether heterogeneous.

Puerto Rican Taíno/Boricua activism takes place in a context that has historically abounded with other social movements—student, ecological, antimilitary, proindependence—which leads to questions about the intersections and alliances that have formed, are forming, and will form among these varieties of social activism. How might these potential connections influence Taíno/Boricua activism now and in the future? How do personal relationships affect the possibility for such partnerships? Reviews of trends in the study of social movements often focus on understanding why and how particular social actors come to organize sufficiently around particular issues in order to mobilize as a larger group (Holland, Fox, and Daro 2008; Franceschet 2004; Gongaware 2003; Nash

2005; Salman and Willem 2009; Wolford 2006). Work in the last decade has increasingly attended to how "ephemeral and factionalized" (Edelman 2001, 310) such groupings are. Indigenous activism is no different. The lack of cohesion and the fluidity of alliances and quarrels among Taíno/Boricua groups complicate their functioning as a united movement. And given the diverse and sometimes conflicting identifications of individual social actors who represent a variety of social practices, traditions, and beliefs, some members have to juggle their religious affiliations with their ethnic Taíno/Boricua identifications. Many Taíno/Boricua activists are Christian, and while a few people, mostly Catholic, have no trouble integrating their religious identity with their Taíno/Boricua identity, other people, mostly Lutheran and Pentecostal, struggle to do so. On one occasion, for example, Yarey attempted to bring her Taíno language program to a Lutheran school and found that some teachers and parents presumed that Taíno ceremonies were un-Christian and, therefore, diabolical. The school rejected Yarey's program, and after that experience, Yarey was always careful to tell teachers and parents that her program was cultural and not religious. But there are many who find Taíno/Boricua spirituality to be an important aspect of their identification as Taíno/Boricua, and it would be interesting to investigate the parallels between Taíno/Boricua spirituality and Santería or spiritism (*espiritismo*), especially because Santería is related to African spiritual practices, and many Taíno/Boricua consider espiritismo to have many Indigenous influences.

Linguistic anthropology has much to offer the study of activism and social movements in its attention to the way people interactionally negotiate alignments in order to make unified claims. Though Taíno/Boricua activists may draw from their ethnic identifications to make claims about sacred sites and sociocultural revitalization, their activism is not just about identity; their alignments are also about sympathy and similarity. The success of Taíno/Boricua claims depends on the activists' ability to come together to achieve larger shared goals despite disagreements among them. This means that sometimes, groups such as the LGTK and CGT may have to ignore the differences in how they approach language recovery and activism in favor of presenting a united front at a national symposium. A consideration of the linguistic and discursive strategies used to interrupt institutionally sanctioned hierarchies exposes how national ideologies and historical trajectories manifest interactionally in people's expectations, where these ideologies can be disrupted and reconfigured. Such reconfiguring on an everyday level and at different sites of social interaction could ensure, for example, the Taíno/Boricua people's right to defend and become custodians of sacred ceremonial and burial sites such as Caguana and Jácanas.

—

This book has been my attempt to make sense of the life trajectories and histories I encountered throughout my research. I have not aimed to make these histories coherent or unambiguous; instead, I wanted to examine how they emerged and materialized interactionally. Through my own interactions with Taíno activists, with Boricuas, and with Jíbaros, my expectations were recalibrated, broadened, and complicated. Throughout, I have attempted to indicate those moments when I too was interpellated, when I was being resocialized. My analyses have been informed by these experiences.

I grounded my work in the historical specificities of Puerto Rico not because Taíno/Boricua Indigenous groups only exist there (they exist across the Greater Antilles) but because it was important to look at how race became visible or veiled, centralized or trivialized in the historically specific terms under which the Taíno/Boricua groups I spent time with were analyzed and assessed. Racial politics in the Caribbean, and specifically Puerto Rico, have been slightly distinct from racial politics in mainland Latin America. In many continental Latin American countries, the exclusion and scrutiny of hypervisible Indigenous populations and the concomitant erasure of Black populations were accomplished through ideologies of mestizaje, discriminatory state polices, and everyday prejudices. In Puerto Rico, however, Blackness, made interactionally visible, has been discriminated against and trivialized, while Indigeneity has been erased and imagined as long extinct through genocide. As an extinct population, the Taíno have been celebrated as a shared, essential, and fundamental part of the island's heritage, imagined as beautiful, noble, and kind.

While the national discourse surrounding the historically imagined Taíno/Boricua constitutes them as romanticized figures, the actual people who identify as Taíno/Boricua today often do not fit the noble (and extinct) figurations of Taíno/Boricuaness as portrayed in school textbooks. Contemporary Taíno/Boricua do not claim to live in isolated, untouched, pre-Columbian villages wearing naguas while hunting and gathering their food. And not all of the contemporary Taíno/Boricua look like textbook Taíno, nor do they all look or act like each other. Some present-day Taíno/Boricua are lighter skinned, some are darker skinned; some have straighter hair, others have curlier hair; some live in rural areas, others live in more urban areas; some are uneducated, others have advanced degrees. They are a diverse group of people. What unites them, allows them to engage in community building and recognize each other, is a particular way of seeing the world that resulted from generations of family narratives passed down to them. They counter questions about their visible continuity, their language, and their practices by explaining that the breaks in transmission are a result of the colonial enterprises that forced them to hide, that removed their modes of survival and made them adapt to new economic circumstances by migrating to where their families could make a living. That is, they contend that their marginalization and discursive erasure made them hidden in plain sight. They assert that their different looks and physical characteristics reflect long-standing Taíno/Boricua practices of adopting previously non-Taíno/Boricua as Taíno/Boricua in ways that allowed cultural and ethnic continuity while also being inclusive of racial mixture. By attempting to understand race and ethnicity in Puerto Rican terms, I have highlighted the racial, ethnic, cultural, and political terrain upon which claims to being Taíno/Boricua take place. It is precisely this discursive and ideological space that I wanted to make explicit in order to better understand the dynamics of racial and ethnic identification more broadly.

Puerto Rican Taíno/Boricua attempts to claim a contemporary identity are not about silencing or denying all other narratives told about the island but about contesting settler-colonial narratives that erase Taíno presence on the island, inserting heterogeneity into the island's pasts and futures. The Taíno/Boricua claims are compelling, in part, for what they tell us about identity and identification, nationalism and belonging, and history and narrative more broadly. Their stories resist being pulled into a unitary, cogent, and intellectually predetermined history of the Puerto Rican nation. Their presence unsettles the hegemony of a singular history of Puerto Rico, of a singular way of belonging to the Puerto Rican nation, of a single way of identifying as Puerto Rican. However, their claims also reflect those histories, nationalisms, and ideologies of identity in complex ways. The contested epistemologies at play are key to understanding how Taíno/Boricua form their political subjectivities and how they envision what is possible and act upon their envisioned futures. More broadly, the Taíno/Boricua case shows how assuming a universal objective narrative and shared epistemological stance produces discursive impasses by erasing the sometimes incompatible ways and sources of knowing that create knowledge and subjectivities themselves. At stake is not only what we know but how we come to know it and become ourselves through our ways of knowing.

Initially, this project emerged out of a desire to understand Puerto Rico, its history, and its people; the process of research and writing brought to light new questions and new areas for examination. My goal has been to share what I saw and heard among the people who were generous enough to let me spend time with them in order to construct a platform from which to see Taíno/Boricua as complex humans rather than as symbols of a host of beliefs and feelings that others project onto them. Observing the Taíno/Boricua as they worked to be recognized as such, to create community and recognize others as also Indigenous, revealed heterogeneous threads of discourse, which, as David Samuels exhorts, demand that we "find meaning in unresolved ambiguity as well as clarity, in disjunctures as well as resonances" (2001, 295). In searching out ambiguity and incongruity, we witness moments when people attempt to make themselves legible to others, audible against a cacophony of voices—moments when unpredictable forms of understanding and transformation become possible.

Acknowledgments

This work has been long in the making. Several years ago in a meeting about a final paper proposal on jibaridad in Puerto Rico for a graduate seminar at the University of Michigan, Tom Trautmann asked if there were any Indigenous movements on the island. After responding with a resolute *no*, I remembered that the previous summer, I had read an article about a group of people claiming to be Taíno protesting the management of the Caguana ceremonial site in Utuado, Puerto Rico. It was this query and my own response to it that led to the questions that would ultimately inform this dissertation project. I want to thank him for asking that initial question.

Barb Meek has been an exceptional teacher, mentor, advisor, and friend. During my many years at Michigan and after, Barb has guided me in thinking about language, Indigeneity, field methods, and analysis. I feel deeply fortunate to have had her exceptional input and her unwavering support throughout all of my academic career. Barb, I thank you for being a role model of integrity and inquisitive scholarship.

The time spent in Bruce Mannheim's office hours and courses were essential to the maturation in my thinking about language, culture, and society in the Spanish-speaking world and beyond. I thank Judy Irvine for her attentive readings, which offered direction to my analyses when I did not know where to go next. Ruth Behar's insightful comments helped me think more broadly about my project, allowing me to see how my concerns were relevant to a broader audience. Y muchas gracias a Lawrence LaFountain-Stokes, who with his broad smile and discerning readings helped me contextualize my work in light of Puerto Rican and Caribbean literature. I am also grateful to all of the Linguistic Anthropology Lab readers at the University of Michigan who took the time to read and give me feedback on those first tortured drafts of what would become the dissertation this book is based on, especially Kate Graber and Elana Resnick. Your comments were deeply appreciated. I am also grateful for funding from the Wenner-Gren Foundation and the University of Michigan, which made my fieldwork possible. Funding from the American Anthropological Association Minority Dissertation Award allowed me to write and complete the dissertation on which this book is based.

To all my friends at the University of Michigan with whom I shared countless hours studying for courses and for prelims, writing grant proposals, and talking about the challenges of fieldwork, who later thoughtfully read drafts of the chapters and presentations and whose input has lingered in my thinking and approaches—I truly am grateful for all your support. Anna Genina, Jessica Rolston-Smith, Kirstin Swagman, Claire Insel, Christina P. Davis, Laura C. Brown, Xochitl Ruiz, Sonia N. Das, Purvi Mehta, Bridget Guarasci, Sara Feldman, Heloise Finch, and Keri Allen—thank you for being a friend. Ed Renollet, Nasia Atique, Nur, Ahmed, Ayeesha, and Mary and the little ones to come—thank you for being my Ann Arbor family and for opening up the warmth of your home to me.

In the field, I was lucky enough to reconnect with friends from my childhood who showed me the island in new ways. Gracias a Raquel Pérez Rodríguez y Sharon López Lugo por ser siempre amigas en todo el sentido de la palabra. Sarah Spiegel, Aaron Parsons, Judah, and Huck—having you guys in Puerto Rico while doing my research was a blessing, and I'm grateful that you were there! And to the new friends who always offered me a time and place to rest, thanks to Roberto Colón. And for always being there when I needed someone to talk to, I thank Toni Calbert, Carol Garvan, and Laura Wells. Y claro, no me puedo olvidar de Anel, saber que tomamos estos caminos erráticos juntas siempre ha sido una fuente de fortaleza para mi. ¡Gracias por siempre ser mi comadre! (Y por leer mis *papers*, ayudarme a traducir, hablar de nuestras teorías . . .)

At the University of South Carolina, I have been fortunate to encounter current and future colleagues who have helped me rethink the reach of my work and offered me support as a scholar. Thanks to Jennifer Reynolds, Elaine Chun, Kim Simmons, Courtney Lewis, Tracey Weldon, and Sharon DeWitte for your friendship and brilliance. As a whole, the anthropology department at the University of South Carolina has been a wonderful and supportive place to grow as a scholar. I also want to thank the student members of the SocioLingAnth Lab for all of your wonderful insights and conversations. During my time in Colombia, Paolo Von Nuremburg, Katrina Walsemann, and Kristen Puckett, you have been wonderful friends and sounding boards for the struggles in this process—thanks for the food and drinks! I have workshopped ideas that have made themselves into this book with a wonderful group of unparalleled Latinx scholars. Pat Zavella, Aimeé Villareal, Gina Pérez, Alex Chávez, Jonathan Rosa, Gilberto Rosas, Santiago Guerra, Andrea Bolívar, and Ana Aparicio—thanks to each of you for helping me see connections and relevances that I had missed and taken for granted. I also want to thank Yolanda Martínez-San Miguel for reaching out to me to consider Rutgers for this book, which helped remind me that there might be a broader audience for this work. And many thanks to Kim Guinta for being patient as I worked to polish and complete this book for publication. Beth Marino was a truly brilliant and wonderful editor who helped me be clearer in my writing and argument.

Comments and feedback from audiences and discussants at the American Anthropological Association Annual Meetings, Canadian Anthropology Society Annual Conference, and the Caribbean Studies Association Annual Conference have been indispensable to my thinking and in widening the scope of conversations this work has engaged in. I am especially thankful to Anthony Webster, Deborah Thomas, Inmaculada García-Sánchez, Susan Philips, and Michelle Daveluy for their thoughtful feedback of different presentations that would become the basis for the chapters in this book.

And no fieldwork happens without people who are willing to admit a relative stranger into their lives. Estoy sumamente agradecida a Valeriana Rodríguez por ser mentora y ejemplo, a Elba Lugo por su energía y generosidad, a Margarita Nogueras por ser un ser tan bondadoso y sereno, a Carlalynne Meléndez por su brío y optimismo, a Papo, Joanna, Nancy, Frank, Tuján, José, David, Daniel, y todos los demás Taíno/Boricuas que permitieron que entrara a sus vidas y escribiera sobre ellos. Sé que nunca haré justicia a la riqueza de sus vidas, pero espero que este trabajo tenga en ello algo para cada uno de ustedes.

A mi familia, gracias por darme la confianza de echar pa'lante, sabiendo que siempre tengo un hogar con gente que quiero y que me quiere. Les agradezco por celebrar mis triunfos aún más que yo, y por ser mi refugio cuando necesito recoger mis fuerzas. Mami, Daddy, Allen, Eric, Liza, y Zoelle, los amo. A todos mis abuelos, que ya no están, gracias por inspirarme a buscar y saber más allá de lo que es obvio. Los extraño con el alma.

Jonathan Comish, thank you for reading each page of my dissertation—more than once. For making me food and coffee. For picking up the laundry and cleaning the litter boxes. For the thoughtful reading and editing of my work. For caring for me and our children, Mateo and Isaac, who inspire me to be a better version of myself every day. Los amo también, always and forever. To all, thank you y muchas, muchas gracias desde lo más profundo de mi corazón.

Some parts of this manuscript have been reproduced with permission from previous articles:

Feliciano-Santos, Sherina. 2017a. "How Do You Speak Taíno? Indigenous Activism and Linguistic Practices in Puerto Rico." *Journal of Linguistic Anthropology* 27 (1): 4–21. https://doi.org/10.1111/jola.12139.

———. 2017b. "Prophetic Repairs: Narrative and Social Action among Puerto Rican Taíno." *Language & Communication* 56: 19–32. https://doi .org/10.1016/j.langcom.2017.03.001.

———. 2019. "Negotiation of Ethnoracial Configurations among Puerto Rican Taíno Activists." *Ethnic and Racial Studies* 42 (7): 1149–1167. https://doi.org/10.1080/01419870.2018.1480789.

Feliciano-Santos, Sherina, and Barbra A. Meek. 2012. "Interactional Surveillance and Self-Censorship in Encounters of Dominion." *Journal of Anthropological Research* 68 (3): 373–397. https://doi.org/10.3998/jar .0521004.0068.305.

Glossary

areyto—A ceremonial dance

behique—A spiritual and medical specialist

bohío—A typical conical shaped straw home

Boricua—A person Borikén

Borikén—Puerto Rico's Indigenous name

cacica—Marked female form for "chieftan"

cacique—Chieftan

Canjíbaro—Name used by persons who ascribe to a Mayan genealogy for Indigenous Boricuas

indio—In Puerto Rico, used to describe people who are or look Indigenous according to local evaluative criteria

jíbaro—Can be used in distinct ways, but most often describes rural peasants in Puerto Rico

Jíbaro-Boricua—Another name used by persons who ascribe to a Mayan genealogy for Indigenous Boricuas

Taíno—Name used by persons who ascribe to an Arawakan genealogy for Indigenous Boricuas (This is also the most commonly used term.)

Taíno/Boricua—Term used throughout the book to be inclusive of Indigenous people in Puerto Rico who claim either Mayan or Arawakan genealogies

Notes

Introduction

1. Taíno/Boricua groups are found in Puerto Rico and the United States (other Taíno groups are also found in Cuba, the Dominican Republic, and Jamaica). Their trajectories as activist organizations can be traced to the U.S. political identity and Puerto Rican anticolonial movements of the 1970s. I found that New York–based groups and Puerto Rican groups often form alliances, which are made and often broken over disagreements regarding authority over representations of Taíno history, political structure, public behavior, and project investments.

2. Most Taíno I interviewed found *neo-Taíno* problematic. They argued that *neo-Taíno* made their claims seem less authentic and that it highlighted discontinuity, rather than continuity, with pre-Columbian Caribbean Indigenous peoples.

3. Yarey gave me permission to use her real Taíno name. When not otherwise noted, all names have been changed to protect the identities of the social actors involved. The pseudonyms were chosen based on what each social actor was called by members of their organizations.

4. Vargas-Ramos (2005) reminds us that census data in Puerto Rico fails to capture the full richness of local categories of assessing physical appearances and ethnic and/or racial affiliations.

5. To distinguish the two uses of the term, I use the uppercase *J* in *Jíbaro* to refer to the archetype and the lower case *j* in *jíbaro* in reference to actual populations thus identified.

1. The Stakes of Being Taíno

1. Between 1917 and 1948, attempts to teach students in English and to impose U.S. models of decency upon the local population were met with disdain, leading to the rise of nationalist and anti-U.S. movements in the thirties and forties. However, these movements resulted in much controversy and in the 1937 massacre, ordered by the U.S.-appointed governor, of Puerto Rican nationalists on a Palm Sunday in the southern town of Ponce. While Luis Muñoz Marín, the first popularly elected governor of Puerto Rico, had been proindependence as well, his project can be understood as an attempt to reconcile the reality of the colonial relationship with the United States with local national identity and pride. The success of his project is apparent—approximately half of today's voting population identifies as being part of the PPD (Partido Popular Democrático), and even the pro-statehood party has endorsed a version of statehood they call *estadidad jíbara*, or "Puerto Rican statehood," including the maintenance of Spanish as an official language of Puerto Rico.

2. The Puerto Rican political system is modeled after the United States' three-branch federal system.

3. Luis Muñoz Marín operationalized his political vision through two different programs: Operation Serenity and Operation Bootstrap. The economic efforts on the island were structured through Operation Bootstrap, a series of economic policies and tax subsidies to attract U.S. companies to move their operations to Puerto Rico. Operation Serenity was its moral counterpart—an attempt to restructure Puerto Rican cultural ideas so as to better fit industrialization efforts and to impel people to join the workforce and to restructure the Puerto Rican family and family geography so as to better fit U.S. models of the nuclear family while fomenting calm in the face of infrastructural and economic change and protecting Puerto Rican culture. The project that implemented the cultural goals of this vision was DIVEDCO (Division of Community Education), created through Law 372, which was approved unanimously by the House and the Senate on May 14, 1949. DIVEDCO actualized the aims of this project through its community education mission, drawing from and celebrating selected aspects of Puerto Rican national

culture. The discourse surrounding Operation Serenity made the maintenance of the morals and traditions that were understood to be the essence of Puerto Ricanness the responsibility of each Puerto Rican in the face of rapid industrialization and change (Méndez Velázquez 2005). However, the cultural projects implemented by the Muñoz Marín government also reflected an elite vision of Puerto Rican culture and tradition, which were not always reflective of all Puerto Rican experiences and positionalities (Lloréns 2014).

2. Historical Discourses and Debates about Puerto Rico's Indigenous Trajectory

1. This quote was located in the book's summary on the back jacket.
2. On the issues of what gets left out of the archives that inform much historical work, see Stoler (2010); Wolf (2010 [1982]).
3. For similar arguments concerning the revision of the narrative of Taíno extinction in Cuba, see Yaremko (2009).
4. From "Prophecy of the Morning Star . . . the Story" by Margarita Nogueras Vidal (2007).
5. Abuela Shashira communicated this to me in Spanish, which I wrote in my field notes and translated to English as soon as I was able.

3. Jíbaros and Jibaridades, Ambiguities and Possibilities

1. Though fascinating in itself, a thorough discussion of the Spanish caste system here is beyond the scope of this chapter.
2. Interestingly, the term as it was used in this image does capture how many understand the island's current racial makeup—namely, as a mixture of African, Spanish, and Indian ethnoracial heritages.
3. Before the eighteenth century, there is a dearth of written documentation on this topic specifically and concerning Puerto Rico more generally. By the eighteenth century, the social and physical distance between island elites and the rural populations already becomes apparent.
4. Berkhofer (1978) discusses early Spanish encounters with the Taíno Arawak Indians and exposes how the trope of the noble savage was established early in the process of conquest. Sometimes virtuous,

sometimes deficient in civilization, sometimes both, the descriptions of the Taíno (and later jíbaro) were drenched with the image of the noble savage—a people lacking civilization, somehow both innocent and immoral.

5. For more on the travel writing genre in the colonial Caribbean, see Hulme (2004)

6. Compare with how Native American figures in the United States were deployed in "misrule traditions" as a mode of social protest (Deloria 1999, 12).

7. Lomawaima and McCarty (2002); Adams (1995); and Szasz (1999) discuss similar educational practices in American Indian education beginning in the early twentieth century in both the United States and Puerto Rico—an explicit policy of assimilating Native Americans and Puerto Ricans, transforming them into "Americans," though such efforts were often fraught with ambivalence.

8. A *fogón* refers to an outside cooking fire, typically consisting of three rocks that sustain a large pot and wood charcoal to fire the pot.

4. Impossible Identities

1. I particularly look to the interdisciplinary work of psychologists Peggy Miller and Heidi Fung and anthropologist Michele Koven, which considers how narrative as a medium of socialization has a role in "reproducing and anchoring identities" and as a medium of "innovation and transformation" enables social actors to "reenvision their lives" (2007, 596).

2. For more on debates regarding mtDNA evidence among Taíno and popular misunderstandings of this research, see Benn Torres (2014, 2018); Guitar, Ferbel-Azcarate, and Estevez (2006); Haslip-Viera (2013); Jobling, Rasteiro, and Wetton (2016); Martínez-Cruzado et al. (2001).

3. A popular form of music among Puerto Rican youth, it combines aspects of rap, reggae, and Caribbean rhythms—including, according to Yarey, Taíno beats. For more on reggaeton music, see Rivera, Marshall, and Pacini Hernandez (2009).

4. *Baquiné* refers to a special category of religious funerary wake that is celebrated for children and has been documented throughout

Afro-Caribbean populations, including in Puerto Rico (Alvarez Nazario 1961). It is described as a "modality of sung rosary." Sung rosaries (*rosarios cantaos*) are a traditional practice where the rosary and its prayers are sung.

5. Both arguments (for reggaeton and Indigenous continuity in Puerto Rico) refute the logic that traditional practices and peoples are lost because they have changed or that new practices cannot, at the same time, be traditional.

5. (Re)Constructing Heritage

1. Additionally, the program was presented in a way that fed into nationally circulating nationalistic concepts of language teaching and learning in Puerto Rico. For example, Yarey once commented about "como los muchachos pronunciaban el Arauco era mejor que el inglés" (August 29, 2007, personal communication; how the kids pronounced the Arawakan was better than English). This led her to a discussion of how this may be because the Taíno language is less foreign to Puerto Rican youth than English.

2. On issues related to language reclamation and revitalization more generally, see Errington (2003); Hinton (2001); Hinton and Ahlers (1999); Hinton and Hale (2001); R. Moore (2006); Wong (1999).

3. On similar questions, see Dementi-Leonard and Gilmore (1999); Eisenlohr (2004b); Moore and Tlen (2007).

4. The Taíno Nation is the organization's actual name.

5. Oscar Lamourt Valentín, known as Oki, graduated with a BA in sociolinguistics from Iowa State University in the '60s or '70s. A continuing studies course given by Uahtibili Báez Santiago and Huana Naboli Martínez Prieto at the University of Puerto Rico–Utuado Campus, Introducción al Lenguaje Taíno, describes Oki as follows (with my translation given below):

Al presente no se ha publicado estudio etimológico alguno sobre la lengua nativa en Puerto Rico. El único estudio lingüístico documentado existente fue realizado por el Sr. Oscar Lamourt Valentín, antropólogo y lingüísta lareño, quien aprende las lenguas maya de los pueblos tzeltal y lacandón, mientras convive con ellos, y al descubrir la relación de estas lenguas con la nuestra, comienza y documenta el primer estudio etimológico existente de la lengua nativa boricua. Descubre que nuestra lengua, no taína ni arahuaca, es una de las lenguas mayas, la del pueblo Chib'al'o o Jíbaro, como se conoce hoy en su forma transliterada por el español.

As of the present [time], no etymological studies of the Puerto Rican Native tongue have been published. The only existing documented linguistic study was realized by Mr. Oscar Lamourt Valentín, anthropologist and linguist from Lares, who learned the Mayan tongues from the Tzeltal and Lancandon peoples while he lived with them, and in discovering the relation of these tongues with our own, [he] begins and documents the first existing etymological study of or native Boricua language. He discovers that our language, not Taíno or Arawakan, is one of the Mayan tongues, of the Chib'al'o or Jíbaro peoples, as known in its transliterated version in Spanish.

6. He continues,

This is a very curious condition of things because there is no secret in their regards being agglutinative polysyllabic root elements combined grammatically, so that each term is a grammatical coherent product of the language . . . which remarkably escape identification when of course integrity is surfeit since intentionality is to be supposed.

One should also observe that a European language is made to assume the place of a pre-columbian language, which is even more strange yet, since the same things can be repeated over again, if you can get away with it the first time by employing the term preamerican, as if everything past . . . was future. (Lamourt Valentín n.d., 1)

7. These are all sixteenth-century chroniclers.

8. Perhaps these links to Mayan language and culture serve to associate the island's Indigenous population with a historically documented, prestigious, and powerful Indigenous group, or it might be related to the documented forced migration and displacement of Indigenous persons throughout South America and Mesoamerica and the Caribbean, including Puerto Rico, in the sixteenth and seventeenth centuries.

9. These are the research consultants' actual names, as requested by the participants.

10. Groups that (broadly) claimed Arawakan genealogies would travel to meet other Arawakan Indigenous groups, such as LGTK's visit to the Kalinago in the Caribbean and the TN's visit to Lokono groups in Guyana. Tito Guajataca of the MIJB was unable to afford a visit to Yucatán, but he was taking a correspondence course to learn the language. Groups based in the United States also often cooperated with U.S.-based Native American groups.

6. How Do You See the World as a Taíno? Conceptualizing the Taíno Gaze

1. In *The Order of Things*, Foucault writes about resemblances with respect to their role in sixteenth-century epistemes. He argues that such a logic of resemblances as tied to making meaning "provides all investigation with an assurance that everything will find its mirror and its macrocosmic justification on another and larger scale; it affirms, inversely, that the visible order of the highest spheres will be reflected in the darkest depths of the earth" (1994, 31), which is helpful in understanding the logic that may undergird analyses such as Robinson's.

2. For further discussion, see Silverstein (1976); Urciuoli (2003); Harkness (2010).

7. Protest, Surveillance, and Ceremony

1. Such political surveillance has its roots in McCarthyism and the Cold War–era blacklisting that took place under the FBI's Counter Intelligence Program (COINTELPRO), which, under the directives of

J. Edgar Hoover, conducted investigations and attempted to disrupt what were deemed potentially subversive groups between 1956 and 1971, including many civil rights groups, women's rights groups, communist and socialist organizations, and groups protesting the Vietnam War.

2. What follow are the relevant sections of the Ground Archaeological Heritage Protection Act, Law 112 of July 20, 1988:

SECTION 5—Within ninety (90) days from the date this law becomes valid, all natural or legal persons and all Government agencies and instrumentalities, including its public corporations and municipalities, are obligated to effectively notify the Council by letter, of all material, structures or sites that are under their ownership, possession or custody, which may be of Puerto Rican archeological interest according to the provisions of SECTION 1 of this Act. It is also required to notify the Council within thirty (30) days from the date in which the discovery of any goods of archaeological interest located near the surface that are prone to being declared of public utility, as stated in SECTION 1 of this Act. . . .

SECTION 9—As of the enactment of this law, no natural or legal person, government agency, public corporation or municipality may sell or exchange, transfer, alter, take possession, transfer, or take out of the territory of the Commonwealth of Puerto Rico any property or object that constitutes part of the Puerto Rican archeological land heritage, according to the provisions of SECTION 1 of this Act, without sending notice to the Council and having obtained their permission to carry out the corresponding procedures.

3. Translated from "quienes excluyen a la Ley 112 del proceso bajo Ley 106 del Advisory Council, no son las instituciones federales no los funcionarios federales locales propiamente, sino funcionarios de tercer rango del Estado Libre Asociado de Puerto Rico en su interpretación 'a capricho' de la Ley 106" (Medina-Carrillo 2007).

4. See K. Basso (1996) for a discussion of links between landscape and social narratives.

References

Abbad y Lasierra, Iñigo. 1959 [1778]. *Historia geográfica, civil y natural de la isla de San Juan Bautista de Puerto Rico*. Edited by Isabel Gutiérrez del Arroyo. San Juan: Editorial de la Universidad de Puerto Rico.

Acevedo, Gregory. 2004. "Neither Here nor There." *Journal of Immigrant & Refugee Services* 2 (1/2): 69–85.

Adams, David Wallace. 1995. *Education for Extinction: American Indians and the Boarding School Experience, 1875–1928*. Lawrence: University Press of Kansas.

Agha, Asif. 2005. "Voice, Footing, Enregisterment." *Journal of Linguistic Anthropology* 15 (1): 38–59.

Ahlers, Jocelyn C. 2006. "Framing Discourse." *Journal of Linguistic Anthropology* 16 (1): 58–75.

———. 2014. "Linguistic Variation and Time Travel: Barrier, or Border-Crossing?" *Language & Communication* 38:33–43.

———. 2017. "Native California Languages as Semiotic Resources in the Performance of Identity." *Journal of Linguistic Anthropology* 27 (1): 40–53.

Alegría, Ricardo E. 1969. *Descubrimiento, conquista y colonización de Puerto Rico, 1493–1599*. San Juan: Colecciones de Estudios Puertorriqueños.

Alonso, Manuel A. 1970 [1845]. *El Gíbaro*. San Juan: Instituto de Cultura Puertorriqueña.

Alvarez Nazario, Manuel. 1961. *El elemento afronegroide en el español de Puerto Rico: Contribución al estudio del negro en América (Vol. 1)*. San Juan: Instituto de Cultura Puertorriqueña.

———. 1996. *Arqueología lingüística: Estudios modernos dirigidos al rescate y reconstrucción del arahuaco taíno*. San Juan: Editorial de la Universidad de Puerto Rico.

Amery, Rob. 2016. *Warraparna Kaurna! Reclaiming an Australian Language*. Adelaide: University of Adelaide Press.

Anderson, Mark. 2007. "When Afro Becomes (like) Indigenous: Garifuna and Afro-Indigenous Politics in Honduras." *Journal of Latin American and Caribbean Anthropology* 12 (2): 384–413.

Anonymous. 1814. "El Gívaro Paciente: Lo que pasa en los campos." *Diario Económico de Puerto Rico*, no. 41 (June 17): 351–353.

Anzaldúa, Gloria. 1987. *Borderlands—La Frontera: The New Mestiza*. San Francisco: Aunt Lute.

Arrom, Juan Jose. 2000 [1980]. *Estudios de Lexicología Antillana*. San Juan: Editorial de la Universidad de Puerto Rico.

Asad, Talal. 1991. "Afterword: From the History of Colonial Anthropology to the Anthropology of Western Hegemony." In *Colonial Situations: Essays on the Contextualization of Ethnographic Knowledge*, edited by George W. Stocking, 314–324. Madison: University of Wisconsin Press.

Asamblea Legislativa de Puerto Rico. 1988. Ley de protección del patrimonio arqueológico terrestre de Puerto Rico. Ley 112 del 20 de julio de 1988 (según enmendada 2003).

Austin, John Langshaw. 1975. *How to Do Things with Words*. Oxford: Oxford University Press.

Ayala, Cesar. 2000. "Uncovering Secret Files: Political Persecution in Puerto Rico." *Against the Current* 15 (1): 41–43.

Báez Santiago, Uahtibili, and Huana Naboli Martínez Prieto. 2008. *"Puerto Rico": La Gran Mentira*. Camuy, PR: MOVIJIBO.

Basso, Ellen B. 2009. "Ordeals of Language." In *Culture, Rhetoric, and the Vicissitudes of Life*, edited by Michael Carrithers, 121–137. New York: Berghahn Books.

Basso, Keith. 1996. *Wisdom Sits in Places: Landscape and Language among the Western Apache*. Albuquerque: University of New Mexico Press.

Bauman, Richard, and Charles L. Briggs. 1990. "Poetics and Performances as Critical Perspectives on Language and Social Life." *Annual Review of Anthropology* 19 (1): 59–88.

Behar, Ruth. 1993. *Translated Woman: Crossing the Border with Esperanza's Story*. 10th anniversary ed. Boston: Beacon Press.

Bender, Margaret. 2008. "Indexicality, Voice, and Context in the Distribution of Cherokee Scripts." *International Journal of the Sociology of Language* 192:91–103.

Benítez-Rojo, Antonio. 1996. *The Repeating Island: The Caribbean and the Postmodern Perspective*. Durham: Duke University Press.

Benn Torres, Jada. 2014. "Prospecting the Past: Genetic Perspectives on the Extinction and Survival of Indigenous Peoples of the Caribbean." *New Genetics and Society* 33 (1): 21–41.

———. 2018. "'Reparational' Genetics: Genomic Data and the Case for Reparations in the Caribbean." *Genealogy* 2 (1): 7.

Berkhofer, Robert F. 1978. *The White Man's Indian: Images of the American Indian from Columbus to the Present*. 1st ed. New York: Knopf.

Berman Santana, Déborah. 2005. "Indigenous Identity and the Struggle for Independence in Puerto Rico." In *Sovereignty Matters: Locations of Contestation and Possibility in Indigenous Struggles for Self-Determination*, edited by Joanne Barker, 211–223. Lincoln: University of Nebraska Press.

Bofill Calero, Jaime O. 2014. "Bomba, danza, calipso y merengue: Creación del espacio social en las fiestas de Santiago Apóstol de Loíza." *Latin American Music Review / Revista de Música Latinoamericana* 35 (1): 115–138.

Bonilla, Yarimar, and Marisol Lebrón, eds. 2019. *Aftershocks of Disaster: Puerto Rico before and after the Storm*. Chicago: Haymarket.

Bonilla-Silva, Eduardo. 2006. *Racism without Racists: Color-Blind Racism and the Persistence of Racial Inequality in the United States*. Lanham: Rowman & Littlefield.

Borrero, Roberto Mucaro. 2001. "Rethinking Taíno: A Taíno Perspective." In *Taíno Revival: Critical Perspectives on Puerto Rican Identity and Cultural Politics*, edited by Gabriel Haslip-Viera, 139–160. Princeton: Markus Wiener.

Bosque Pérez, Ramón, and José Javier Colón Morera. 1997. *Las carpetas: Persecución política y derechos civiles en Puerto Rico; Ensayos y documentos*. San Juan: Centro para la Investigación y Promoción de los Derechos Civiles.

Bourdieu, Pierre. 1999. *Language and Symbolic Power*. Edited by John Thompson, translated by Gino Raymond and Matthew Adamson. Reprint ed. Cambridge: Harvard University Press.

Brau, Salvador. 1983 [1917]. *Historia de Puerto Rico*. New York: D. Appleton and Company.

Brusi Gil de Lamadrid, Rima, and Isar Godreau. 2007. "¿Somos Indígenas?" *Diálogo*, March–April, 10–11.

Bucholtz, Mary, and Kira Hall. 2005. "Identity and Interaction: A Sociocultural Linguistic Approach." *Discourse Studies* 7 (4/5): 585–614.

———. 2009. "Locating Identity in Language." In *Language and Identities*, edited by Carmen Llamas and Dominic Watt, 18–28. Edinburgh: Edinburgh University Press.

Caban, Pedro. 2017. "Puerto Rico and PROMESA: Reaffirming Colonialism." *New Politics Journal* 14 (3): 120–125.

Castanha, Anthony. 2004. "Adventures in Caribbean Indigeneity Centering on Resistance, Survival and Presence in Borikén (Puerto Rico)." PhD diss., University of Hawai'i.

———. 2008. "Adventures in Indigenous Caribbean Resistance, Survival and Presence in Borikén (Puerto Rico)." Native American and Indigenous Studies Conference. Athens, GA: University of Georgia. Unpublished manuscript.

———. 2011. *The Myth of Indigenous Caribbean Extinction: Continuity and Reclamation in Borikén (Puerto Rico)*. London: Palgrave Macmillan.

Chatterjee, Partha. 1993. *The Nation and Its Fragments: Colonial and Postcolonial Histories*. Princeton: Princeton University Press.

Choksi, Nishaant. 2015. "Surface Politics: Scaling Multiscriptality in an Indian Village Market." *Journal of Linguistic Anthropology* 25 (1): 1–24.

Clifford, James. 2013. *Returns: Becoming Indigenous in the Twenty-First Century*. Cambridge: Harvard University Press.

Clifford, James, and George E. Marcus. 1986. *Writing Culture: The Poetics and Politics of Ethnography*. Berkeley: University of California Press.

Collins, James. 2014 [1998]. *Understanding Tolowa Histories: Western Hegemonies and Native American Responses*. New York: Routledge.

Collins, Patricia Hill. 1986. "Learning from the Outsider Within: The Sociological Significance of Black Feminist Thought." *Social Problems* 33 (6): s14–s32.

Coll y Toste, Cayetano. 2011. *Prehistoria de Puerto Rico*. San Juan: CreateSpace Independent Publishing Platform.

Colón Peña, Martin Stuart. 2001. *Voces taínas de boriquén*. San Juan: Publicaciones Educativas Puertorriqueñas.

Conklin, Beth A. 1997. "Body Paint, Feathers, and VCRs: Aesthetics and Authenticity in Amazonian Activism." *American Ethnologist* 24 (4): 711–737.

Córdova, Nathaniel I. 2005. "In His Image and Likeness: The Puerto Rican Jíbaro as Political Icon." *CENTRO: Journal of the Center for Puerto Rican Studies* 17 (2): 170–191.

Cortés, Jason. 2018. "Puerto Rico: Hurricane Maria and the Promise of Disposability." *Capitalism Nature Socialism* 29 (3): 1–8.

Cruz, María Acosta. 2014. *Dream Nation: Puerto Rican Culture and the Fictions of Independence*. New Brunswick: Rutgers University Press.

Curet, Luis Antonio. 2015. "Indigenous Revival, Indigeneity, and the Jíbaro in Borikén." *CENTRO: Journal of the Center for Puerto Rican Studies* 27 (1): 206–247.

———. 1992. "House Structure and Cultural Change in the Caribbean: Three Case Studies from Puerto Rico." *Latin American Antiquity* 3 (2): 160–174.

Curtis, Katherine J., and Francisco Scarano. 2011. "Puerto Rico's Population Padrones, 1779–1802." *Latin American Research Review* 46 (2): 200–213.

Das, Sonia N. 2011. "Rewriting the Past and Reimagining the Future: The Social Life of a Tamil Heritage Language Industry." *American Ethnologist* 38 (4): 774–789.

Dávila, Arlene. 2001. "Local/Diasporic Taínos: Towards a Cultural Politics of Memory, Reality, and Imagery." In *Taíno Revival: Critical Perspectives on Puerto Rican Identity and Cultural Politics*, edited by Gabriel Haslip-Viera, 33–53. Princeton: Markus Wiener.

Dávila, Tuján. 2001. *¡Batey!* Self-published.

Davis, Christina P. 2020. *The Struggle for a Multilingual Future: Youth and Education in Sri Lanka*. Oxford: Oxford University Press.

Davis, Jenny L. 2017. "Resisting Rhetorics of Language Endangerment: Reclamation through Indigenous Language Survivance." *Language Documentation and Description* 14:37–58.

de la Cadena, Marisol, and Orin Starn. 2009. "Indigeneity: Problematics, Experiences and Agendas in the New Millennium." *Tabula Rasa* (10): 191–224.

de las Casas, Bartolomé. 1974 [1552]. *The Devastation of the Indies: A Brief Account*. Baltimore: Johns Hopkins University Press.

Delgado, Juan Manuel. 1977. "¿Dónde están nuestros indios?" *El Nuevo Día*, November 19, 1977, 14–15.

Deloria, Philip J. 1999. *Playing Indian*. Rev. ed. New Haven: Yale University Press.

Dementi-Leonard, Beth, and Perry Gilmore. 1999. "Language Revitalization and Identity in Social Context: A Community-Based Athabascan Language Preservation Project in Western Interior Alaska." *Anthropology & Education Quarterly* 30 (1): 37–55.

Dinzey-Flores, Zaire Zenit. 2013. *Locked In, Locked Out: Gated Communities in a Puerto Rican City*. Philadelphia: University of Pennsylvania Press.

Dippie, Brian W. 1982. *The Vanishing American: White Attitudes and U.S. Indian Policy*. Lawrence: University Press of Kansas.

Dirlik, Arif. 1996. "The Past as Legacy and Project: Postcolonial Criticism in the Perspective of Indigenous Historicism." *American Indian Culture and Research Journal* 20 (2): 1–31.

Duany, Jorge. 2002a. "Mobile Livelihoods: The Sociocultural Practices of Circular Migrants between Puerto Rico and the United States." *International Migration Review* 36 (2): 355–388.

———. 2002b. *The Puerto Rican Nation on the Move: Identities on the Island and in the United States*. Chapel Hill: University of North Carolina Press.

DuBord, Elise. 2007. "La Mancha del Plátano: Language Policy and the Construction of Puerto Rican National Identity in the 1940s." *Spanish in Context* 4 (2): 241–262.

Duranti, Alessandro. 2004. "Transcription Conventions." Last modified July 18, 2019. http://www.sscnet.ucla.edu/anthro/faculty/duranti/audvis/annotate.htm.

Edelman, Marc. 2001. "Social Movements: Changing Paradigms and Forms of Politics." *Annual Review of Anthropology* 30 (1): 285–317.

Eisenlohr, Patrick. 2004a. "Register Levels of Ethno-national Purity: The Ethnicization of Language and Community in Mauritius." *Language in Society* 33 (1): 59–80.

———. 2004b. "Temporalities of Community: Ancestral Language, Pilgrimage, and Diasporic Belonging in Mauritius." *Journal of Linguistic Anthropology* 14 (1): 81–98.

————. 2006. *Little India: Diaspora, Time, and Ethnolinguistic Belonging in Hindu Mauritius*. Berkeley: University of California Press.

El Vocero. 2007. "DESCRUBREN poblado taíno." October 19, 2007, Front page.

Empson, William. 1966 [1930]. *Seven Types of Ambiguity*. New York: New Directions.

Errington, Joseph. 2001. "Colonial Linguistics." *Annual Review of Anthropology* 30 (1): 19–39.

————. 2003. "Getting Language Rights: The Rhetorics of Language Endangerment and Loss." *American Anthropologist* 105 (4): 723–732.

Feliciano, Zadia M., and Andrew Green. 2017. "US Multinationals in Puerto Rico and the Repeal of Section 936 Tax Exemption for U.S. Corporations." Working Paper 23681, National Bureau of Economic Research.

Feliciano-Santos, Sherina. 2017. "Prophetic Repairs: Narrative and Social Action among Puerto Rican Taíno." *Language & Communication* 56:19–32.

Fernández Méndez, Eugenio. 1976. *Las encomiendas y esclavitud de los indios de Puerto Rico, 1508–1550*. Río Piedras: Editorial Universitaria, Universidad de Puerto Rico.

————. 1995a. *Crónicas de Puerto Rico: Desde la conquista hasta nuestros días, 1493–1955*. 7th ed. San Juan: Ediciones "El Cemi" Editorial Universitaria, Universidad de Puerto Rico.

————. 1995b. *Proceso histórico de la conquista de Puerto Rico, 1508–1640*. San Juan: Ediciones El Cemí.

Field, Margaret. 2001. "Triadic Directives in Navajo Language Socialization." *Language in Society* 30 (2): 249–263.

Figueroa, Loida. 1971. *Breve historia de Puerto Rico: Desde sus comienzos hasta 1800*. San Juan: Editorial Edil.

Fitzgerald, Kathleen J. 2007. *Beyond White Ethnicity: Developing a Sociological Understanding of Native American Identity Reclamation*. Lanham: Lexington Books.

Flores, Juan, John Attinasi, and Pedro Pedraza. 1981. "'La Carreta Made a U-Turn': Puerto Rican Language and Culture in the United States." *Daedalus* 110 (2): 193–217.

Forte, Maximilian Christian. 2005. "Extinction: Historical Trope of Anti-Indigeneity in the Caribbean." *Issues in Caribbean Amerindian Studies* 4 (4).

Foucault, Michel. 1980. *Power/Knowledge: Selected Interviews and Other Writings, 1972–1977*. New York: Pantheon.

———. 1994. *The Order of Things: An Archaeology of the Human Sciences*. Reissue ed. New York: Vintage.

———. 1995. *Discipline and Punish: The Birth of the Prison*. Translated by Alan Sheridan. New York: Vintage.

Franceschet, Susan. 2004. "Explaining Social Movement Outcomes: Collective Action Frames and Strategic Choices in First- and Second-Wave Feminism in Chile." *Comparative Political Studies* 37 (5): 499–530.

Gal, Susan. 2005. "Language Ideologies Compared." *Journal of Linguistic Anthropology* 15 (1): 23–37.

Gal, Susan, and Kathryn A. Woolard. 1995. "Constructing Languages and Publics: Authority and Representation." *Pragmatics* 5 (2): 129–138.

Galarza, Sujey M. 2007. "Complicating Taíno Identifications among Puerto Ricans: Rearticulations of the Taíno Trope within Nationalist Identification Debates in Puerto Rico." Master's thesis, State University of New York at Binghamton.

Gallie, W. B. 1969 [1956]. "Essentially Contested Concepts." In *The Importance of Language*, edited by Max Black, 121–136. Ithaca: Cornell University Press.

Giddens, Anthony. 1976. *New Rules of Sociological Method: A Positive Critique of Interpretative Sociologies*. London: Hutchinson.

———. 1977. *Studies in Social and Political Theory*. New York: Basic Books.

Giddens, Anthony, and Philip Cassell. 1993. *The Giddens Reader*. Palo Alto: Stanford University Press.

Godreau, Isar P. 2008. "Slippery Semantics: Race Talk and Everyday Uses of Racial Terminology in Puerto Rico." *CENTRO: Journal of the Center for Puerto Rican Studies* 20 (2): 5–33.

———. 2015. *Scripts of Blackness: Race, Cultural Nationalism, and U.S. Colonialism in Puerto Rico*. Champaign: University of Illinois Press.

Godreau, Isar P., Mariolga Reyes Cruz, Mariluz Franco Ortiz, and Sherry Cuadrado. 2008. "The Lessons of Slavery: Discourses of Slavery, Mestizaje, and Blanqueamiento in an Elementary School in Puerto Rico." *American Ethnologist* 35 (1): 115–135.

Goebel, Zane. 2010. "Identity and Social Conduct in a Transient Multilingual Setting." *Language in Society* 39 (2): 203–240.

Goffman, Erving. 1962. *Asylums: Essays on the Social Situation of Mental Patients and Other Inmates.* 1st ed. Chicago: Aldine Press.

———. 1974. *Frame Analysis: An Essay on the Organization of Experience.* Cambridge: Harvard University Press.

Golash-Boza, Tanya, and Eduardo Bonilla-Silva. 2013. "Rethinking Race, Racism, Identity and Ideology in Latin America." *Ethnic and Racial Studies* 36 (10): 1485–1489.

Goldstein, Alyosha. 2016. "Promises Are Over: Puerto Rico and the Ends of Decolonization." *Theory & Event* 19 (4). https://www.muse.jhu.edu/article/633271.

Gómez Acevedo, Labor, and Manuel Ballesteros Gaibrois. 1978. *Culturas indígenas de Puerto Rico.* Madrid: Samarán.

———. 1993. *Vida y cultura precolombinas de Puerto Rico.* San Juan: Editorial Cultural.

Gongaware, Timothy B. 2003. "Collective Memories and Collective Identities: Maintaining Unity in Native American Educational Social Movements." *Journal of Contemporary Ethnography* 32 (5): 483–520.

Gonzales, Angela. 1998. "The (Re)Articulation of American Indian Identity: Maintaining Boundaries and Regulating Access to Ethnically Tied Resources." *American Indian Culture and Research Journal* 22 (4): 199–225.

González, Christina M. 2015. "A Piece Not the Puzzle: Genetics and Affirmations of Taíno Identity Among Puerto Ricans." *GeneWatch* 28 (2): 14–17.

———. 2018. "Abuelas, Ancestors and Atabey: The Spirit of Taíno Resurgence." *American Indian Magazine* 19 (3). https://www.americanindianmagazine.org/story/abuelas-ancestors-and-atabey-spirit-taino-resurgence.

Gonzalez, Jose L. 1980. *El pais de cuatro pisos y otros ensayos.* Río Piedras: Ediciones Huracán.

Graham, Laura. 2002. "How Should an Indian Speak? Amazonian Indians and the Symbolic Politics of Language in the Global Public Sphere." In *Indigenous Movements, Self-Representation, and the State in Latin America,* edited by Kay B. Warren and Jean E. Jackson, 181–228. Austin: University of Texas Press.

Granberry, Julian, and Gary Vescelius. 2004. *Languages of the Pre-Columbian Antilles.* Tuscaloosa: University of Alabama Press.

Gravlee, Clarence C. 2005. "Ethnic Classification in Southeastern Puerto Rico: The Cultural Model of 'Color.'" *Social Forces* 83 (3): 949–970.

Green, Melanie C., Jeffrey J. Strange, and Timothy C. Brock. 2003. *Narrative Impact: Social and Cognitive Foundations*. New York: Psychology Press.

Green, Rayna. 1988. "The Tribe Called Wannabee: Playing Indian in America and Europe." *Folklore* 99 (1): 30–55.

Grosz, Elizabeth A. 1999. *Becomings: Explorations in Time, Memory, and Futures*. Ithaca: Cornell University Press.

Guerra, Lillian. 1998. *Popular Expression and National Identity in Puerto Rico: The Struggle for Self, Community, and Nation*. Gainesville: University Press of Florida.

Guitar, Lynne. 2002. "Documenting the Myth of Taíno Extinction." *Kacike: Journal of Caribbean Amerindian History and Anthropology*, December. https://archive.org/stream/KacikeJournal_34/GuitarEnglish_djvu.txt.

Guitar, Lynne, P. Ferbel-Azcarate, and Jorge Estevez. 2006. "Ocama- Daca Taíno (Hear Me, I Am Taíno): Taíno Survival on Hispaniola, Focusing on the Dominican Republic." In *Indigenous Resurgence in the Contemporary Caribbean: Amerindian Survival and Revival*, edited by Maximiliano Forte, 41–67. New York: Peter Lang.

Gumperz, John. 1992. "Contextualization and Understanding." In *Rethinking Context: Language as an Interactive Phenomenon*, Studies on the Social and Cultural Foundations of Language 11, edited by Alessandro Duranti and Charles Goodwin, 229–252. Cambridge: Cambridge University Press.

Haley, Brian D., and Larry R. Wilcoxon. 1997. "Anthropology and the Making of Chumash Tradition." *Current Anthropology* 38 (5): 761–794.

———. 2005. "How Spaniards Became Chumash and Other Tales of Ethnogenesis." *American Anthropologist* 107 (3): 432–445.

Harkness, Nicholas. 2010. "Words in Motion and the Semiotics of the Unseen in Two Korean Churches." *Language & Communication* 30 (2): 139–158.

Haslip-Viera, Gabriel, ed. 2001. *Taíno Revival: Critical Perspectives on Puerto Rican Identity and Cultural Politics*. Princeton: Markus Wiener.

———. 2009. "Changed Identities: A Racial Portrait of Two Extended Families, 1909–Present." *CENTRO: Journal of the Center for Puerto Rican Studies* 21 (1): 37–51.

———. 2013. *Race, Identity and Indigenous Politics: Puerto Rican Neo-Taínos in the Diaspora and the Island.* CreateSpace Independent Publishing Platform.

———. 2014. *Race, Identity, and Indigenous Politics: Puerto Rican Neo-Taínos in the Diaspora and the Island.* New York: Latino Studies Press.

———. 2019. *Indigenous Revivalism in the Evolving Spanish-Speaking Caribbean and Its Diaspora at the Beginning of the Third Decade of the Twenty-First Century.* New York: Latino Studies Press.

Hathaway, Michael. 2010. "The Emergence of Indigeneity: Public Intellectuals and an Indigenous Space in Southwest China." *Cultural Anthropology* 25 (2): 301–333.

Hernández Hiraldo, Samiri. 2006. "'If God Were Black and from Loíza': Managing Identities in a Puerto Rican Seaside Town." *Latin American Perspectives* 33 (1): 66–82.

Hill, Jane H. 2002. "'Expert Rhetorics' in Advocacy for Endangered Languages: Who Is Listening, and What Do They Hear?" *Journal of Linguistic Anthropology* 12 (2): 119–133.

Hinton, Leanne. 2001. "Language Revitalization: An Overview." In *The Green Book of Language Revitalization in Practice*, edited by Leanne Hinton and Kenneth Hale, 3–18. San Diego: Academic Press.

Hinton, Leanne, and Jocelyn Ahlers. 1999. "The Issue of 'Authenticity' in California Language Restoration." *Anthropology & Education Quarterly* 30 (1): 56–67.

Hinton, Leanne, and Ken Hale. 2001. *The Green Book of Language Revitalization in Practice.* San Diego: Academic Press.

Holland, Dorothy, Gretchen Fox, and Vinci Daro. 2008. "Social Movements and Collective Identity: A Decentered, Dialogic View." *Anthropological Quarterly* 81 (1): 95–126.

Holmquist, Jonathan Carl. 2005. "Social Stratification in Women's Speech in Rural Puerto Rico: A Study of Five Phonological Features." In *Selected Proceedings of the Second Workshop on Spanish Sociolinguistics*, edited by Lofti Sayahi and Maurice Westmoreland, 109–119. Somerville: Cascadilla Proceedings Project.

hooks, bell. 2000 [1984]. *Feminist Theory: From Margin to Center.* London: Pluto Press.

———. 2014 [1981]. *Ain't I a Woman? Black Women and Feminism.* 2nd ed. New York: Routledge.

Hulme, Peter. 2004. "'The Silent Language of the Face': The Perception of Indigenous Difference in Travel Writing about the Caribbean." In *Perspectives on Travel Writing*, edited by Glenn Hooper and Tim Youngs, 85–98. Aldershot: Ashgate.

Inoue, Miyako. 2002. "Gender, Language, and Modernity: Toward an Effective History of Japanese Women's Language." *American Ethnologist* 29 (2): 392–422.

Irvine, Judith T. 2004. "Say When: Temporalities in Language Ideology." *Journal of Linguistic Anthropology* 14 (1): 99–109.

———. 2005. "Commentary." *Journal of Linguistic Anthropology* 15 (1): 72–80.

———. 2008. "Subjected Words: African Linguistics and the Colonial Encounter." *Language & Communication* 28 (4): 323–343.

Irvine, Judith T., and Susan Gal. 2000. "Language Ideology and Linguistic Differentiation." In *Regimes of Language: Ideologies, Politics, and Identities*, edited by Paul Kroskrity, 35–83. Santa Fe: School of American Research Press.

Jackson, Jean E., and Kay B. Warren. 2002. *Indigenous Movements, Self-Representation, and the State in Latin America*. Austin: University of Texas Press.

Jackson, Shona N. 2012. *Creole Indigeneity: Between Myth and Nation in the Caribbean*. Minneapolis: University of Minnesota Press.

Jaffe, Alexandra Mystra. 1999. *Ideologies in Action: Language Politics on Corsica*. Berlin: Walter de Gruyter.

Jaffe, Alexandra Mystra, Jannis Androutsopoulos, Mark Sebba, and Sally Johnson. 2012. *Orthography as Social Action: Scripts, Spelling, Identity and Power*. Berlin: Walter de Gruyter.

Jobling, Mark A., Rita Rasteiro, and Jon H. Wetton. 2016. "In the Blood: The Myth and Reality of Genetic Markers of Identity." *Ethnic and Racial Studies* 39 (2): 142–161.

Keegan, William F., and Lisabeth A. Carlson. 2010. *Talking Taíno: Caribbean Natural History from a Native Perspective*. Tuscaloosa: University of Alabama Press.

Kenny, Michael G. 1999. "A Place for Memory: The Interface between Individual and Collective History." *Comparative Studies in Society and History* 41 (3): 420–437.

Kuilan-Torres, Sandra J. 2005. "No hallan foro los 'indígenas.'" *El Nuevo Día*, July 30, 2005, 65.

LaFountain-Stokes, Lawrence M. 2007. "Queer Ducks, Puerto Rican Patos, and Jewish American Feygelekh: Birds and the Cultural Representation of Homosexuality." *CENTRO: Journal of the Center for Puerto Rican Studies* 19 (1): 192–229.

Lamourt Valentín, Oscar. n.d. "The Extrapolation and the Limits of Language." Unpublished Manuscript. Printed on paper.

Lawrence, Bonita. 2004. *Real Indians and Others: Mixed-Blood Urban Native Peoples and Indigenous Nationhood*. Lincoln: University of Nebraska Press.

LeBrón, Marisol. 2016a. "Mano Dura Contra el Crimen and Premature Death in Puerto Rico." In *Policing the Planet: Why the Policing Crisis Led to Black Lives Matter*, edited by Jordan T. Camp and Christina Heatherton, 95–107. New York: Verso.

———. 2016b. "People before Debt." *NACLA Report on the Americas* 48 (2): 115–117.

Ledru, André Pierre. 2013 [1797]. *Viaje a la isla de Puerto Rico en el año 1797: Ejecutado por una comisión de sabios franceses, de orden de su gobierno bajo la dirección del capitán Nicolás Baudín, con objeto de hacer indagaciones y colecciones relativas a la historia natural*. Edited by Libia M. González López. San Juan: Historiador Oficial de Puerto Rico.

Leonard, Wesley. 2007. "Miami Language Reclamation in the Home: A Case Study." PhD diss., University of California, Berkeley. *EScholarship*, January 1, 2007. http://escholarship.org/uc/item/1c4779gb.

Lingis, Alphonso. 1999. "Innocence." In *Becomings: Explorations in Time, Memory, and Futures*, edited by Elizabeth A. Grosz, 201–216. Ithaca: Cornell University Press.

Lloréns, Hilda. 2014. *Imaging the Great Puerto Rican Family: Framing Nation, Race, and Gender during the American Century*. Lanham: Lexington Books.

———. 2018a. "Identity Practices: Racial Passing, Gender, and Racial Purity in Puerto Rico." *Afro-Hispanic Review* 37 (1): 29–47.

———. 2018b. "Imaging Disaster: Puerto Rico through the Eye of Hurricane María." *Transforming Anthropology* 26 (2): 136–156.

Lloréns, Hilda, Carlos G. García-Quijano, and Isar P. Godreau. 2017. "Racismo en Puerto Rico: Surveying Perceptions of Racism." *CENTRO: Journal of the Center for Puerto Rican Studies* 29 (3): 154–183.

Lomawaima, K. Tsianina, and Teresa L. McCarty. 2002. "When Tribal Sovereignty Challenges Democracy: American Indian Education and the Democratic Ideal." *American Educational Research Journal* 39 (2): 279–305.

López, Irene. 2008. "Puerto Rican Phenotype: Understanding Its Historical Underpinnings and Psychological Associations." *Hispanic Journal of Behavioral Sciences* 30 (2): 161–180.

López Yustos, Alfonso. 1997. *Historia documental de la educación en Puerto Rico*. San Juan: Publicaciones Puertorriqueñas.

Lorde, Audre. 2012 [1984]. *Sister Outsider: Essays and Speeches*. Berkeley: Crossing Press.

Macdonald, Sharon. 1997. *Reimagining Culture: Histories, Identities and the Gaelic Renaissance*. Oxford: Berg.

Makepeace, Anne, dir. 2010. *We Still Live Here (Âs Nutayuneân)*. Oley: Bullfrog Films.

Malaret Yordán, Augusto. 1932. "¿Por qué llamamos jíbaros a nuestros campesinos?" *El Mundo*, January 23.

Maldonado, Ileana. 2001 [1998]. *Coloreando y aprendiendo con Katsí*. San Juan: Editorial de la Universidad de Puerto Rico.

Mannheim, Bruce. 1998. "A Nation Surrounded." In *Native Traditions in the Postconquest World: A Symposium at Dumbarton Oaks, 2nd through 4th October 1992*, edited by Elizabeth Hill Boone and Tom Cummins, 383–420. Washington, D.C.: Dumbarton Oaks. https://trove.nla.gov.au/version/26638373.

Martínez-Cruzado, J. C., G. Toro-Labrador, V. Ho-Fung, M. A Estévez-Montero, A. Lobaina-Manzanet, D. A. Padovani-Claudio, H. Sánchez-Cruz, P. Ortiz-Bermúdez, and A. Sánchez-Crespo. 2001. "Mitochondrial DNA Analysis Reveals Substantial Native American Ancestry in Puerto Rico." *Human Biology* 73 (4): 491–511.

Martínez-San Miguel, Yolanda. 2011. "Taíno Warriors? Strategies for Recovering Indigenous Voices in Colonial and Contemporary Hispanic Caribbean Discourses." *CENTRO: Journal of the Center for Puerto Rican Studies* 23 (1): 197–215.

Martinez-Valentin, José E. 2003. *Más de cien años de carpeteo en Puerto Rico.* Caguas: n.p.

Medina-Carrillo, Norma. 2007. "Quién permitió la destrucción del yacimiento en ponce?" *Claridad. 8–14 de noviembre de 2007* (2855): 4–6.

Meek, Barbra A. 2012. *We Are Our Language: An Ethnography of Language Revitalization in a Northern Athabaskan Community.* Tucson: University of Arizona Press.

——. 2014. "'She Can Do It in English Too': Acts of Intimacy and Boundary-Making in Language Revitalization." *Language & Communication* 38:73–82.

Méndez Ballester, Manuel. 1979 [1965]. *Bienvenido, Don Goyito: Comedia en Tres Actos.* San Juan: Ediciones Gaviota.

Méndez Velázquez, Anel. 2005. "Cultural Nationalism and the Policing of Gender and Sexuality in Puerto Rico, 1930s–1970s." Master's thesis, John W. Draper Master's Program in Humanities and Social Thought, New York University.

Miller, Peggy J., Heidi Fung, and Michele Koven. 2007. "Narrative Reverberations: How Participation in Narrative Practices Co-creates Persons and Cultures." In *Handbook of Cultural Psychology,* edited by S. Kitayama and D. Cohen, 595–614. New York: Guilford Press.

Mintz, Sidney. 2005. "Ethnic Difference, Plantation Sameness." In *Ethnicity in the Caribbean: Essays in Honor of Harry Hoetink,* edited by Gert Osstindie, 39–52. Amsterdam: Amsterdam University Press.

Montero, Mayra. 2005. "Espejitos." *El Nuevo Día,* Revista Domingo, August 21, 2005, 3.

Moore, Patrick, and Daniel Tlen. 2007. "Indigenous Linguistics and Land Claims: The Semiotic Projection of Athabaskan Directionals in Elijah Smith's Radio Work." *Journal of Linguistic Anthropology* 17 (2): 266–286.

Moore, Robert E. 2006. "Disappearing, Inc.: Glimpsing the Sublime in the Politics of Access to Endangered Languages." *Language & Communication* 26 (3–4): 296–315.

Moraga, Cherríe, and Gloria Anzaldúa, eds. 1981. *This Bridge Called My Back: Writings by Radical Women of Color.* London: Persephone Press.

Moreno Alonso, Manuel. 1983 [1745]. "De Cádiz a Veracruz en 1745." *Historiografía y Bibliografía Americanistas* 27:17–41.

Muratti, Daliana. 2005. *Borikén para niños.* Hato Rey: Publicaciones Puertorriqueñas.

Nash, Catherine. 2005. "Geographies of Relatedness." *Transactions of the Institute of British Geographers* 30 (4): 449–462.

Navarro Tomás, Tomás. 1966. *El español en Puerto Rico: Contribución a la geografía lingüística hispanoamericana.* Río Piedras: Editorial Universitaria, Universidad de Puerto Rico.

Nazario, Manuel Álvarez. 1961. *El elemento afronegroide en el español de Puerto Rico: Contribución al estudio del negro en América.* San Juan: Instituto de Cultura Puertorriqueña.

Negrón de Montilla, Aida. 1975. *Americanization in Puerto Rico and the Public-School System, 1900–1930.* 2nd ed. Río Piedras: Editorial Universitaria, Universidad de Puerto Rico.

Nevins, M. Eleanor. 2010. "Intertextuality and Misunderstanding." *Language & Communication* 30 (1): 1–6.

Newell, Sasha. 2009. "Enregistering Modernity, Bluffing Criminality: How Nouchi Speech Reinvented (and Fractured) the Nation." *Journal of Linguistic Anthropology* 19 (2): 157–184.

Nogueras Vidal, Margarita. 2007. *Profecia de Aura Surey . . . El Cuento / Prophecy of the Morning Star . . . the Story.* Jayuya: Independently published and printed.

O'Brien, Jean M. 2010. *Firsting and Lasting: Writing Indians Out of Existence in New England.* Minneapolis: University of Minnesota Press.

Ochs, Elinor, and Lisa Capps. 2009. *Living Narrative: Creating Lives in Everyday Storytelling.* Cambridge: Harvard University Press.

Ó hIfearnáin, Tadhg. 2014. "Sociolinguistic Vitality of Manx after Extreme Language Shift: Authenticity without Traditional Native Speakers." *International Journal of the Sociology of Language* 2015 (231): 45–62.

Pagán Jimenez, Jaime R., and Reniel Rodríguez Ramos. 2008. "Toward the Liberation of Archaeological Praxis in a 'Postcolonial Colony': The Case of Puerto Rico." In *Archaeology and the Postcolonial Critique*, edited by Matthew Liebmann, 53–72. Lanham: Rowman Altamira.

Pagliai, Valentina. 2009. "Conversational Agreement and Racial Formation Processes." *Language in Society* 38 (5): 549–579.

Pané, Fray Ramon. 1999 [c. 1496]. *An Account of the Antiquities of the Indians: A New Edition, with an Introductory Study, Notes, and Appendices by José Juan Arrom.* Durham: Duke University Press.

Parker, Franklin, and Betty June Parker, eds. 1978. *Education in Puerto Rico and of Puerto Ricans in the U.S.A.: Abstracts of American Doctoral Dissertations.* San Juan: Inter American University Press.

Paschel, Tianna S. 2016. *Becoming Black Political Subjects: Movements and Ethnoracial Rights in Colombia and Brazil.* Princeton: Princeton University Press.

Pedreira, Antonio Salvador. 1935. *La actualidad del jíbaro.* Edited by Ramón Méndez Quiñones. Río Piedras: Editorial Universitaria, Universidad de Puerto Rico.

Pérez, Gina. 2004. *The Near Northwest Side Story: Migration, Displacement, and Puerto Rican Families.* Berkeley: University of California Press.

Perley, Bernard. 2011. *Defying Maliseet Language Death: Emergent Vitalities of Language, Culture, and Identity in Eastern Canada.* Lincoln: University of Nebraska Press.

———. 2012. "Zombie Linguistics: Experts, Endangered Languages and the Curse of Undead Voices." *Anthropological Forum* 22 (2): 133–149.

Philips, Susan U. 2004. "The Organization of Ideological Diversity in Discourse: Modern and Neotraditional Visions of the Tongan State." *American Ethnologist* 31 (2): 231–250.

Picó, Fernando. 1986. *Historia general de Puerto Rico.* San Juan: Ediciones Huracán.

Poitevin, René Francisco. 2000. "Political Surveillance, State Repression, and Class Resistance: The Puerto Rican Experience." *Social Justice* 27 (3): 89–100.

Povinelli, Elizabeth A. 2002. *The Cunning of Recognition: Indigenous Alterities and the Making of Australian Multiculturalism.* Durham: Duke University Press.

———. 2011. *Economies of Abandonment: Social Belonging and Endurance in Late Liberalism.* Durham: Duke University Press.

Rampton, Ben. 2011. "Style Contrasts, Migration and Social Class." *Journal of Pragmatics* 43 (5): 1236–1250.

Redman, Peter. 2005. "The Narrative Formation of Identity Revisited: Narrative Construction, Agency and the Unconscious." *Narrative Inquiry* 15 (1): 25–44.

Rindstedt, Camilla, and Karin Aronsson. 2002. "Growing Up Monolingual in a Bilingual Community: The Quichua Revitalization Paradox." *Language in Society* 31 (5): 721–742.

Rivera, Raquel Z. 1997. "Rapping Two Versions of the Same Requiem." In *Puerto Rican Jam: Rethinking Colonialism and Nationalism*, edited by Frances Negrón-Muntaner and Ramón Grosfoguel, 243–256. Minneapolis: University of Minnesota Press.

Rivera, Raquel Z., Wayne Marshall, and Deborah Pacini Hernandez, eds. 2009. *Reggaeton*. Durham: Duke University Press.

Rivera-Lassén. 2006. "En busca de Iguanaboina." *El Nievo Día*. La Revista, November 19, 2006, 12–13.

Rivera-Rideau, Petra R. 2013. "From Carolina to Loíza: Race, Place and Puerto Rican Racial Democracy." *Identities* 20 (5): 616–632.

Roberts, Peter. 1999. "The (Re)Construction of the Concept of 'Indio' in the National Identities of Cuba, the Dominican Republic, and Puerto Rico." In *Caribe 2000: Definiciones, identidades y culturas regionales y/o nacionales*, edited by Lowell Fiet and Janette Becerra, 99–120. San Juan: Editorial Universitaria, Universidad de Puerto Rico.

Rodríguez, Jorge. 2005. "Persistencia indígena en novela 'El último sonido del Caracol.'" *El Vocero de Puerto Rico*, August, Sección Escenario.

Rodríguez-Burns, Francisco. 2007. "A partir de enero en el sureste de la isla enseñanza taína a más de 20 escuelas." *Primera Hora*, December 8, 2007, 9.

Rodríguez-Díaz, Carlos E. 2018. "Maria in Puerto Rico: Natural Disaster in a Colonial Archipelago." *American Journal of Public Health* 108 (1): 30–32.

Rosa, Jonathan. 2016. "Racializing Language, Regimenting Latinas/os: Chronotope, Social Tense, and American Raciolinguistic Futures." *Language & Communication, Fashions of Speaking and the Temporalities of Self-Fashioning* 46:106–17.

Roth-Gordon, Jennifer. 2009. "The Language That Came Down the Hill: Slang, Crime, and Citizenship in Rio de Janeiro." *American Anthropologist* 111 (1): 57–68.

Rouse, Irving. 1993. *The Taínos: Rise and Decline of the People Who Greeted Columbus*. Reissue ed. New Haven: Yale University Press.

Salman, Ton, and Assies Willem. 2009. "Anthropology and the Study of Social Movements." In *Handbook of Social Movements across Disciplines*, Handbooks of Sociology and Social Research, edited by Bert

Klandermans and Conny Roggeband, 2010 ed., 205–265. New York: Springer.

Samuels, David. 2001. "Indeterminacy and History in Britton Goode's Western Apache Placenames: Ambiguous Identity on the San Carlos Apache Reservation." *American Ethnologist* 28 (2): 277–302.

Santiago, Esmeralda. 1993. *When I Was Puerto Rican: A Memoir.* New York: Vintage.

Scarano, Francisco A. 1989. "Congregate and Control: The Peasantry and Labor Coercion in Puerto Rico before the Age of Sugar, 1750–1820." *Nieuwe West-Indische Gids / New West Indian Guide* 63 (1/2): 23–40.

———. 1993. *Puerto Rico: Cinco siglos de historia.* San Juan: McGraw-Hill.

———. 1996. "The Jíbaro Masquerade and the Subaltern Politics of Creole Identity Formation in Puerto Rico, 1745–1823." *American Historical Review* 101 (5): 1398–1431.

———. 1999. "Desear el jíbaro: Metáforas de la identidad puertorriqueña en la transición imperial." *Islas e Imperios / Islands and Empires* 2:65–74.

Shulist, Sarah. 2016. "Language Revitalization and the Future of Ethnolinguistic Identity." *Language & Communication* 100 (47): 94–99.

Silverstein, Michael. 1976. "Shifters, Linguistic Categories, and Cultural Description." In *Meaning in Anthropology*, edited by Keith H. Basso, Henry A. Selby, and School of American Research, 11–55. Albuquerque: University of New Mexico Press.

———. 1979. "Language Structure and Linguistic Ideology." In *The Elements: A Parasession on Linguistic Units and Levels*, 193–247. Chicago: Chicago Linguistic Society.

———. 1993. "Metapragmatic Discourse and Metapragmatic Function." In *Reflexive Language*, edited by John A. Lucy, 33–58. Cambridge: Cambridge University Press.

Silverstein, Michael, and Greg Urban, eds. 1996. *Natural Histories of Discourse.* Chicago: University of Chicago Press.

Solórzano García, Melissa. 2007. "Reafirma ICP el poder de proteger las excavaciones." *El Nuevo Día*, October 31, 2007, 16.

Stanley, Liz, and Sue Wise. 2013. "Method, Methodology and Epistemology in Feminist Research Processes." In *Feminist Praxis (RLE Feminist Theory): Research, Theory and Epistemology in Feminist Sociology*, edited by Liz Stanley, 20–60. New York: Routledge.

Steiner, Stan. 1974. *The Islands: The Worlds of the Puerto Ricans.* 1st ed. New York: Harper & Row.

Steinmetz, George. 1992. "Reflections on the Role of Social Narratives in Working-Class Formation: Narrative Theory in the Social Sciences." *Social Science History* 16 (3): 489–516.

Stevens-Arroyo, Antonio M. 2006. *Cave of the Jagua: The Mythological World of the Taínos.* Scranton: University of Scranton Press.

Stivers, Tanya, and Makoto Hayashi. 2010. "Transformative Answers: One Way to Resist a Question's Constraints." *Language in Society* 39 (1): 1–25.

Stoler, Ann Laura. 2008. "Epistemic Politics: Ontologies of Colonial Common Sense." *Philosophical Forum* 39 (3): 349–361.

———. 2010. *Along the Archival Grain: Epistemic Anxieties and Colonial Common Sense.* Princeton: Princeton University Press.

Suárez-Findlay, Eileen J. 2000. *Imposing Decency: The Politics of Sexuality and Race in Puerto Rico, 1870–1920.* Durham: Duke University Press.

Swinehart, Karl F. and Kathryn Graber. 2012. "Tongue-Tied Territories: Languages and Publics in Stateless Nations." *Language & Communication* 32 (2): 95–97.

Szasz, Margaret Connell. 1999. *Education and the American Indian: The Road to Self-Determination since 1928.* 3rd ed. Albuquerque: University of New Mexico Press.

Taussig, Michael T. 1986. *Shamanism, Colonialism, and the Wild Man: A Study in Terror and Healing.* Chicago: University of Chicago Press.

Tedlock, Dennis, and Bruce Mannheim, eds. 1995. *The Dialogic Emergence of Culture.* Champaign: University of Illinois Press.

Thompson, Donald. 2005. "Film Music and Community Development in Rural Puerto Rico: The DIVEDCO Program (1948–91)." *Latin American Music Review* 26 (1): 102–114.

Tirado, Amilcar, dir. 1967. *La buena herencia.* Film documentary. San Juan: DIVEDCO.

Torres, Arlene. 1998. "La Gran Familia Puertorriqueña 'Ej Prieta de Beldá' (The Great Puerto Rican Family Is Really Really Black)." In *Blackness in Latin America and the Caribbean: Eastern South America and the Caribbean,* edited by Norman E. Whitten and Arlene Torres, 285–306. Bloomington: Indiana University Press.

Torres-Robles, Carmen L. 1999. "La mitificación y desmitificación del jíbaro como símbolo de la identidad nacional puertorriqueña." *Bilingual Review / La Revista Bilingüe* 24 (3): 241–253.

Trechter, Sara. 2001. "White between the Lines: Ethnic Positioning in Lakhota Discourse." *Journal of Linguistic Anthropology* 11 (1): 22–35.

Trías Monge, José. 1997. *Puerto Rico: The Trials of the Oldest Colony in the World*. New Haven: Yale University Press.

Trouillot, Michel Rolph. 1995. *Silencing the Past: Power and the Production of History*. Boston: Beacon Press.

Urciuoli, Bonnie. 2003. "Excellence, Leadership, Skills, Diversity: Marketing Liberal Arts Education." *Language & Communication* 23 (3/4): 385–408.

———. 2010. "Entextualizing Diversity: Semiotic Incoherence in Institutional Discourse." *Language & Communication* 30 (1): 48–57.

Urla, Jacqueline. 1988. "Ethnic Protest and Social Planning: A Look at Basque Language Revival." *Cultural Anthropology* 3 (4): 379–394.

———. 1993. "Cultural Politics in an Age of Statistics: Numbers, Nations, and the Making of Basque Identity." *American Ethnologist* 20 (4): 818–843.

Urrutía, Rubén. 2010. "El Taíno vive." *El Nuevo Día*, Online edition, October 10, 2010. https://www.elnuevodia.com/noticias/locales/nota/eltainovive-795837/.

U.S. Census Bureau. 2012. *2010 Census of Population and Housing, Summary Population and Housing Characteristics, CPH-1-53, Puerto Rico*. Washington, D.C.: U.S. Government Printing Office.

Vales, Luis E. González. 1988. "El Diario Económico de Puerto Rico: Manifestación puertorriqueña de la prensa económica española." *Estudios de historia social y económica de América* (3–4): 123–134.

Valle Atiles, Francisco del. 1995 [1887]. "El campesino puertorriqueño: Condiciones intelectuales y morales." Reprinted in *Crónicas de Puerto Rico: Desde la conquista hasta nuestros días, 1493–1955*. 7th ed. Edited by Eugenio Fernández Méndez, 505–540. San Juan: Ediciones "El Cemi" Editorial Universitaria, Universidad de Puerto Rico.

Vargas-Ramos, Carlos. 2005. "Black, Trigueño, White . . . ? Shifting Racial Identification among Puerto Ricans." *Du Bois Review: Social Science Research on Race* 2 (2): 267–285.

Wagenheim, Kal, and Piri Thomas. 1970. *Puerto Rico: A Profile*. Westport: Praeger.

Wagenheim, Olga Jiménez de. 1998. *Puerto Rico: An Interpretive History from Pre-Columbian Times to 1900*. Princeton: Markus Wiener.

Webster, Anthony K. 2010. "On Intimate Grammars with Examples from Navajo English, Navlish, and Navajo." *Journal of Anthropological Research* 66 (2): 187–208.

———. 2012. "'Don't Talk about It': Navajo Poets and Their Ordeals of Language." *Journal of Anthropological Research* 68 (3): 399–414.

———. 2015. *Intimate Grammars: An Ethnography of Navajo Poetry*. Tucson: University of Arizona Press.

Wolf, Eric R. 2010 [1982]. *Europe and the People without History*. 2nd ed. Berkeley: University of California Press.

Wolford, Wendy. 2006. "The Difference Ethnography Can Make: Understanding Social Mobilization and Development in the Brazilian Northeast." *Qualitative Sociology* 29 (3): 335–352.

Wong, Laiana. 1999. "Authenticity and the Revitalization of Hawaiian." *Anthropology & Education Quarterly* 30 (1): 94–115.

Woolard, Kathryn A. 2002. "Bernardo de Aldrete and the Morisco Problem: A Study in Early Modern Spanish Language Ideology." *Comparative Studies in Society and History* 44 (3): 446–480.

Wright, Robin M., and Jonathan D. Hill. 1986. "History, Ritual, and Myth: Nineteenth Century Millenarian Movements in the Northwest Amazon." *Ethnohistory* 33 (1): 31–54.

Yaremko, Jason M. 2009. "'Obvious Indian'—Missionaries, Anthropologists, and the 'Wild Indians' of Cuba: Representations of the Amerindian Presence in Cuba." *Ethnohistory* 56 (3): 449–477.

Zenker, Olaf. 2014. "Linguistic Relativity and Dialectical Idiomatization: Language Ideologies and Second Language Acquisition in the Irish Language Revival of Northern Ireland." *Journal of Linguistic Anthropology* 24 (1): 63–83.

Zenón Cruz, Isabelo. 1975. *Narciso descubre su trasero (el negro en la cultura puertorriqueña)*. Vol. 2. San Juan: Editorial Furidi.

Zentella, Ana Celia. 1990. "Returned Migration, Language, and Identity: Puerto Rican Bilinguals in Dos Worlds/Two Mundos." *International Journal of the Sociology of Language* 84:81–100.

Index

Page numbers followed by *f* and *t* refer to figures and tables, respectively.

CGT. *See* Consejo General de Taínos
Cherokee scripts, 105–106
Chib'al'o-Boricua. *See* Jíbaro-Boricua
Christianity, 52, 129, 167, 178
Coll y Toste, Cayetano, 129
"color blindness," 78
Consejo General de Taínos (CGT;
General Council of Taíno), 40, 41, 149;
activism by, 141, 153–154, 158–165, 169,
173; ceremonies of, 139–140, 170; communication and, 137–138, 151; history of,
4–5; language and, 103, 136–137; meaning making and, 148, 152; strategies of,
171; United Nations and, 172–173
"contemporary Spaniards," 151–152
continuity, xviii; cultural, 180; Indigenous,
44, 63; linguistic, xix; Taíno, 94
Córdova, Nathaniel I., 61
Council of the Indies, 34
Counter Intelligence Program
(COINTELPRO), 197–198n1
countersurveillance, 161, 164

Dávila, Arlene, 78
Davis, Jenny, 101
de las Casas, Bartolomé, 33, 117, 122
delegitimization, 81
Delgado, Juan Manuel, 37, 39
Deloria, Philip J., 13
del Valle Atiles, Francisco, 55–57
Departamento de Recursos Naturales
y Ambientales (DRNA; Depart-
ment of Natural and Environmental
Resources), 154, 156, 158, 159–160,
161–165
Department of Public Instruction, 77
Diálogo, 76
diaspora, 7, 16–17, 174, 176
difference, 13, 20, 81, 106
Dinzey-Flores, Zaire Zenit, 79
Division of Community Education
(DIVEDCO), 42, 62, 77, 192–193n3
DNA, 72, 85, 175–176. *See also* mitochon-
drial DNA
Dominican Republic, 121, 122

DRNA. *See* Departamento de Recursos
Naturales y Ambientales

Economies of Abandonment (Povinelli), 22
education; erasure and, 69; for jíbaros, 62,
schoolbooks, 33, 43, 47, 180; by Taíno
groups, 82–94; under U.S. rule, 68–70.
See also schools
ELA. *See* Estado Libre Asociado
elites, xv, 15, 63, 64; use of Jíbaro archetype, 57, 58*f*, 60
emergence, 12, 14, 18
Empson, William, 18–19
encomienda system, 33, 38
English language, 16–17, 192n1; as foreign,
103, 163, 195n1
epistemologies of possibility, 12, 23
erasure, 30, 37, 63, 170, 181; discursive, 180;
language and, 19, 101
"Espejitos" ("Little mirrors"; Montero), 75
Estado Libre Asociado (ELA), 77
ethnography, 3, 14, 79–80, 139
ethnoracial regimes, 2
exclusion, 17, 37, 63, 179
extinction narrative, 2, 11, 12, 31, 176;
challenging of, 18
Eyeri language, 121–125

Federal Bureau of Investigation (FBI),
155, 197–198n1
Felipe II, king of Spain, 34
feminist theory, 20, 21–22
Figueroa, Loida, 35
Foucault, Michel, 171; *The Order of Things*,
197n1 (chap. 6)
Free Associated State Commonwealth
of Puerto Rico. *See* Estado Libre
Asociado
Fung, Heidi, 194n1

Gal, Susan, 19
genealogy, 1, 79, 113, 134; linguistic, 99,
100, 132, 134–135. *See also* Arawakan
genealogy; Mayan genealogy; Taíno:
genealogy and

Movement), 5, 65; indigeneity and, 114, 115; language and, 99, 113, 117, 132, 133, 172

mtDNA. *See* mitochondrial DNA

Muñoz Marín, Luis, 61, 192n1, 192–193n3

music, 56, 78, 90–93, 194n3

Naguaké, 172, 173

National Historic Preservation Act (NHPA), 156–157

nationalism, 181; cultural, 2, 17, 77; Puerto Rican, 12, 43, 60, 192n1

National Museum of the American Indian, New York City, New York, xvii, 18, 173–174

Native American Graves Protection and Repatriation Act (NAGPRA), 157

"Native Language as Identity Marker" (NLIM) style, 112

nature: meaning in, 136–137, 138, 140, 144–148; messages of spirits in, 168, 169–170

neo-Chumash, 12–13

New South Associates, Stone Mountain, Georgia, 155–157

New York City, New York, 17, 70, 113, 174, 191n1

NHPA. *See* National Historic Preservation Act

noble savage, 56, 193–194n4 (chap. 3)

Nogueras Vidal, Margarita, 40

Nuevo Día, El, 75, 177

O'Brien, Jean, 101

Oficina de Estatal de Conservación Histórica (OECH; State Office of Historic Preservation), 154, 156

Oki. *See* Lamourt Valentín, Oscar

Operation Bootstrap, 192–193n3

Operation Serenity, 192–193n3

oral history. *See* history: oral

Order of Things, The (Foucault), 197n1 (chap. 6)

O'Reilly, Alexander, 35

Our Father prayer, translation of, 129–131

Pagán Jiménez, Jaime R., 77

Pané, Ramón, 117, 122

pardos (free colored people), 35–36

Partido Popular Democrático (PPD; Popular Democratic Party), 61, 192n1

Paschel, Tianna, 81

Pedreira, Antonio Salvador, 60–61

Perley, Bernard, 14

Permanent Forum on Indigenous Issues, United Nations, 70, 170

phenotypes, 38, 80

pictographs, 104, 148

Ponce de León, Juan, 33

Popular Democratic Party. *See* Partido Popular Democrático

Povinelli, Elizabeth A., 14, 23; *Economies of Abandonment*, 22

PPD. *See* Partido Popular Democrático

Primera Hora, 106

profecía, la (prophecy). *See* Aura Surey, prophecy of

Puente del Indio, Vega Baja, Puerto Rico, 29

Puerto Rican Institute of Culture. *See* Instituto de Cultura Puertorriqueña

Puerto Ricanness, 3, 17, 26, 73, 192–193n3; jibaridad as, 103; Jíbaro as archetype of, 48, 59, 61; racial triad and, 83–84

Puerto Rico: ancestry in, 32; contemporary understandings of, 151–152; cultural traditions, 90–93; demographics of, 6, 35–36, 60, 191n4; discourses of, 2–3; double colonization of, 69; geography of, 34, 38, 118; hegemonies in, xv, 12, 17; history of, xv–xvi, 15–17, 30, 114, 181; literature of, 57; national myth of, 77, 78; racial politics in, 179–180; U.S. takeover of, 15–16, 78

racial blending, 78, 88, 176

racial continuum, 79, 80

racial discourses, 81

racial dynamics, 77

racial ideologies, 49, 77, 78–79, 83

racialization, xii–xiii, 21, 72, 78–79, 80

racial politics, 179

racial triad, 2–3, 76, 77–78, 84; indigeneity and, 88

reappropriation, 169

reemergence, 14, 40, 41

reggaetón, 91–93, 194n3

relatedness, 25–26, 117

Repeating Island, The (Benítez-Rojo), 2

revitalization: cultural, 106; linguistic, 30, 102; sociocultural, 178

Rindstedt, Camilla, 138

Rivera-Rideau, Petra R., 79

Rodríguez Ramos, Reniel, 77

Salcedo, Diego, 33

Samuels, David, 181–182

Santiago, Esmeralda, *When I Was a Puerto Rican*, 62–63

Scarano, Francisco A., 52, 56–57

schools: Americanization and, 16, 194n7; as colonization systems, 39–40; education about Taíno, 82–94, 104–107. *See also* education

semiotic ambiguity, 12, 18–19

settler colonialism, xv, 15, 21; narratives of, 31, 181

slavery, 31, 33

Spain, 15, 33, 34–35, 109, 152

Spanish language, 111–112, 118, 119*t*, 133; Indigenous influence on, 100, 116; as national language, 16–17, 192n1; preferred to English, 103; subversion of, 109–110. *See also* Jíbaro Spanish

speech registers, 65, 66–67, 68

spelling, 59, 110, 116, 123

spiritism (espiritismo), 178

spirits, 143, 149, 151; communication with, 111, 139–140; messages of, in nature, 137, 168, 170

spiritual frame (cuadro espiritual), 111

State Office of Historic Preservation. *See* Oficina de Estatal de Conservación Histórica

Steiner, Stan, 35, 44

stereotypes, 68, 75–76; appearance and, 84–85, 88

surveillance, 154–155, 161, 163, 164–165, 170–171, 197–198n1

Taboas Cruz, Liliana, 176–177

Taíney language, 113, 120–127, 133, 172; teaching of, 127–132

Taíno: contemporary understanding of, 77–78, 151–152; in conventional histories, 32–36; demographics of, 6; erasure of, 170, 181; genealogy and, 71–72, 80, 85–86, 175; identification as, 11–12, 25–26, 105; as legacy, 17, 42–43, 78; as national symbol, 17; practices of, 42, 82, 102, 125, 138; presumption of extinction, xv, xvi, 5, 19, 32, 44; rejection of term, 1, 113, 114, 115, 116; resurgence of, 11; terminology of, 6

Taíno activism, 19, 80, 170–171, 177–179; archaeology and, 75–76, 157–165; organization of, 6–7, 173

"Taíno: A Symposium in Conversation with the Movement," 173, 174–176

Taíno/Boricua: activism by, 1, 73, 100, 134, 147, 191n1; criticism of, 77, 95; erasure of, 37; extinction narrative, 2, 29–30; historical imagining of, 180; identification as, 1, 77, 181; as identity category, 94, 134; language and, 133–134; presumption of extinction, 1; terminology of, 1, 6; trajectories of, 23

Taíno/Boricua heritage, 3, 95

Taíno/Boricua mobilization, 2–3, 77, 80

Taíno/Boricuaness, 3, 180

Taíno/Boricua survival, 38; denial of, 30; oral history and, 31, 39

Taíno communication, 137–138, 140–141, 152, 165

Taíno consciousness, 149, 151

Taíno gaze, 140, 141, 145, 151

Taíno language, 99–102, 111–112, 132–134, 136–137, 195n1; origins of, 133, 195–196n5; orthography of, 101, 104, 105*f*, 109–111, 110*f*; reconstruction of, 112, 118, 120;

signs and, 148; tokens of, 99, 104–107, 137; vocabulary of, 107–109, 133

Taíno mobilization, xv, 12, 19, 24, 81, 174

Taíno Nation (TN), 99, 113, 120–127, 132, 133–134, 172; teaching by, 127–132, 133

Taíno: Native Heritage and Identity in the Caribbean (National Museum of the American Indian), xvii, 18, 173–174

Taínoness, 6, 70, 103, 136, 164

Taíno scripts, 133; Guaka-Kú, 109–111, 110*f*, 111*f*, 112; LGTK, 104–107, 105*f. See also* Taíno language: orthography of

Taínos: La última tribu (Taínos: The last tribe; López), xviii

Taíno spirituality, 40, 93, 144–147, 149–151, 178

Taíno survival, 104, 138, 152, 173; conventional history and, xvi, 37, 40; cultural, 175, 176; discourses of, 12, 34; erasure of, 55–56; narratives of, xviii–xix

temporality, 21–22, 23

TN. *See* Taíno Nation

Translated Woman (Behar), 64

Trechter, Sara, 139

United Confederation of Taíno People (UCTP), 70

United Nations, 70, 170, 172

United States: archaeology and, 154, 156–157; as corrupting influence, 127;

diaspora in, 7, 16–17, 174; language and, 17, 103; relationship with Puerto Rico, 174, 192n1; schools and, 16, 39, 194n7; takeover of Puerto Rico, 15–16, 78

University of Puerto Rico (UPR), San Juan, Puerto Rico, 76, 133, 156

U.S. Army Corps of Engineers (USACE), 154, 155, 156

Vargas-Ramos, Carlos, 191n4

Vocero, El, 155

Warren, Kay B., 15

ways of knowing, 23, 151, 181

ways of seeing, 151, 171

Webster, Anthony, 103

When I Was a Puerto Rican (Santiago), 62–63

Whiteness, 62, 139

Whites, 35, 36; Jíbaros represented as, 47, 61–62

White supremacy, 21

Wilcoxon, Larry R., 12–13

Woman of Caguana, 141–142

Wright, Robin, 41

Yucatec Mayan language, 5, 101, 113, 117, 132–133

Zenker, Olaf, 101

About the Author

SHERINA FELICIANO-SANTOS is an associate professor of anthropology at the University of South Carolina. She is a linguistic anthropologist who investigates how language, interaction, and history mediate racial, ethnic, and national belonging in a globalizing context, specifically with attention to Puerto Rico and the United States.